Infinite
Possibilities

Infinite
Possibilities

THE ART OF LIVING YOUR DREAMS

MIKE DOOLEY

ATRIA BOOKS
New York London Toronto Sydney

BEYOND WORDS
Hillsboro, Oregon

ATRIA BOOKS
A Division of Simon & Schuster, Inc.
1230 Avenue of the Americas
New York, NY 10020

BEYOND WORDS
20827 N.W. Cornell Road, Suite 500
Hillsboro, Oregon 97124-9808

Managing editor: Lindsay S. Brown
Editor: Julie Knowles
Copyeditor: Jennifer Weaver-Neist
Design: Devon Smith
Composition: William H. Brunson Typography Services

First Atria Books/Beyond Words hardcover edition September 2009

ATRIA BOOKS and colophon are trademarks of Simon & Schuster, Inc.
Beyond Words Publishing is a division of Simon & Schuster, Inc.

Manufactured in the United States of America

ISBN: 978-1-58270-226-1

To Mom

and

To all who have taken the time to write of your gratitude for the original twelve-hour audio version of this book during the past nine years. You often ask me if I have any idea how much my work means to you, but I wonder if you have any idea how much your encouragement has meant to me.

Contents

Preface   ix

Acknowledgments   xi

Introduction: An Adventurer's Guide to the Jungles of
    Time and Space   xiii

1   Thoughts Become Things   1

2   Beliefs   27

3   Blessed Emotions   53

4   Life Is Waiting for You   77

5   Gifts from Heaven   103

6   Magical Universe   123

7   The Elixir of Life   151

8   Abundance, Health, and Harmony   163

9   Relationships   193

10   Tools and Techniques   223

11   Questions and Answers   249

12   The Meaning of Life   265

Epilogue   275

More on Mike   277

Recommended Reading   279

Preface

There could be no better time than now, at this crossroads in history, to finally learn the truth about who you really are and all you're capable of. Please don't let the title of this book mislead you. Just as it's about learning of your power, it is also about learning of your responsibilities. It shares exactly how to operate within the framework of these two pillars so that you can move through the affairs of the world, discovering opportunity where others have only found closed doors. This is a time of change and upheaval: the old is giving way to the new, naiveté is giving way to truth, and spirituality is about to take on an entirely new meaning. Those who learn of their greatness, honor their passions, and accept responsibility for their own happiness will usher in a golden age that will dwarf any experienced in history. There's never been a more exciting time to be alive.

I began writing the chapters that follow on January 1, 2001, as the script for the audio program that would become the genesis of this book. Only weeks before, I'd announced to my email list that it would be offered in twelve one-hour installments during the coming calendar year, to be delivered at the first of each month. I was late.

I was also scared. I was starting my working life over, this time as a full-time writer, and at a loss to explain why I even had to begin a new career, except, of course, there was no money coming in. But I knew a few things about life and its mechanics—of our divinity and power, of holding to a dream and physically moving with it.

Since then, *Infinite Possibilities* has gone on to become one of the bestselling audio programs on the internet and in the self-improvement world. It's led to speaking engagements all over the globe, being featured in the bestselling book and DVD *The Secret*, and the creation of *Notes from the Universe*, the daily email I now send to a list that's grown to over three hundred thousand people in 182 countries, reminding them of how worthy they are, how powerful they are, and how much they deserve.

What I discovered yet again is that remembering my true place in life—understanding my role in its creation and demonstrating such understandings through thought, word, and deed—is always enough to change *everything*. In spite of their surroundings, even when unable to explain recent events and how "I created this mess," through *understanding* life's truths, people can still begin using what they already have, starting from wherever they are, to blast forward and improve their fortunes immeasurably.

This is what *Infinite Possibilities* promises: an understanding of your divine powers, a roadmap for harnessing life's ultimate "absolute," and a reminder of the infinite grace and perfection that always embraces us. You needn't explain what's led you here today—why the relationship didn't work out, why the business never took off, or why the diet didn't succeed—nor must the world be in harmony and governments honorable, in order for you to learn who you really are and to understand all the possibilities that still lie before you. Yet, as has always been true for me, once change begins sweeping into your life and a new chapter is written, you'll be able to glance back with relative ease at the commotion that preceded the turning point and see the order and beauty in all that unfolded, as well as your hand in its creation and the purpose it served.

To the life of your dreams,
September 8, 2009

Acknowledgments

J believe a number of people have been tapped by the Universe in the past nine years, summoned by my dreams and actions, to inspire me, challenge me, or kick me in the butt, and their arrival into my life was choreographed to make this book as good as it could be and released exactly when it should be. While I won't share who did what, I'd like to thank them all from the bottom of my heart:

> *Mom, for giving me the gift to dream and to believe in myself. Joe Vitale, author and marketing dynamo, for being the first to "discover me" (after Mom) by spreading the word and becoming a friend many years before either of us reached the mainstream. Rhonda Byrne, producer and author of* The Secret, *for being the second to "reach out." I'll never forget when she and her fabulous sister, Glenda, greeted me one fine morning in Chicago to tell me of her vision for bringing "joy to billions" and her wish to include me in the caper. Cynthia Black, publisher at Beyond Words, for being the third person to emerge from the "unseen," believing I had something to offer, after which her fantastic partner, Richard Cohn, and the rest of her amazing team at Beyond Words—specifically, Lindsay Brown, Marie Hix,*

Acknowledgments

Devon Smith, and Danielle Marshall—enthusiastically jumped on board. Judith Curr, publisher at Atria, for her supernatural gut instincts. Julie Knowles, editor, for taking me to the pavement with her calculated skepticism. Eric Rayman for his brilliance and integrity as one of the finest attorneys I may ever know. And Hope Koppelman, Danika Burr, Jesse Mazur, Paola Malicki, Amanda Reid, Carrie-anne Larmore, Crystal Floyd, and Kody Kasper for their priceless contributions to the business of TUT and our combined vision of "Global Domination"!

Introduction

*N*ot long ago, in the nether reaches of ad infinitum, there formed a council of fearless explorers—adventurers much like you—who had become bored with perfection, infinity, and unending bliss. Whatever it was they wanted, they got. However they wanted to change, they did, and whatever they wanted to be, they became. Their existence had become so "same old, same old" that they hardly felt like the great Adventurers they were. It wasn't enough, they agreed; something had to be done. So, being who they were, they decided to invent an entirely new dimension for their reality.

Well, new dimensions, even for these Adventurers, don't get invented very often, so you can imagine their excitement as they began to explore the vast new possibilities that suddenly lay before them. And this dimension was especially exciting because it made possible the previously unthinkable ability of being in just one place, without being everywhere else at once.

You see, back then, in the nether reaches of ad infinitum, there was only the here and now; nothing else existed. These poor explorers never had anywhere to go because they were already everywhere! What their new dimension did was enable them to dim their awareness of everywhere else enough to focus on being a single "somewhere" at a time.

And now that they could create somewheres, they found they could each devise secret patterns among their somewheres to play games and conduct experiments. In fact, they did this so often that they began referring to this new dimension as the Secret Pattern Adventure for Creative Enlightenment, or SPACE for short.

SPACE became the new frontier, with lots of possibilities for exploration, fun, and games. And perhaps the most remarkable phenomenon about SPACE was the startling discovery that it could be filled with their thoughts: whenever their thoughts were focused and concentrated within their SPACE, they became dense and appeared solid!

They discovered that they could think big or small, red or blue, hard or soft—whatever they imagined—and their thoughts would then become the same "thing" in SPACE! These Adventurers had discovered that their thoughts could be projected into this SPACE of theirs, where they would then appear as objects, and they quickly came to realize that they could Manifest Any Thought That Existed into Reality, so in no time at all (mostly because time had not yet been invented), MATTER began to fill their SPACE! Matter, of course, was the acronym for Manifest Any Thought That Existed into Reality. (These Adventurers, as you can tell, loved acronyms.)

Creativity soared as they dabbled, first creating stars and planets and then mountains and oceans. Everything they dreamed of came to life in an explosion of light, color, and sound that stretched their imagination to the very edges of their SPACE.

It was all incredibly exciting, except, deep down inside, they knew that something was missing. As spectacular as their new worlds were, they themselves, the creators of everything, remained on the outside looking in.

The Adventurers began to ponder how they could become part of the mysterious, enchanting, material worlds they'd created, and in their wondering they asked, "If our MATTER is simply occupied SPACE, and deep down we know that we're really still everywhere else at once ... hmmm ... could we possibly exist in the very same SPACE that holds our MATTER?"

Well, of course they could, and as they thought it, they did it, taking up residence "inside" their MATTER, just as if it were a "somewhere," by dimming their awareness of everywhere else.

Now, to make things even more interesting, right about then a new game called "hide-and-seek" was being invented, and, as could be predicted, the Adventurers scurried about and hid themselves inside their creations, where they would not likely be found. They Hid Under Matter Animated in the Now, because "now" was still all there was (since time had not yet been invented), and henceforth referred to themselves as being HUMAN when they were in hiding.

It was a great idea, this hiding under MATTER—so great, in fact, that no one was ever found! So despite their joy in having found a new game to play, they were no longer aware of one another's discoveries. Big problem.

This prompted a call to go out for the need to Trace one another In Material Existence; thus TIME was born finally! The games resumed, reunions were planned, and the fun really began—that is, until everyone had pretty much "been there, done that!"

Another idea was needed, and given the Adventurers' track record, it didn't take them long to come up with one. What if, they thought, we all venture out together, in HUMAN form, into the same SPACE at the exact same TIME? Whoa! This idea was so monumental, so profound, so colossal that it sent a big bang booming throughout all creation, and it has since been compared to the invention of light itself.

Well, by now it should be obvious that these Adventurers weren't your normal, everyday kind of Adventurers. They were creative Adventurers on a mission—to have as much fun as could possibly be imagined—and to that end, as you well know, they've been wildly successful, though they have met up with a few wrinkles that are still being ironed out.

For instance, once TIME was invented, they spent so much of it playing as a creation among their creations that they began to lose themselves. For example, during their unending games of hide-and-seek, they stayed HUMAN for so long, not wanting to be found, that they actually began to forget they were also "everywhere else" at once.

Many more began to forget that they were even Adventurers, and as TIME marched on, they fell into a deeper and deeper trance. In fact, so far did they fall that they began to feel trapped within their bodies and helpless among their creations. No longer did they notice that they themselves were the ones crafting the objects and events of their lives with their thoughts, though this didn't change; instead they saw these "things" as something to contend with.

Unfortunately, a direct result of this naiveté led to their first taste of FEAR, which was felt whenever they Failed to Experience the Actual Reality before them. A scary thing, they soon found out. No fun at all! And worse, a whole horde of emotions sprang to life with their every misunderstanding.

Never in any reality have such lofty beings plunged into such great despair. Terror, anger, sadness, and guilt were rampant. It was a travesty through and through until, little by little, there began a great healing—not from on high or any other such place (though some still say it was a Mystically Incited Reality Adjustment Concealed by Loving Entities); it was a healing that had transpired from within; life ministering to life itself—perhaps a MIRACLE either way.

It turns out that the Adventurers were learning from their emotions. For example, if FEAR stems from the Failure to Experience the Actual Reality before you, then at least it serves as an unmistakable warning (to the one doing the "fearing") that his or her thinking has strayed from the truth.

And there was even more good news about these emotions. It turned out they could also be warm and fuzzy, funny and silly, and even wild and crazy! And it was their passage through all the emotions, happy and sad, that brought the "Illustrious Ones" (as they came to be called) their greatest achievement: an inner Pleasure Experienced by Accepting all Creation as it Exists, or inner PEACE. Mastered by so few, as it requires a deep under-standing of the perfection that exists within everything, every moment, every place, and in everyone, no matter what!

By now, in the present day, all forms of awareness, from everywhere ever thought of, have heard about SPACE, TIME, and the brilliant Adventurers who created it all. And those who drop by for a look at this lit-tle corner of creation are so astounded by what they find that they are changed forever.

It's not just the splendor of the planets nor the raging life that thrives upon them, nor even the bold and outrageous thoughts that continue to perpetuate them all that astound visitors. Observers are left speechless and are downright humbled by the few who have returned from the adven-ture—those Adventurers who have actually found themselves.

These are the Illustrious Ones whose glowing radiance and divine illumination reflect an understanding rooted in the unshakable knowledge that all things and events are born of thought, that in TIME and SPACE it's all good, and that everything, everywhere, always is One.

Only by losing themselves and serving their illusions could these Adventurers then be driven emotionally—by their burning desires—to reclaim and know the depths of their own divinity. By truly understanding their reality, they've become the inspiration and the ideal for all to follow.

Having just shared all that, it is a bit amazing to us that more have not joined the ranks of the Illustrious Ones. Certainly to each his (or her) own; it's just that they're all still so caught up in this most awesome adventure of theirs that it seems they really couldn't care less about "everywhere else"!

Perhaps you understand them better. Still, to us at least, it seems a shame that such inexhaustible energy and creative genius is being so thoroughly neglected. If they could—and we assure you, they can—just for an instant, glimpse their greater reality and see themselves as the omniscient, unlimited, fun-loving gladiators they've always been, it would so radically change everything! Not that they should "return." Heavens, no. We just think that they may have a better ... "TIME," shall we say, if reminded that they themselves are creators. Don't you think?

By the way, we've blown the lid clear off your little charade—FOUND YOU!

Now, let's get this party started ...

**You have but to direct your thinking
to direct your experience.**

In many ways, this is a true story. Actually, it's *our* story and it's more factual than fictional: We were among the illustrious architects who dreamed up time and space—the eyes and ears of God—and we're now alive in our own creation to experience our divinity in ways that it could not otherwise be experienced. We are the very reason the sun rises each day. And grasping this premise, instinctively if not intellectually, you should, therefore, be able to see just how worthy you are of any other dream you may care to conjure up. There's no one outside of yourself who has anything to do with it; you're not here to be tested and judged. You have but to direct your thinking to direct your experience. It's that easy.

You are one of the original Adventurers—unlimited, fearless, and divine—not merely a human being. You are an adventurer just being human.

Unfortunately, most of our fellow cohorts are still "lost in space," with virtually everything in our society telling us, reminding us, and insisting that we are limited, aging "creatures," living lives between luck and fate in a hard, unforgiving world. The truth, however (and this will likely ring bells in your heart of hearts), is that we are infinite and powerful, fun-loving gladiators of the Universe, with eternity before us and the power of our thoughts to help shape it.

We create our own realities, our own fate, and our own luck. That is how powerful we are, and that is how powerful *you* are. And to offset all the contradictory thinking of the media and masses, you need to hear this kind of message as often as you hear all the others.

This book was written with such a message. It's a book on the nature of reality—a reality that is simple, organized, and, above all, knowable. My aim throughout is to explain exactly how you fit into this reality, and then to remind you of how powerful you are, of how far you can reach, and of how much you deserve so that you can begin thriving as the giant you are in this oasis among the stars. You have indeed been endowed with the gift to make your dreams come true.

Blood, sweat, and tears aren't what it takes to create real change. Instead, it's your imagination, beliefs, and expectations that draw you into the action, circumstances, and "coincidences" that make dream manifestation inevitable. This isn't wishful thinking. It's the way things have always been in the jungles of time and space, the illusionary dimension that is both our laboratory and playground. Here our *thoughts become things*, our word is our wand, and we can learn of our divinity by witnessing the daily miracles we perform, effortlessly crafting spirit into circumstance as we perpetuate the material world we share. You don't necessarily need more education, more connections, or more lucky breaks. You just need to understand the principles and concepts that every prophet and mystic has shared since the beginning of time—principles that have nothing to do with religion and everything to do with the truth about who we really are, why we're here, and the magic at our disposal.

Your dreams are not yours by accident. You have them for many reasons, not the least of which is to make them come true. Your dreams are meant to be—if you do your part. This can seem like a mighty tall order when you don't fully understand what your part is or the processes that make dreams come true, especially while the whole world wants you to believe that suffering and sacrifice pave the road to success. With greater understanding, however, you'll find that nothing could possibly be easier than the way life *really* works.

There is nothing you can't do, nothing you can't have, and nothing you can't be.

You are guided, you do have the power, and the Universe is actually conspiring on your behalf.

This book reviews the principles and concepts that can give you flight. These principles are now at play in your own life, whether you know what they are or not, and these principles are incredibly easy to use. By identifying, understanding, and harnessing them, you will access the power that can literally turn wishes into reality.

Consider today's so-called successful people. Are they smarter than you? Are they more deserving? Have they paid greater dues? No. Whether through intelligence or naiveté (often the latter, but it doesn't make *any* difference), they're actually living in ways that engage life's principles so that the Universe begins serving them.

The good news is that such people are proof that anyone else can do the same. And understanding this, you'll have an advantage: you'll understand your successes and therefore won't have to live in fear that they could ever be taken away from you.

My mission is to help you look within, to discover how unlimited you are, and to help you find the keys to "the Kingdom." What you then decide to do with those keys will be up to you.

In the following pages, I aim to brush up against your own deep, long-forgotten memories that have been yearning to be exercised, thought about, and rediscovered. There's the old adage about it being better to teach someone to fish than to give him or her a fish, and in this book, I intend to remind you (more than teach you) of your divine nature and limitless capabilities so that you can achieve your own happiness and fulfillment.

If someone were tell to you the truth about life, reality, and the powers you possessed, would you recognize it as the truth? If someone were to offer you the key to the kingdom of your wildest dreams, would you accept it? I think you would.

Know ye not that ye are gods?

Psalms 82:6, John 10:34

1

Thoughts Become Things

*F*rom as far back as I can remember, until I was a young adult, I used to think that everyone knew something I didn't. I felt like the perennial outsider. They, like me, weren't aware of what it was, and they didn't seem to notice that I was without it. But to me, the difference was painful. Life's "little things" seemed second nature to others, whereas I felt I had to fake that I knew what was going on. I felt awkwardly different, which led to an overwhelming desire to question what most people seem to take for granted: a desire to know what this life is about.

In the beginning, my search for answers revolved around the issues of life, death, and the powers of the mind. But from this search arose other intriguing mysteries concerning time, space, heaven, hell, hypnosis, UFOs, ghosts, ESP, the dream state, reincarnation, and the like. Early on, I had drawn basic conclusions that explained each mystery, but they were just hunches. For example, I remember telling my mother when I was about thirteen that time and space couldn't really exist as we've defined them, and that neither could hell or a God that wasn't One with all things, living and inanimate. My sense was that He or She or Whatever was not just inside us all, but that no part of our experience could ever be anything less than 100 percent "God."

I didn't realize it at the time, but my desire to "know" had put me on an inner path toward understanding; my thinking was beginning

1

to attract similar thinking. It was as if my questions were slowly answering themselves, opening my eyes to the insights that I now know are latent within each of us. As I walked this path of seeking, the questions I dwelled upon were somehow answered. I was never sure just when my answers had arrived. I only sensed, sometime after "illumination" on the subject, that an intuitive knowing had been imparted when I wasn't paying close attention. The point of sharing this is to reveal that the answers I was receiving came from within, which is exactly where your answers reside as well.

I was raised Catholic, baptized and confirmed, but I found many of the teachings, rules, and rituals contradictory and, more importantly, inconsistent with the conclusions I had intuitively deduced. I've always believed, for example, that each of us is really doing his or her best, given our own understandings, misunderstandings, and upbringings. Therefore, if divine judgment were to be passed on a life—and I don't believe it is—sin could only ever be regarded as an honest "mistake" caused by deeply misunderstanding the nature of our reality, not a demerit system that leads to eternal damnation.

Wouldn't a loving Father, I reasoned, have more compassion than to seek revenge on His comparatively feeble children who are temporarily blinded by the illusions of time and space? Even human parents are far more understanding of their own flesh and blood than the "Father" portrayed in most religions. Sin, and its past and present connotations, must have been a term derived by man, I concluded, not by an understanding, all-knowing God. Then and now I believe that our so-called sins should simply serve us as teachers, not as tormentors.

So, while raised amidst traditional religious views, I also needed explanations that made sense, and just as importantly, I've always believed such explanations were attainable. Rather than simply dismissing what didn't make sense to me about my Catholic upbringing, I looked for similarities between what they taught and what I felt, deduced, or rationally understood, and once "my bucket" was full, I looked beyond religion and into myself to begin drawing conclusions about life, dreams, and happiness. For example, I believe that Jesus was here to tell us (as many other wise teachers have) that we are all "children of God." Jesus taught that we all can do the things He did: believe and you shall receive; knock and it will be answered; on Earth as it is in heaven; ye are Gods. I believe that there are no sins, there is no evil, and there is no hell other than what exists in our own minds, and that Jesus came to Earth to be a living example of these teachings, to show a better way to His fellow travelers during a dark time in history—when limiting beliefs were so ingrained in the culture that few people could even imagine expanding their thoughts, and thereby their world. This kind of thinking isn't new. The conclusions I've drawn parallel truths that have been shared by different religions and spiritual philosophies as old as history, all of which remind us of our power, magnificence, and divinity. And when we understand our time and space reality from this perspective as Creators ourselves, we finally begin to grasp the immense power we wield to shape our lives.

Our so-called sins should simply serve us as teachers, not as tormentors.

In spite of feeling like an outsider throughout most of my childhood and even much of my adult life, today I feel fantastically blessed to possess my perspectives and grateful for the alienation I've felt most of my life—a life that has led me to you. And because I still consider myself a student and an adventurer, I believe my life's mission is remarkably similar to yours: to begin *applying* this wisdom of the ages, these timeless truths concerning the nature of reality, so as to consciously direct and craft my own happy and fulfilling reality.

The Greatest Adventure of All

I believe that you and I are presently in the middle of an *adventure* like no other. There's no question that life is dangerous enough to be considered an adventure; none of us know for sure if we'll even live to see another sunrise. And every single day comes loaded with its own brand new and exciting experiences. Traveling to faraway places like Cairo or Istanbul is fascinating, but even from the comfort of your own home, there's more romance, exhilaration, and challenge in a life well lived. Adding still more to the adventure, each and every day, contains an abundance of the unknown.

And isn't it the unknown, the uncertainties, that makes an adventure an adventure? We all have hopes, dreams, worries, and fears, yet these all stem from the uncertainty in our lives. With just the slightest reflection, one can quickly see that it's this very uncertainty that makes it all *worthwhile*. If you were given a magic pen and every morning you could write down exactly what you wanted to have happen to you that day, knowing it would always happen, do you realize how *miserably* boring your life would become? After all, how many times could you win the lottery and still be thrilled?

And in life, no matter where we find ourselves—Katmandu or Nairobi—the best things are indeed free. Life's greatest pleasures are an endless list: a child's laughter, a lover's embrace, playing tug-of-war with your dog, swimming, listening to music, eating, hiking, watching the rain, planting a tree, sitting in front of a fire, talking with friends—and they're all free! It *is* a wonderful life, and these kinds of delights are usually sprinkled throughout all our day-to-day adventures.

Perhaps what makes this adventure *most* extraordinary is that we each have the power to conceive and achieve our own wildest dreams. After all, what would be the point of an adventure if we didn't have some control over its outcome, or if we couldn't choose the pleasures or the lessons that we'd derive from it? You might argue that because of the unknown, you can't know all that the future holds, but without even reading another word in this book you *already* know that you *can* choose to set goals and begin moving toward them, to great effect.

In life, you are the pilot or the divemaster of your destiny; every day you get to choose the line of work you're in, the relationships you will or won't foster, and whether or not you'll embrace your disappointments to glean from them their priceless, hard-earned lessons. And these decisions, combined with our attitudes, our beliefs, and, of course, the use of our imagination, carry us through all our personal journeys and point squarely at the "safaris" that await us tomorrow.

Getting Your Groove On

So how do you maximize your adventure through time and space? Two simple steps: First, *understand* the adventure. As an analogy, you wouldn't try to drive a car until you first understood how it operates and the rules of the road. Secondly, begin *living* the adventure. To draw from the same analogy, once you've learned about your car and the road, it still remains up to you to get into the driver's seat, turn the key, put it in gear, and go! In other words, *apply* your understandings, which, as I said earlier, is what you and I now have in common as the mission of our lives.

Amazingly, most people seem to think that just because they're alive they automatically know all there is to know about living. People just don't stop *to think* that there might be more than they already know. It hasn't occurred to them that "things" might not be as they seem—*and they're not*! Fortunately, it only takes a little new thinking to begin seeing things as they really are and to radically change everything.

And when it comes right down to it, could anything be easier than thinking? And what could be more rewarding? After all, isn't every major breakthrough, discovery, or personal revelation only a thought away? In fact, the next shocking invention that changes the course of our civilization does not lie far off in the future. It isn't a million or a billion dollars away, or a person or a corporation away. It exists *just a thought away* from right here and now; it's just a thought away from the thoughts we now entertain—the very thoughts you are now thinking.

For instance, first came the thought that people should be able to travel through the air and *then* came the reality: aviation. First came the thought that electrical energies should be manageable and *then* came the reality of electricity. And first come goals, such as falling in love, buying a home, and landing a job, and then—*click, click, click*—dreams start coming true.

Actually, with much of the world still in "survival mode," even right here in the United States, it's both forgivable and understandable that more people haven't extended a little new thinking to the experiences we share and end up taking for granted. Yet times are swiftly changing, and as the world is about to discover, the truth about our power has been just beneath our noses since the dawn of time.

Be Careful What You Wish For

Have you ever heard someone say, "Be careful what you wish for, because you just might get it"? I'll bet you have. We all have. And you know what else? I'll bet you believe it's true or at least you do to some degree, don't you?

But how or why could it be true? Have you thought about that? What mysterious *principle* might be at play here that could turn a wish into reality? You're probably not superstitious, so what is it? What's the reason you believe this may work?

You've likely heard about the power of positive thinking or the new buzzwords (thanks largely to the bestselling DVD and book *The Secret*) "the Law of Attraction." But have you ever stopped to wonder what powers positive thinking or the Law of Attraction? *Something* does! And I'm sure you've heard about the art of visualization too. You've probably even tried it, and maybe you've got some great stories to tell about its success. But have you ever stopped to wonder how or why it works?

All these concepts pretty much say the same thing, but why do people on every continent believe in them without ever questioning their logistics?

Something's going on here. Something big—really BIG. My mother likes to say, "Where there's smoke, there's fire," and what's going on here is of such a magnitude that the flames dwarf any other fire ever known to humankind. But just what is it that's going on? And if there *is* something, wouldn't it be worth some digging or some new thinking to uncover it, understand it, and then harness it? Wouldn't the effort warrant virtually any sacrifice or commitment? You bet it would!

Thoughts Become Things

In three short, life-changing, never-to-be-forgotten words, the answer to what's going on—and to what we've been missing—is, "Thoughts become things!" That's it. *Thoughts become things*! This is the underlying *principle* that turns a wish into reality. It's what powers positive thinking and gives rise to the Law of Attraction, and it's why visualizations work.

Thoughts become things is the reason dreams and nightmares come true, because the thoughts we think *literally* become the "things" and events of our life. This principle is immutable and is as reliable as gravity itself—not just sometimes but all the time, and not just with our positive thoughts but with the other ones too. In fact, we can't ever turn it off.

All of this is awesome news because every minute of every day we get to choose just what we'll think. Of course, our words and our actions are also supremely important, and much will be said about each in the chapters that follow, yet both are nothing more than an extension of our thoughts. *Our words and our actions are merely our thoughts given wings.* Our thoughts are where *everything* begins. With this principle, you can bring virtually anything you can imagine into your life, and it's not just limited to attracting material things. You can also imagine more love, more joy, and more laughter.

Our lives evidence that thoughts actually have properties like those that belong to any material element, and such properties give rise to principles and laws. It's just that these properties, until recently, have escaped the observation of our scientists, engineers, and even most philosophers because they're obviously invisible to our physical sensory perception and the typical tools of observation. Fortunately, for those who need scientific proof, quantum science is now picking up where Albert Einstein left off in explaining the properties of thoughts and the effect the observer has on his or her experiments. But with or without scientific proof, in the simplest of terms, there is no one who can deny that thoughts exist. And for anything to exist, mustn't it have principles, traits, and characteristics?

My message, and that of countless teachers throughout the ages (though each in their own words), is that once a thought is thought, it's as if it's instantaneously endowed with its own power and will to become physical or, just as miraculously, to begin attracting its nearest equivalent (hence the Law of Attraction). It's as if it's given a single, solitary mission: to manifest into its thinker's life, within time and space. If you think thoughts of material things, your thoughts will become those material things. And if you think thoughts of events or circumstances, your thoughts will rearrange the players and the props of your life, predisposing you to those events or circumstances. *The only mitigating factors are your other thoughts*, which can take on a variety of "shades," which are typically referred to as your beliefs, expectations, anticipation, and intentions, to name a few. If you think thoughts of love or hate or of other emotions, your thoughts will shift around the *material* circumstances of your life so that you will experience those thought-of emotions over and over again.

Caveats?

Here are some of the attributes of this principle you should be aware of. It doesn't matter what your thoughts are, or whether they serve you or not, or whether they're "good" or not, or whether they're fair or not. Thoughts, vis-à-vis this principle, are like gravity in that they don't discern or judge *what* you're thinking; they just exist. *So it's up to us to choose our thoughts wisely!*

As creators, thinking is literally our only point of influence on the world and life's magic. Contrary to the views we inherited as children, such as "a thought's just a thought, abstract and ethereal; what's real is the chair, the table, and the food on your plate," it turns out the opposite is true. Our thoughts are what is "real"; they're the starting point of all that will become tangible in our lives—pre-matter, if you will—while the "things of time and space" are the reflection of what has previously been thought, individually and en masse, and are little more than a mirage. Accordingly, *nothing* plays a greater role in how we construct our fortunes and misfortunes than the thoughts we choose to think.

When it comes to thoughts about other people, we *can* "miraculously" attract those *who possess similar thoughts and complementary dreams*—potential partners in love or in business, clients, customers, and so on—with stunning accuracy and precision while simultaneously repelling others. We *cannot*, however, insist on any *particular person* behaving in a particular way. We simply cannot manipulate others with our thoughts, and most fortunately, nor can they manipulate us. Influence, sometimes; manipulate, never. The other person or people must be in alignment or agreement with our thoughts for there to be a partnership, a friendship, or even an adversarial relationship, but with a cast of over seven billion people on the planet to choose from, and our interconnectedness with them all through our innate divinity, we can always find *exactly* what we're looking for as long as we don't insist upon who it is. So when it comes to thinking thoughts about specific others, try this: take them out of the picture and instead imagine how you want to feel or the end result of whatever it is you really want.

For instance, if you want to redirect an old lover back into your life, don't think of that person; simply imagine the love you want to feel and share. Let your thoughts bring you what you really want—in this case, the feeling of love with the "right" person, not a specific person. I can hear the cries of protest already, saying that it really is a specific person missing from your life as well as the love you shared with them. I know how tough this shift from "other" to "self" can be, so I'll give it more explanation a bit later. For now, let me just say that if you're really hung up on a particular "someone," then there's *something* you're missing. There's something you're misunderstanding about your fabulous self, your magical world, or the infinite possibilities that remain for the happiest, most romantic years of your life. And perhaps the reason that specific person is no longer in your life, or is out of your realm of influence, is so that you will be led to finding the truth about what you've been misunderstanding, clearing the way for someone even more ideally suited to you than you can presently imagine.

Here's the good news: whatever it is you're missing, it's only a thought away and infinitely closer to you than that specific someone and infinitely easier for you to attain. And once you think it, look out, world, because the love you're missing will quickly flood into your life again unlike anything you've felt before, which is exactly what you have to look forward to!

Nothing plays a greater role in how we construct our fortunes and misfortunes than the thoughts we choose to think.

Let me give you an example of how to best use your thoughts in order to possibly influence a specific person. Let's say you want to improve how your child is doing in school. The best thing to do is to picture in your mind your child wildly happy, fulfilled, laughing, and confident—which is what you're really after anyway, right? This is far more effective than thinking of specific things happening to or for your child, such as grades going up or seeing him or her excel in any particular endeavor. What we're really after is happiness, either for ourselves or for others, and that's easy to imagine: *see* smiling faces, *feel* warm embraces, and *hear* praise and congratulations.

In all these imaginings, you want to leave out the details of how something will happen. The manifestation process always works quickly and harmoniously, just as air bubbles from the bottom of the sea always find the fastest way to the surface, unless we get in their way. Your thoughts, like the air bubbles, have their own default setting to manifest as quickly as possible, *tempered only by your other thoughts.* For instance, if you start off with demands such as "I'll only be truly happy when so-and-so does such-and-such," you shut the door on all the other ways you could be equally happy. Surrender the "hows" even as you continue living your normal life—knocking on doors, turning over stones—by not insisting upon which doors open or which stones possess your solution *but only upon the end result you desire.*

The Evidence

You'd probably like a little proof that *thoughts become things*, right? That's easy. Very easy. But since you can't see or follow a thought once it's been thought of, you have to look elsewhere for the evidence of its existence. And the best place to look is all around you. Here's some proof from my life:

The first time I can remember coming face-to-face with *thoughts become things* was when I was a nine-year-old kid taking horseback-riding lessons in Cherry Hill, New Jersey, though I didn't understand then just what was going on. My mother used to take my sister and me to riding class every weekend, where we'd learn to post, trot, and canter. After six weeks of classes, we had our first horse show. To this very day, I can remember vividly how the judges lined us up, six young competitors on our ponies in the middle of the ring, before announcing who had won the show. Upon hearing my name called out first, I was so excited that I almost fell off my little steed … until I realized it was because I had just won the green ribbon for having placed six out of six!

Well, I was resilient and I kept on riding (actually, I think it was because Mom made me keep riding), and before long, our second horse show neared. This time I asked Mom, "How do I win? Mom, I want to win." And she replied, "Mike, do three things: First, ride with your heels down. Second, ride with your shoulders back. And third, every night before you go to bed, pray and ask God to help you do your best." What a great way to put it!

I was psyched. The guru of my life had spoken and told me all I had to do to win. I even remember that during the week that preceded the second show, I actually looked forward each day to the evenings when I could have my conversation with God about winning. And on show day I did, going from worst to first in my little class of riders. Now I don't like to brag (obviously), but ever since then I've won a lot more blue ribbons, literally and figuratively, in a wide variety of endeavors.

Yet today, when I look back to that one week preceding the second horse show, I realize that something else happened every single night during my conversations with God—something I now believe made *all* the difference. During my five- or ten-minute prayers, I was *thinking thoughts of victory*. I could see that blue ribbon in my mind's eye, not the green one. I could hear my name being called last, not first. And I imagined myself receiving that trophy with the little horsey on top. Every night, I was intently visualizing and thinking about winning, *and those thoughts came to pass.*

The next time I knowingly encountered this principle of *thoughts become things* came shortly after graduating from college. I had been hired by Price Waterhouse (P.W.), now Price-WaterhouseCoopers, which at the time was considered the Tiffany's of what used to be the "Big Eight" accounting firms and, to this day, a famous, highly regarded, worldwide operation. Unfortunately for me, my first three months with P.W. were a nightmare. I couldn't do anything right. Everything I touched seemed to unravel. I was a walking disaster, and in that short time, I had accumulated five or six evaluations for each of the major corporate audits I had worked on. The gist of each was the same: "Mike Dooley ... *must* improve."

I don't think I can actually convey to you what an awful episode in my life that was. I was fraught with fear from morning to night that I would be fired from my first job in the real world—a job that had taken months of pounding the pavement to get and a job that I had made sure everyone I had ever known knew I had ...

I remember coming home one day (I was still living with my mother at the time), walking into the living room, and telling Mom with absolute certainty that I was going to get fired. Now, by that time in my life I was already onto the idea of *thoughts become things*, yet it wasn't until I heard myself say, "Mom, I'm going to get fired ... I know I'm going to get fired," that the proverbial light went on. Suddenly I realized the dire *thoughts* I'd been thinking virtually nonstop over the past few months—thoughts that were only making matters much worse.

I immediately went to the living room couch, laid down, closed my eyes, and began visualizing. Now, this may not sound too difficult, but when you're a bad auditor, just *how* do you imagine yourself behaving as a good auditor? After all, a bad auditor doesn't know what a good auditor does, or he wouldn't be a bad auditor!

Here's what I visualized, and it's what you can visualize whenever you don't know *how* to achieve an end result: I simply thought *exclusively* of the end result, not giving one moment's thought to *how* I would get there. I didn't close my eyes and see myself performing audits I didn't know how to perform. Instead, I saw myself walking up and down the hallways of P.W. beaming with joy, thrilled to be alive, and happy to be at work. I saw myself saying "Hi!" to all the partners and staff, and in my mind's eye I saw them actually saying "Hi" back to me (which, at that time, wasn't happening). From that day on, as soon as I got home from work each day, I did my little visualization exercise.

Three weeks later the phone in the office staff area rang. Even though there were fifteen of us working as entry-level audit staffers, I knew the call was for me because I was the only one not assigned to an audit team out in the field ... And not only was the call for me but it was from the head of human resources. As sweat beaded on my forehead and my heart began pounding, he told me that the firm's tax department was shorthanded going into its busiest season of the year, and with some hesitation he added that the audit department "wouldn't mind" loaning me to the tax department.

No, this wasn't good news! Like all new auditors, the tax department struck me as a terrifyingly complex place, a whole other world, but I had no choice. I was loaned to the tax department.

Yet in what seemed like no time at all, I *was* walking up and down the hallways of P.W. just beaming with joy. It turned out that the tax department loved me, and I loved being in the tax department. My short-term loan became a permanent transfer, and from that day forward my career at P.W. took off.

I simply thought *exclusively* of the end result, not giving one moment's thought to *how* I would get there.

Finally, no longer under the guillotine of fear that I would be fired from my first job in the "real" world, I was at last able to start thinking *thoughts* about thriving instead of just surviving. And one of the things I did back then, to help me *think thoughts* about thriving, was create a little scrapbook to help me visualize every conceivable detail of my dreamed-of life. Very simply, I took some blank white sheets of copy machine paper (compliments of P.W., no doubt), and on each page I pasted a photograph of something I wanted, usually cut from advertisements in magazines.

The photos included fancy watches, nice homes, condominiums, expensive cars, and international destinations such as London, Paris, Hong Kong, and Tokyo. Traveling abroad was actually one of my long-range goals, mainly because I had no reason to believe I could do it as a young man fresh out of college. But I figured that since I was crafting my dream life, I might as well include it all. Wow, was I wrong! Completely underestimating the incredible power of thought.

Dreams Do Come True

Ten months later, while attending a P.W. training session in Reston, Virginia, I learned for the first time that every year the firm offered a few foreign assignments to select individuals. This session was at the very end of November that year, just a few days before Thanksgiving. Six weeks later, just after the start of the New Year, I was based and living in the sunny capital city of ... Riyadh, Saudi Arabia.

Now, this may not sound like a dream come true to you, and I have to admit that I hadn't pasted any photos of the Middle East into my scrapbook, nor had I even *heard* of Riyadh six weeks before calling it "home." But I *had* been visualizing the end result I was after—my dreamed-of life—and looking back, I don't think anything else, all other things considered, could have gotten me there quicker.

During my stay in Saudi Arabia, I accumulated enough vacation, "banked" overtime, and floating holidays to have three months of paid time off. Plus, the assignment included hardship pay and an airfare allowance for home leave every six months, which I could use to go anywhere in the world that I wanted. And I wanted!

I traveled around the world twice, visiting every city and country on this planet that I had ever dreamed of in Africa, Asia, and the South Seas. And my heart nearly missed a beat one morning while having breakfast at the Regent Hotel in Kowloon, Hong Kong. Oblivious in one moment, thunderstruck in the next, looking up from my coffee through the two-story plate-glass windows that surrounded me, suddenly I recognized that I was sitting in front of the exact same view of Hong Kong Island that I had cut and pasted into my little scrapbook just two years earlier.

When my tour of duty in the Middle East was finished, I received my first-choice city for repatriation. I bought a really cool condo in downtown Boston, and I walked through Faneuil Hall to and from work every day. Eighteen months later, upon receiving notice of my impending promotion to manager, a distinction revered second only to becoming a partner, I decided to move on and follow another dream: to become an entrepreneur. The only problem was that I had no idea *how* to become an entrepreneur or what my business would offer.

My job—our job—is first and foremost to simply define the dream, specifically *the end result*, in every imaginable detail.

Fortunately, my life's lessons by that time had clearly shown me that in order to make a dream come true, you don't have to know *how* it will come true—that in fact the *hows* are the domain of the Universe. My job—our job—is first and foremost to simply define the dream, specifically *the end result*, in every imaginable detail.

So I defined my dream of running my own company, quit P.W., sold my condo, and moved to Orlando, Florida. Within a few months I teamed up with my brother, a graphic artist, and my mother, who's very cool, and we launched TUT Enterprises Inc.: "Totally Unique T-shirts." Over the next ten years, the three of us sold over one million of them.

I could burn through the next eleven chapters telling you more stories of adventures and misadventures that were all preceded by my thoughts and still not tell you everything. But you know who else could do that, don't you? You. Because whether or not you know about this principle doesn't affect how well it works.

Your thoughts have always become the things of your life; they're doing it right now, and they're going to continue doing it for as long as you think them. But maybe, rather than looking at your own life for proof (because sometimes we're not always as objective with ourselves as we'd like to be), look around at the lives of your friends, family members, coworkers, and neighbors to see the evidence of how their fortunes and misfortunes parallel their thinking.

And while you're thinking of other people, think of the ones who currently live in wealth and abundance. If you don't know many wealthy people, think of celebrities or media personalities—rock stars, actors, sales legends—and ask yourself, "What *one thing* do they all have in common (besides cash)?!"

Did they all go to Harvard and get an MBA? I doubt it. Many of my wealthy friends were lucky to finish high school. Were they all born into wealthy, well-connected families? Hardly. At least not the ones I know. Were they all blessed with high IQs, either intellectually or emotionally? Oh, please. We all know a lot of dumb rich people, right? I mean, all you have to do is turn on your television to see them! So what, then, what one thing, besides cash, do they all have in common?

At a minimum, they all believed that "it" could happen to them. And once you believe something, whether justified or not, "right" or "wrong," you cannot help but *think thoughts* along the lines of your beliefs. Our thoughts mirror our beliefs (which we'll talk more about later). And once you've *thought thoughts*, what happens next? They strive to become the things and events of your life. It's the law.

Now think of the wealthy people you know who possess perhaps half, or less than half, of your intelligence, charm, and good looks (I'm sure you can think of someone), yet who earn at least double your salary each year. And ask yourself, why? How could this be? Aren't we all made of the same stuff—flesh and bone with beating hearts and coursing red blood? In fact, there's absolutely nothing different between you and those you think about, nor is there anything different between you and me. We're all exactly the same except for one thing: our thoughts. One life can go "this way" and another "that way," and in the end, won't it always be because of the different thoughts each person chose?

I expect that you're mostly on board, perhaps thinking, "Yeah, it's true. I can buy that. Thoughts do become things, attitude is everything, and we make our own reality; I've always been a positive person." But I don't think you get it—not yet—because I don't think you can yet fathom that there is *never* any exception to this principle. *Thoughts become things*; there are no mitigating factors, there are no exceptions—your thoughts account for every wonderful and "difficult" thing that's ever happened to you. In fact, your thoughts are the only reason that *anything* has ever happened, or not happened, in your life.

Removing Any Doubt

I realize this may sound extreme and hardcore, but I'm deliberately pushing you to your limit. I want you to reach the end of your ability to comprehend this principle and force you to admit that you've got some issues with it. Why? Because by facing our issues, whatever they are, we can then blast through them and better understand the truth. Life is knowable; your questions have answers, but only if you know enough to ask them. Then by fully understanding this principle, we can then put it to use, without doubting ourselves or thinking that perhaps there are other forces at play that might undermine our efforts.

So unless you've previously dwelled on this principle as an "absolute," there are very likely two major obstacles that prevent you from fully comprehending that it's your *thoughts* that *entirely* create your reality.

"Why Haven't I Won the Lottery Yet?"

You could fairly ask, "Well, Mike, if *thoughts become things* is as predictable as gravity, then what about those dreams of ours that have never seen the light of day? Why haven't I won the lottery yet?" The first objection, then, is that there have been things you've wanted in your life—things you've "badly" wanted, things you perhaps *thought about* for months or maybe even years on end—that never came to pass.

The answer is very simple. We never want just one thing, do we? Nor do we ever think just one thought. In fact, scientists now tell us that each and every day of our life we can think more than sixty thousand unique thoughts! Well, whenever we're thinking this many thoughts, isn't there a possibility—even a great likelihood—that some of our thoughts may contradict one another or even be mutually exclusive?

For example, you might yearn for the top spot on the corporate ladder, thinking about it month in and month out, year in and year out; visualizing the corner office; imagining yourself making big decisions and marshalling the "troops." But if at the same time you're thinking these kinds of thoughts you also come home from work each day and greet your spouse with "No one at work has any idea of how valuable I really am," or "No one at work truly appreciates the difference I could make," then those thoughts must also do what all thoughts do: strive to become part of your reality. So the person who thinks he's underappreciated typically *becomes* underappreciated, which is not a very good place to be if you also see yourself climbing to the top of the corporate ladder.

Indeed, there are subtle nuances affecting your manifestations that *may* lead some outcomes to seemingly have an upper hand over other outcomes, yet all these nuances can be summed up in three words: "your other thoughts." And these *other thoughts* on life, people, and happiness perhaps received more repetition, were backed with greater feelings and more expectation, or were acted upon more than the thoughts that have not yet manifested.

To give you another example, let's say that you now regularly visualize living in wealth and abundance, imagining yourself living in a big house, driving a fancy car, and traveling the world in style. Yet if all your life, and still to this day, you've believed and thought (whether you realize it or not) that people with money are not spiritual people or that big money means big problems ... well, you can't have your cake and eat it too! Money is either wonderful and good and you want some or it's bad and evil and you want to avoid it. Entertaining thoughts from both camps can put you somewhere in the middle, simply stagnating with neither too much nor too little.

So you see, it's possible that your thoughts may conflict with one another without you even being aware of it. I'll talk more about how to pin down your thoughts and get focused later, but the point right now is that it's because of such conflicts that there have been times in your life that you did not get what you wanted. Nevertheless, the thoughts that did "win out" were also yours. The lesson here is that just because you haven't always received what you most wanted doesn't mean you didn't get what you were thinking about. The reason some of your thoughts have not yet come to pass is because *other thoughts of yours have*, and they got in the way.

"Whose Thoughts Were Those?!"

The second major obstacle likely preventing you from fully understanding that your *thoughts become things* comes from the fact that throughout your life there have been unexpected things that you *did* get—experiences you've had, some pleasant and others sworn to secrecy, that you never, ever thought about ahead of time. Now, you might want to ask, "Well, Mike Dooley, if *thoughts become things* is as predictable as gravity, *whose* thoughts were those?!"

Here's an example of how this works. I like to visit South Beach, Miami, for short weekend getaways. I love the energy in Miami, its emerging culture, and its diverse people. For me, Orlando is "point A"—my present location—and Miami is "point B"—the goal, the end result, the destination I am *thinking* about. Well, for me to get from point A to point B, there must be a journey. This journey will inevitably be made up of some *unthought-of* territory, such as whether or not traffic will cooperate, where the turnpike might be under construction and detoured, where I'll stop for rest or gas, and what smiling or frowning faces I'll see in the cars I pass or that pass me. Yet all these *unthought-of* experiences in my journey are necessary in order to get me to my destination. And the same kind of *unthought-of* experiences occur on journeys set into motion whenever we think new thoughts.

Whenever you think a new thought, it has to deal with where you currently are in your life in order to take you where your new thinking lies. And in getting you from point A to point B, you'll very often have to be drawn through *unthought-of* territory, which is not to imply that absolutely anything could happen on such journeys. Anything and everything that does happen would be predicated on *all your other thoughts* about life, people, and the journey.

For example, let's say you're thinking thoughts about more love, joy, and laughter coming into your life. To get more or less of anything or to affect any kind of change in your life, your thoughts will need to take you on a journey through time and space, through the material world, so that circumstances can exist for the fruition of your dreams. And how might your thoughts do this?

Well, you might "accidentally" bump into a long-lost friend and renew the friendship, which in turn branches into many more friendships, and you're off! Or you might "coincidentally" find a stray dog or cat that you adopt, who adds immeasurably to the joy in your life for years to come. Alternatively, through a string of what appear to be "misfortunes," you might be forced to relocate to an entirely new town that you subsequently adore.

You see, whenever something unexpected or *unthought of* falls onto our path, it's *always* a stepping stone in a journey to a "place" that we have been thinking about, because in time and space, as you well know, there are no accidents and coincidences.

For accidents and coincidences to exist, we'd be robbed of our power; it couldn't then be said that we have dominion over all things or that we are divine, supernatural creators; there'd have to be caveats for luck or mistakes or fate. It would mean that we could only be cocreators of our most intimate and personal experiences. It would mean that anything could happen next, in spite of our best efforts—in fact, in spite of our existence at all. Just as a chain can only be as strong as its weakest link, for a reality to exist where we might at times be without even .0001 percent of our incredible power, it would mean, at times, we'd have 0 percent power. And even if for only a few seconds of our entire life we might have zero power (and those seconds could randomly appear at key pivotal times or crossroads), the effect could approximate having zero power throughout our entire life, *perhaps defeating the entire point of our existence.* No way. Life is far too amazing, majestic, and perfect for accidents and coincidences to exist that would rob us of our freedom, glory, and power.

On the other end of the analytical spectrum, however, just because "everything matters" doesn't translate into "everything has profound meaning." It all matters in the sense that every thought, word, and feeling of ours lends itself to creation. However, any particular thought, such as "My friends are usually late," "@#$% happens," or "Guys lie," may or may not have a meaningful impact on your life, given all your other thoughts, some of which may contradict these statements. For example, while stubbing your toe in the middle of the night would never be an "accident," neither would it necessarily have a profound meaning. Its significance and meaning would depend on the confluence of all your thoughts, profound and trite alike.

**Whenever something unexpected or
unthought of falls onto our path, it's *always*
a stepping stone in a journey to a "place"
that we have been thinking about.**

Where to Begin?

Working with your thoughts means becoming aware of your thoughts and knowing what they are. Sometimes this can be a daunting task, particularly when you realize that all day long you're thinking away without ever really thinking about what you're thinking about! And then there are those hidden beliefs of yours—beliefs you don't even know you have—that are responsible for generating their own nearly invisible thoughts. Yikes! Where to begin?

Just do what you can. Your life is already filled with challenges, right? At work or at home, no matter what you do, you're always dealing with the unexpected, and frankly, it's not always easy. We've all been through times when we wished we could just quit that job or relationship, walk away, and never look back, but most of the time we don't. Why?

We don't because we know that no matter how challenging certain situations can be, their rewards, or the anticipated upside for seeing them through, are greater. We know that if we at least do what we can, things will get better; they *always* do. And the same is true when it comes to working with your thoughts. You just do it! You do what you can.

Visualization: Pictures (or Feelings) in Your Mind

If you can begin to grasp that your world does indeed revolve around the thoughts you choose, then it becomes a no-brainer to realize that at least sometimes, preferably daily, it would be helpful to deliberately "think" the kind of thoughts you'd like to experience. I recommend starting with visualization, as anyone can set aside five minutes a day to visualize and it doesn't cost a thing. Here are four rules I follow that help me visualize:

1. *Don't overdo it.* Never visualize for more than five minutes at a time, because it's too easy to start daydreaming and get sidetracked if you try to do it longer. It's better to have an intense five minutes than a poor fifteen or thirty; quality is far more important than quantity. When I visualized five minutes a day about turning around my career at P.W., that five minutes was up against all-day-long worrying and fretting about getting fired, yet it won out. The reason those five minutes prevailed despite the huge imbalance is because of our natural inclination to succeed (there's more about this in chapter 6, "Magical Universe"), which makes visualizing all the more powerful.

2. *Be gentle with yourself.* Go easy. Have patience. Don't get mad at yourself if you find your thoughts turning negative or if you find that you sometimes worry throughout the day. I know what it's like: You're driving down the road, having an argument with someone in your mind, or you're worried that things aren't going as well as you'd like at work or at home. When you start becoming aware of your thinking, you'll start catching yourself a lot more often with some pretty surprising thoughts, and this can even happen while you visualize. That's okay! At least you're becoming aware in ways that you never were before, and this is a great starting point. Even when I was visualizing happily walking up and down the hallways of P.W., *I would still catch myself worrying about getting fired.* What did I do? What *could* I do? I just did what I could: I pressed on with my visualizing and did my best—and it was enough.

3. *Feel the joy.* If you want to really energize and supercharge your thoughts, add emotion to them. Not all thoughts are the same. True, they all strive to become things, but apart from that, thoughts have different intensity levels; emotion is what turns up the volume. *Emotion is pure power*, and when combined with visualizing, it makes things happen a whole lot faster. Feel the emotions related to whatever it is you want. Feel the excitement, the joy, the pleasure, the victory, or whatever it is that will accompany your thoughts' manifestation.

Audience members often ask me what they should do if they are unable to see images in their mind's eye. I tell them not to worry, as they're perhaps even at an advantage. I tell them to drop the images entirely in exchange for clarity on the *feelings* they wish to feel. The more you can feel the joy, the faster the physical details of your life will fall into place yielding your manifestation.

4. *Don't visualize more than once or twice a day.* First of all, your life and happiness spring from the present, not the future, and by dwelling too much on your hopes for tomorrow, you could easily begin taking for granted all that you already have to be happy about. Secondly, if you dwell too much on your dreams coming true, you may become more and more aware, or conscious, of the difference between where you are today and where you want to go. The distance between where you now are and where you want to be may seem overwhelming, and you may begin to doubt yourself, lose confidence, and quit visualizing altogether.

What Would You Wish For?

This principle of *thoughts become things* is the be-all and end-all of how to live the life of your dreams. It's really the only rule that matters, and understanding its existence is the first step in mastering your life and living your dreams. You don't have to understand *how* it really works. You just have to understand that it *does* work. Unfailingly. Never lose sight of that. Never let it go. And as you keep this understanding in the forefront of your mind, proof of its existence will surface in your life, and you'll realize that it's been there all along.

> *Emotion is pure power*, **and when combined with visualizing, it makes things happen a whole lot faster.**

Your awareness of this principle, substantiated with your own evidence that it works, will empower you; you'll believe in yourself and in your inherent ability to deliberately change the course of your life. You'll pursue your dreams with a greater confidence than you have ever felt before. Why? Because you'll understand that the number one requirement for their realization is simply that you dream them! And what could be easier than that?

Now, before this chapter ends, I want to ask you a question, and I want you to be completely selfish when you answer it.

If you could have just one wish granted—any wish, anything you can imagine—what would you wish for? Would you wish for a billion dollars? Would you wish for health? Would you wish for love? Would you wish for a million more wishes? What would you wish for?

Well, if you have read carefully, *really carefully*, and you now truly understand that your thoughts become the things and events of your life, then I know what you wished for. There's really only one thing you would logically wish for. I know that you would wish for things to be exactly as they are now, so that you could remain alive in a kingdom that you rule with the thoughts you choose to think, and where you have indeed been given dominion over all things ... right? Because you now understand that living as a creation, among your own creations as we do here in the jungles of time and space, is as good as it gets.

Thoughts become things! There are no preconditions, there is no hidden agenda, and there are no unknown variables working against you in this Garden of Eden, this paradise amongst paradises, where each of us is indeed master of our destiny.

2

Beliefs

*A*nything that affects our thinking affects our lives. And nothing else affects our thinking more than our beliefs. In this chapter, I'll touch on the fundamentals of how our beliefs shape our thoughts and thus our world.

Thinking Is Believing

Day in and day out, we're always unavoidably thinking thoughts, and surprisingly, we're hardly aware of what most of them are. Yet as we perpetually think these thoughts, we also perpetually visualize, anticipate, expect, and, ultimately, manifest the life we lead. We unconsciously yet effortlessly breathe life into all our experiences, giving little, if any, attention to our thoughts and the mechanics involved. And so it should be. But what we ought to at least become aware of is that it's our normal everyday thoughts and wandering imagination that compose most of our thoughts, so it's these thoughts that are responsible for bringing about most of our experiences.

So the billion-dollar question is, "How can I direct the stream of my countless daily thoughts so they work to serve my needs and desires?" And the billion-dollar answer is, "By aligning your beliefs with the life of your dreams."

As one believes, so shall one think.

In other words, to master your thoughts and imagination, and therefore your life and destiny, you must first master their captain—your beliefs. By ensuring that your beliefs about reality and your place in it are in alignment with your dreams, you can rest assured that you will naturally and automatically be thinking the "good" thoughts, even when you're not paying attention. And these in turn will become the things and events of your life.

Believing Is Thinking

To begin with, what are beliefs? Let me give you a few examples by asking you some simple questions that can be answered with two or three descriptive words. First, what do you think of people in general? For instance, are they kind, trustworthy, and good-hearted, or are they shallow, naive, and lazy? Okay. Now, what do you think of life in general? Is it easy, hard, exciting, or boring? And good health? Is it elusive or predictable, and do you have it or do you wish you did? And tell me about yourself. Are you creative, stubborn, determined, carefree, or disappointed?

No matter how you answered those questions, you've just shared with me some of your beliefs. Here's the catch: you think your answers are simply innocent observations about your reality and yourself, but instead they've actually helped *create* your reality. If you think life is hard, for example, it becomes hard. It *wasn't* hard to begin with, not until you started thinking it was. Over time, however, you stopped seeing this observation as "your opinion" and began seeing it as a fact of life, and thus the belief was born.

We have thousands of beliefs. They're not all undesirable, but they do become the *de facto* police officers of our thoughts. They create rules for our thinking, and these rules are the most rigid ones we live by. You see, apart from what would be a very short list of life's "absolutes," or "Truths of Being," there are almost no rules. Here's a brief list of these absolutes, or truths, which I have deduced from my own life experiences and observations:

The Truths of Being: Life's Absolutes

We are all One (of One, of God, divine, interconnected). Nothing can exist outside of God or be "non-God." To be non-God, where would it come from; *what would it be made of?* This is perhaps the most basic, most obvious truth. It's easy to deduce with the slightest contemplation, leading to the obvious conclusion, espoused by many religions, that there has only ever been, and therefore could only ever be, One God. All that is seen, and all that is unseen, is pure God. Every grain of sand, the vacuums of space, every thought, *every one of us*, is pure God. It's only been our virtually exclusive reliance upon our physical senses to interpret reality and to pass judgment that makes this tricky to grasp, and that leads us to want to see everything in duality. We see life as either/or, as black or white, causing some to assume that if there's a God, there must be something opposite of God. There isn't; there can't be.

Thoughts become things (We are Creators). Literally, our thoughts, *being pure God* for the prior truth, have an energy and a "life force" all their own. Our thoughts are "alive," aware, and active. This is not to imply they have humanlike characteristics, just as we don't generally ascribe such characteristics to a zebra or a rose (even though both are pure God), but our thoughts have their own brand of awareness and their own characteristics and properties of consciousness. Within time and space, one such property is that our thoughts immediately, "intelligently," seek to be physically manifested. Seen through the prism of time: God becomes consciousness, becomes awareness, becomes thought, becomes matter—such transformations neither diminish "It," nor make "It" any less God.

Life (Consciousness, God, energy; we ourselves) is eternal. We are the creators of this illusory dimension of time (Einstein himself called it relative), so we must exist "before" it and we will exist "after" it. Granted, this may again stretch those who rely exclusively upon their physical senses to interpret reality, but doesn't our mere essence, our mere existence, being clearly independent of our physical bodies (evidenced by the nighttime dream state, *countless* near-death and out-of-body reports, and our stream of waking consciousness, none of which can logically be the product of our cells, atoms, and molecules) make this obvious? And if our awareness is independent of our body, it must then be independent of space and therefore independent of time. (Time is simply an attribute, or a measure, of space; they are one and the same, like an X and a Y axis that creates a plane. Without time, you cannot have space and vice versa.)

There is only Love (There is only God). Similar to, if not the same as, the first truth, this phraseology allows us to introduce the concept of love. Mustn't some form of love—divine love, undoubtedly far beyond what we practice as human love—be the motivation and reason behind *all* reality? Without love, which is a form of caring, why bother creating worlds and developing consciousness? Furthermore, when it comes to infinite Divine Intelligence, or the Creator of all "things," could there possibly exist even the tiniest pocket in reality that was forgotten, tainted, or miscreated into anything that wasn't full of divine love? This brings us to the next truth.

It's all good (Everything is exactly as it "should" be). Again, similar to prior truths above yet stated this way, this absolute allows for another concept to be addressed: "chance." In Divine Mind, even while all things remain possible, with infinite possibilities for expansion into unimaginable realms, in the deepest sense, ultimate outcomes, such as growing, learning, and remaining One with Divine Mind after the adventure, were *not* left to chance. There's no possibility for mistake, accident, *should have, maybe,* or *hope so* because the *general* potentials for development were all seen and understood at a higher level before our adventure began. As an analogy, while there exists an infinite number of roads to Rome, none of them change Rome. And just because to us, from our extremely limited perspectives, it seems that bad things happen, in the grandest scheme of things this becomes an impossible conclusion. Further, taking into account that we are pure God, pure energy, eternal, living in an adventure-dreamworld of our own creation, and that *no matter what happens* in this adventure we all return to our celestial source, wiser, whole, enriched, and all powerful. The only conclusion that exists is that "it's" truly *all good.*

This list is not meant to be all inclusive, as each of these truths could have a number of spin-offs, such as those offered in the parentheses, but the list is sufficient to obtain a solid grasp on the nature of our reality and to begin applying our power to fantastic effect. I'd also like to point out that of these truths, only one has a moving part, a variable: Thoughts Become Things. *And look who's thinking now.*

These truths are absolute; they are for us like water is to a fish: indisputable givens. They are immovable. They exist *even in the absence of belief in them,* creating the stage we live our lives upon. Of course, it could be said that these are merely my beliefs, and frankly, I have very little concrete evidence to convince you that they are true, especially since they're not physically measurable. But must something be physically measurable to know *with certainty* of its existence? Is not being able to physically prove you dreamed of a red Corvette last night proof that you didn't? Is it unreasonable to ask that we look at our own lives for evidence of these truths? Is it not evident that my postulated absolutes are each empowering; that I do not have an "agenda" other than to free you from self-imposed limitations; that, unlike many religious doctrines, I exclude no one, under any circumstances, from the beauty of these truths? Do they not resonate deep within you? Have they not been uttered and shared by countless others throughout the ages, using words and metaphors that fit the times?

If this kind of thinking is new for you, you may well have some hesitation in accepting it. But I can tell you that as an extreme student of life, in the past thirty years I have thought of and sought out every imaginable challenge to these absolutes. And with time, and through expanding my own thinking wildly outside of the box, they have withstood every assault; moreover, I can use them to understand and handily explain any life scenario.

**To master your thoughts and imagination,
and therefore your life and destiny, you must first
master their captain—your beliefs.**

Within these truths—actually, *because* of these truths—we are limitless in virtually any way we can imagine unless we *believe* otherwise, and then, suddenly, we've got rules, limits, and conditions. Even while these absolutes will not bend (because they don't bend), the experiences and manifestations they make possible *have* to.

The tricky aspect of beliefs is that, without our even knowing it, they limit what we "allow" ourselves to think and, therefore, what we can then manifest into our lives. They obscure the fact that "things" could be different. For instance, if you believe that life's deepest secrets can't be or aren't meant to be known by mortal minds, then not only will you not dwell on life's meaning and block out new thoughts that could have drawn such answers to you, but your perceptions of what you do observe in life will be tunneled by your belief, zeroing you in on only the evidence that supports your theory.

You might even say to yourself that you're open to contradictory evidence, yet if you don't *believe* it could exist based on your first belief, any "evidence" will be diminished and rationalized away. So your beliefs act like filters through which your every thought must be sifted, but these filters are invisible—invisible but not unknowable.

Beliefs Rule

Let's pretend that beliefs are like tinted sunglasses and that your vision through those glasses represents the thoughts you entertain through the filters of your beliefs. Doesn't everything look different, colorwise, when you put on those glasses? Yet after you have them on awhile, you don't even know you're wearing them. In fact, it's hard to remember what things looked like without them, and the only way to remember is to take them off.

Continuing this analogy, let's imagine that everyone in the world wears sunglasses and that no two people have exactly the same tint; everyone is wearing something different. Some wear BluBlocker sunglasses that make everything look yellow, while some wear red blockers, green blockers, and *billions* of varieties in between. Now, does the fact that everyone is wearing different sunglasses have any effect on reality, on what people see, or just on *how* they see it? Isn't it possible that some people will see colors—even "things"— that are impossible for others to see? And isn't it often easier to see the glasses others wear than it is to see our own? I think you get the idea.

Beliefs are exactly the same in this regard. Most of the time we don't even know we have them, let alone how they're operating, which isn't *necessarily* a bad thing. When our beliefs are in alignment with our dreams, they'll serve us, but if they're not, big problem! Fortunately, beliefs are similar to sunglasses in that we don't have to wear the ones we don't like.

Beliefs create a matrix of sorts, arranging and processing our thoughts, systematically and without judgment, and giving us, in effect, a permission mechanism *to think* or *not to think* along certain lines. For instance, you might want something with all your heart and soul, but without believing it is possible, you simply will not and cannot maintain the *thoughts* necessary to bring it to fruition. This explains why it's your hopes and fears you believe to be the *most plausible* that you usually manifest, because they've been "allowed" the most play in your mind. The thoughts that exist just outside how you define plausible, whether outrageously wonderful or diabolically awful, are generally *not* manifested because they're far too difficult to believe in, and therefore too difficult to clearly imagine and *feel*.

Take a moment to notice what kind of thoughts you think when you're driving your car or running errands. Do you automatically see yourself being interviewed by *Time* magazine? Do you see yourself winning the Nobel Peace Prize? Do you imagine buying a vacation home in some exotic country halfway around the globe? Not likely. Nor, I imagine, do you think about absolute doom and destruction, unending misery and pain, or destitution and poverty. You don't think these thoughts because they're not in alignment with your beliefs, which explains why most people's lives generally stay about the same! We keep thinking the same kinds of thoughts in line with our relatively unchanging beliefs. This is also why the rich get richer and the poor get poorer—not because of a truth about capitalism or a statement about our society, but because they keep thinking the same kinds of thoughts they've always been thinking: either abundance or its lack, *based upon their underlying beliefs*.

Pace Yourself

Let me follow this line of thinking with a suggestion, since virtually all our own beliefs form an interrelated mosaic with themselves: When there's something you want *right away*, don't set your goal too high, because you may not believe in it enough to begin visualizing it properly and regularly. I think you know what I mean. I'm not saying don't dream big, or even huge; I'm just saying pace yourself and give yourself some intermediary goals too.

For example, if right now you're driving a Toyota Corolla, you could probably better imagine owning a Mercedes as your next car than a Lamborghini. Once you get your Mercedes, aim higher and higher. All the while, of course, an exotic import can still be on your list of cars to own one day, though *not necessarily* with an insistence that it be next month. By staging your dreams this way, it's even possible that your dream of eventually owning an "exotic" will enhance your dream of owning a Mercedes, as the Mercedes will be seen as an exciting stepping stone that will make even greater things possible. Plus, if you insist on the Lamborghini first and you don't get it due to a maze of interrelated, conflicting beliefs, then you may just write off visualization altogether as a waste of your time.

Similarly, if you never take vacations but would like to, perhaps begin by imagining yourself at Disney World rather than Luxor, Egypt. If you're sick and bedridden, perhaps imagine yourself gardening, cooking, or shopping, rather than winning marathons. If you're bored and lonely, imagine a friend and a happy outing, rather than walking the red carpet at the Academy Awards.

Follow your feelings when setting goals. Be moderately reasonable *for the short-term goals* and, when you can, strive to understand any emotional resistance you encounter, because this resistance means you've hit some limiting beliefs that need exploring. On the other hand, if you make your goals too easy, they won't inspire you, and your visualizations of them may lack emotion. Inspire yourself, just not to the point of getting psyched out.

Believing Leads to Feeling, and Feeling Makes It Happen Faster

Beliefs also spark emotion, which, as you know from the previous chapter, helps supercharge the power of your thoughts. For instance, when beliefs about a particular "something" are strong enough, anticipation and expectation are aroused, accelerating the manifestation process. When you truly believe in something—good or bad—you repeatedly turn the thought over and over in your mind. With such repetition, you're then almost helplessly drawn to *further* imagine the joy or pain you associate with its manifestation, emotionally making the picture in your mind all the more real. The more real it is, the faster the manifestation.

Eventually, if the belief is strong enough, you'll also begin physically preparing for the manifestation of its related thoughts without even noticing what you're doing. For example, your body is in preparation mode when your adrenaline races before a big event: when you begin noticing new homes before you've even decided to sell your old one; when you start looking for clothes one size smaller or larger than you presently wear; or when you mentally recite, or even talk aloud to yourself, the lines of some anticipated argument.

These are examples of how your beliefs kick your thinking, feeling, and behavioral processes into high gear. And then, because of the underlying principle of *thoughts become things*, look out! Once these images are repeatedly turned over in your mind, combined with the expectation and emotion that have also been sparked by your beliefs, the manifestation of your dream, or the dread, becomes virtually inevitable. It *is* that easy. And here's the kicker: You already do this all day, every day. There's no practice or regimen that needs to be followed. You don't have to start learning something new. You can just keep doing what you've always been doing. But by becoming aware of your miraculous feats of material manipulation, you can begin planting, feeding, and cultivating the thoughts that will blossom into your tomorrows.

You Make Time and Space Look Good!

You are the artist who never sleeps, continually yet unconsciously rearranging the images on your life's canvas with brush strokes of thought, painting as brilliantly or haphazardly as your beliefs allow. And here's the best part: There's nothing magical about the manifestation of thought. It's one of the steadfast principles of time and space, and it operates without exception. It works the same whether you're rich or poor; it works whether you're healthy or sick; *it works whether you know about it or not*. Yet once you know about it, you can then immediately start deliberately using it to your advantage.

Manifesting your thoughts into reality is nothing new, but what is magical is when someone dares to dream—when someone has the courage to think new thoughts, set goals that are presently out of his or her immediate reach, and possess the audacity to believe that they will come to pass.

The Courage to Dream

Thoughts turning into things is how time and space operates. The same rules apply to all, but taking that initial leap from the known into the unknown invokes the secret behind all creation. In one golden moment, when you've given wings to a dream that has only to land, the real work—daring to imagine—is done. The stereotypical beliefs of society and the dogmas of time, which want to confine our thinking to the safety of thoughts already thought, tell us to be conservative, prudent, and careful. But *why*? What is there to be afraid of? We are spiritual beings, eternal beings, and nothing we ever do can change that! Dare to dream, believe in that dream, and then the humdrum process of manifestation begins. Spectacular thoughts take form just as the mundane do, and with the same amount of effort!

You are the artist who never sleeps, continually yet unconsciously rearranging the images on your life's canvas with brush strokes of thought.

Equally amazing as daring to dream is when someone deliberately uses his imagination—his thoughts—as a tool to reach his dreams. I often wonder why more people don't spend time visualizing, despite it being recognized worldwide as a powerful tool. I've come to the conclusion that it's because they simply do not yet understand the principle of *thoughts become things*. So few realize how shockingly powerful their thoughts are and that with the same amount of discipline as it takes for them to brush their teeth each day, they can begin the process of making their dreams come true. Only a few intense minutes are necessary, just once a day, to spark the greatest of material breakthroughs, and it's all in keeping with the rules. Even if it were possible to cheat, could life be any easier than getting what you think about?

The Forbidden Fruit

So where do beliefs come from? Beliefs about anything within time and space actually stem from the Western concept of "original sin," which was this: seeing the illusions of time and space as something independent of ourselves. This means believing that the apple was "real" (demonstrated by biting into it) instead of a reflection of an inner spiritual world from which all experiences first dwell. Because we began seeing the world as separate or independent of ourselves, we decided that for our own safety, comfort, and pleasure we must understand this outer world first. We labeled, categorized, and concluded that life is this, that, and the other thing, and because we thought like that, it *became* like this, that, and the other thing; our time and space beliefs were born. The apple and all such illusions began to take on a "reality" seemingly independent of us, even though we were and still are their unwitting creator and perpetuator—a reality we then needed to react to as we moved through our lives, giving our illusions a power and an independence they could not have without us.

We've failed or forgotten thus far to see ourselves as the creators we are. This means that we're stuck, living within the confines of our beliefs, which we think define the world. In reality however, they define only our thoughts and *perceptions* of the world. And so the "sins" (honest mistakes) of the parent are handed down to the child, generation after generation. As a toddler you adopted the beliefs of those who nurtured and protected you. Just as you consumed the applesauce they fed you daily, so did you unquestioningly accept their beliefs. You had no choice; it was survival. However, as you grew into a young boy or girl and began developing a mind of your own, so too did you begin developing your own beliefs. Not understanding even then that you manifested your thoughts to begin with, you began defining not life itself but what *your* life would become.

Of course, the beliefs of your parents and caretakers, as well as the culture and era you were born into, have a lot to do with your personal beliefs and thus the thoughts you will choose to think and therefore the life you will lead. For instance, if a predominant belief of your family or community was that God lived outside you, or apart from you, and that He judged and punished people, then each time you saw misfortune you'd see it as proof that there was such a God. You'd automatically filter all your experiences through this belief, not even realizing there were any other options. You'd become judgmental of yourself as well, thinking that this is the way of the world. And you'd live with a fear that you weren't measuring up.

Even more shockingly, whenever you encountered evidence that could refute your belief, you would brush it off as unexplainable, or you'd say, "God moves in mysterious ways." It wouldn't matter that in your heart you felt an inexplicable unity with life, or that you sometimes considered yourself to be even more compassionate than your own God, because you'd simply shut out any notions that didn't mesh with your beliefs.

Here's another example: If everyone believed that having wealth and abundance required just the right combination of luck and skill, then it would seem that you, too, must possess just enough skill, at just the right times and in just the right places, in order to come into your own fortune. Because of this thinking, *it would become* a very difficult task. By harboring such a belief, it would become so believable that you would regard it as a fact of life, and you'd begin ignoring the fact that the rich are often ignorant, untalented, or both. You just wouldn't notice their obvious shortcomings—just as they don't notice.

The really good news is that while upbringing can powerfully affect and shape your thoughts, it doesn't mean that you're stuck with those thoughts. You may be stuck with your past, but the future is dependent on what you think here and now, not where you've been.

Beliefs Create Reality

A woman recently approached me after a talk I gave and told me she often wondered at the successes of some of her friends, who are far less spiritual than she (some even greedy in her mind) and completely unaware of life's underlying principles, such as *thoughts become things*. I told her that we all know people like that. These people are gifts in our lives because they serve as irrefutable proof that there's no one sitting around judging us, deciding whether or not we're worthy to have the things we want. We are worthy! *You are worthy!* These people are proof that thoughts *do* become things, no matter who thinks them and no matter why they think them. And here's the best news about people like this: They prove to us that you do not first have to become some kind of perfect, wonderful, selfless "saint" to make progress, grow, and have your dreams come true. You just have to be able to dream and believe in those dreams.

Your beliefs don't just filter your thoughts; they evoke and stimulate your imagination too. The thoughts that either deliberately or unwittingly float through your head each day paint portraits and create scenarios of experiences that await your "arrival." For example, if you've come to believe that people are dishonest and that they'll steal when given the chance, then some of the thoughts you entertain will be affected by this belief. To see this, let's say you're planning a holiday during which your home will be left vacant. While your primary thoughts might be spent planning your travels, your underlying belief about people being dishonest might involuntarily produce mental visions of intruders stealing your belongings while you're away. Of course, this vision, like all the others you entertain, will jockey for its place in time and space, but notice that the belief came first. The belief preceded the mental visualizations of intruders.

In another situation, two people might witness a mugging on a crowded street corner, but when recalling the incident, one might see it as proof of innate human savagery while the other might remember the many caring and concerned bystanders. Both people witnessed the same event, as we witness the events of our lives through the filters of our beliefs, and each drew conclusions from what they saw according to the beliefs they held about reality. Again, their underlying beliefs came first and initiated the thoughts and conclusions that followed. The conclusions then helped validate and reinforce their underlying beliefs.

Up until now you've thought that your beliefs have been defined by your reality, but instead, your reality has been defined by your beliefs. Until now you've given away much of your power to change undesirable circumstances because you've come to think it's you against the world, instead of realizing that *you are your world*. Your world simply mirrors your thoughts, your beliefs, and your expectations, like an echo in a canyon.

What's almost scary is that you can get locked into this syndrome because such beliefs prevent you from imagining beyond their borders. If the Wright brothers hadn't believed human flight was possible, for example, they wouldn't *and couldn't* have spent one minute imagining air travel. Without the belief first, neither the dream nor their plane could have taken off. Your beliefs *permit* or *deny* your dreams.

Seeing the Invisible

Okay, so now you're wondering what your beliefs are and which of them might be limiting. You're also wondering how you can find

41

them if they're really invisible. Well, fear not, because no matter how invisible *they* may be, their results never are.

Much has been said about writing down your beliefs, but this has never really worked for me. I think hunting for beliefs with a pad and paper is like watching the pot that never boils. Plus, I feel I could spend my whole life looking for suspect problem beliefs, some of which I'm not even sure I have, and you know what happens when you start looking for problems—you either find them, and thereby reinforce them with new pictures in your mind, or, if they hadn't existed in the first place, *you start creating them out of thin air* so that you *can* find them. So instead of trying to write down all my beliefs, which, of course, may work just fine for you, I do one of two things: I either "Observe and Dismantle" or I charge ahead with my dreams in an effort to "Bulldoze and Liquefy" any interfering, limiting beliefs.

Observe and Dismantle

Using the Observe and Dismantle approach, I simply do a bit of spying and detective work on myself. I don't do this blatantly, through sessions, or even very consciously. Instead, as I go about my normal daily affairs, I pay close attention to all the things I think, say, and do because these three things reflect what's going on in my mind. If there are limits there, they'll appear in my thoughts, words, and actions.

To give you some examples, have you ever heard yourself say to someone, with a tad bit of envy, "It must be nice"? You're admitting, *even if you're just joking*, that you can't even imagine what it's like having or doing whatever it is, *and you're implying* that you likely won't ever know! Catch yourself the next time you say this, and ask yourself why you believe this object or experience is out of your reach. If you follow your rationale as far as you can into your thoughts, chances are pretty good that you'll bump into your beliefs about it.

Have you ever heard yourself groan when a cashier or techni-
cian adds up a particularly large bill for you? Where's your thinking
then and there? Obviously it's expressing a belief that money is tigh'
or hard to come by, and that the prospect of things changing in thi
regard in the near future is slim to none! And, of course, suc
beliefs, *even when they're accurate reflections of your present ci*
cumstances, will only perpetuate those very circumstances. To spa
change, it must come from within. It must exist in thought, in sp
of the circumstances that presently surround us.

Here's something I've been doing for years whenever I ge
unexpected bill: I say to the person who delivered it, "Phew! C
thing I'm rich!" It usually makes that person laugh, it makes me l:
it takes my mind off any limits, and it's a great affirmation becau
not something I used to believe at every level of my being. By
it again and again, however, it's undoubtedly been one of the
factors contributing to the financial freedom I now enjoy.

Have you ever noticed yourself driving more slowly
gas, price-shopping at the grocery store, or adjusting the
stat in your home to save money? We've all done these
times—myself included—but all these actions typicall'
underlying beliefs in limitation, scarcity, and your inabilit'
and do all you want to have and do. I'm not saying you
be frugal at times, but I am saying that by observing su
iors, you can learn that you have some beliefs about y
that do not reflect the truth. You might say it's not a
your resources really are limited, and I'd agree. But w/
resources limited when your whole life is proof that y
world where your *thoughts become things*? Why are
trouble focusing on wealth and abundance, or convers
you focusing on lack and limits? Of course, the answ
questions may seem elusive or torturously out of yo
for now, just observing the contradictions is what's
yourself in a place of responsibility. Accepting re
what will give you back your power, and we'll tal

"Life Is Waiting for You," about how to counter such behaviors without having to go too far from your comfort zones.

Have you ever wanted something but then caught yourself telling your friends something contradictory? Maybe you really long for a deep and meaningful relationship, but then you hear yourself say something to the effect that relationships never last or that they're unnatural. Or maybe you're trying to lose weight and you're determined to do it, but you hear yourself tell a friend that it makes no difference what you eat, you still can't lose weight. These are more examples of you expressing your so-called invisible beliefs. As I said before, beliefs are no more than opinions about reality. So whenever you catch yourself expressing an opinion, in thought, word, or deed, realize that you've just nailed a belief that's busy building your life around you.

Bulldoze and Liquefy

As silly as the name is, the Bulldoze and Liquefy approach works for me. Very simply, I allow myself to become so empowered by my desires and goals that I can automatically, and effortlessly, Bulldoze and Liquefy any limiting beliefs that might be in my way. How? By reasoning and rationalizing all the reasons why I should have—and deserve—whatever it is that I want, *and then acting the part*. Sometimes I'll even put pen to paper and jot down bullet points of all the reasons why my goal is achievable *and inevitable*.

So rather than first Observing and Dismantling, I physically charge ahead toward whatever it is I want, loaded to the teeth with an understanding about what I'm doing, my place in life, and my heritage as an unlimited eternal creator. These ideals, if held with conviction and *reinforced with action*, will see me through any "attacks" they might encounter from limiting beliefs, invisible or otherwise. And along these lines, I often also think and dwell on the magic of life, the miracles of life, and the grace of my being. By

dwelling on all this perfection, it becomes harder and harder to see myself as limited in any way.

In either approach, what makes this work is that I am ultimately disposing of the old beliefs with a higher *understanding* about myself, my life, and my reality. And one way to arrive at this understanding is by following your thinking and uncovering the rationale for the limiting beliefs you used to live by. If you think money is hard to acquire, ask yourself why, why, why, and compare your answers to the Truths of Being to see how they shrivel up. A higher understanding always has to be there to dissolve old beliefs, and in the light of understanding, limiting beliefs have to disappear, just as the dark disappears when the sun rises. *It's not even necessary, in the end, to know what your limiting beliefs are* as long as you begin to understand and live by the greater truths that surround and support you, particularly in the areas of your life you'd like to see change. Attaining this understanding doesn't have to be a long or drawn-out process. The Truths of Being I've enumerated are so simple. Grasp them. Live them. With illumination comes instant peace and lightning-fast change.

No Dues to Pay

There's no question that limiting beliefs can hold you back, but the reverse is true of empowering beliefs. They can send you through the stratosphere with love, joy, health, and abundance. In either case, your beliefs are like the encased steel girders that support the skyscrapers of your thoughts: invisible but so powerful. Even in the Bible (KJV), Mark 9:23 says that all things are possible with belief, and it adds no caveats! It doesn't say that all things are possible with belief "*if* God says so," or "*if* you're a good person," or "*if* you haven't sinned," or "*if* you pray," or "*if* you deserve." It says all things are possible when you believe! And this is true, because your beliefs draw to themselves all the necessary thoughts to bring your expectations into the physical world. Virtually everything we've ever been told about what it takes to succeed in the world comes a distant second place to beliefs.

Just look at the "success" stories of our time, in any field or profession, and ask yourself these questions: Is there a consistency in their pasts—a religion, formula, ritual, or rite that ensured their success? Were they all goody two-shoes from the right neighborhoods and with morally upstanding parents? Did they all go to college, were they all self-disciplined, and did they all practice, rehearse, and train every day? Did they all have mentors, connections, or lucky breaks? Did they all work lots of overtime?

No, no, no, no, no, no, and no. Their achievements weren't the result of any such dillydallying. They prevailed because they *believed* they would prevail. That's why you know who they are and that's the only reason, even if *they* think otherwise. The connections, circumstances, luck, and coincidences of their life *were drawn to and built around this belief* as they moved with it throughout their affairs.

Whenever you catch yourself expressing an opinion, in thought, word, or deed, realize that you've just nailed a belief that's busy at work building your life around you.

You can't help but make decisions and choose actions based on your beliefs, whatever they are and whether you like it or not, which is why your beliefs are so important.

Look at the accomplished artist, inventor, or tycoon, and think not, "There goes so-and-so, who's talented, innovative, and powerful." Think instead, "There goes someone just like me, who *believes* in his or her talent, inventiveness, and power." You're not lucky or jinxed, protected or abandoned, popular or despised, healthy or sick, wealthy or poor, but you may *believe* you are, and so it will be. We are noth-ing in time and space but thought machines; that's it. We think and our *thoughts become things*. Of course, taking action is absolutely required, but as you'll soon read, our actions usually spring from our beliefs. And in those instances when we don't first possess the beliefs that will throw us into action, we can begin by *deliberately* taking action—baby steps in the direction of our dreams—to begin installing the beliefs we wish to possess (more on this in chapter 4, "Life Is Wait-ing for You").

Living the life of your dreams comes from aligning whatever you want with your beliefs—not virtues, practice, money, patience, connections, tolerance, prayer, meditation, karma, and "goodness" but beliefs and *only beliefs*—particularly the belief in inevitable suc-cess. Most people won't let themselves believe in inevitable success until they feel they live "right," they've received the "proper" educa-tion, they're devoted to their "God," or they're good parents. The truth is that they could have done all those same things and more, much earlier and more often, if only they'd granted themselves the permission to think thoughts of success without the diplomas, age, experience, wisdom, or other dues paid to a coffer requiring only a belief in success.

What's going on when people think they have such bogus dues to pay? They've got rules, some of which are rather obvious, but they all share an even deeper limiting belief, one that again stems from the concept of original sin: thinking that we must first figure out the physical details of exactly *how* our dreams will come true.

We have inner conversations that sound like "I'll start living in abundance once my novel becomes a bestseller." But why limit the infinite avenues of abundance to the lone corridor of selling a novel? And by the same token, why saddle the dream of writing a book with the burden of creating wealth? "I'll be happy once I lose this weight." Sorry, but what does happiness have to do with weight? Nothing—unless we think, say, and believe so. These kinds of self-imposed parameters are the result of a limited belief in our own supernatural abilities, vis-á-vis *thoughts become things*, and they ignore the true magic that belies every new manifestation. This leads us to think we have to logically and physically figure out exactly *how* to bring our dreams to pass, which in effect actually creates restrictions and limitations that need not exist.

We'll tell ourselves that once we get older, we'll slow down a bit and smell the roses, maybe travel some, and enjoy life. But why put off your dreams another moment? I've done a lot of traveling in my life, and it always amazes me when I return home to hear from so many of my friends that they dream of doing such traveling as well. I'm surprised, not because they have this dream but because they aren't acting on it, as I know full well that they have both the financial resources and the available time to do exactly what they claim to be dreaming of doing. Why don't they give it to themselves? It's because they don't believe the rest of their life is in check. It's because they've linked some of their dreams together or they've dreamed up some other limitation. It's as if the sunglasses they're wearing won't allow them to see how livable their dreams are right now!

Whatever it is that you now want, give what you can of it to yourself. And if you feel resistance, follow that wagging tail to the invisible dog it belongs to. Enjoying your life today, by living your dreams to the degree you presently can, is perhaps one of the most powerful things you can do toward expanding your belief system, while disabling limiting, even invisible beliefs.

Advanced Visualization Tips to Bypass Limiting Beliefs

Here are two things you can do to help ensure that a fundamental limiting belief isn't holding you back, even when you don't know what it is:

1. ***When visualizing, always focus on the end result of whatever it is you want.*** Don't let other unrelated images enter your mind about the hows, whys, and wheres of its

attainment. These details should be left entirely out of the picture. Surrender to the vision alone and give your deductive brain a vacation. Remember, air bubbles always know the fastest way to the surface, and your thoughts, when unfettered from your ideas of *how*, always know the fastest way to become the things and events in your life.

2. Don't link your dreams together. Visualize one at a time. If you want abundance, visualize abundance. If you want a bestseller, visualize a bestseller. By focusing on the end result and not making one dream contingent on another, you're freeing the manifestation process from limitation, allowing the invisible forces of imagination to find the absolute shortest distance between your dream and its physical expression.

In the areas of your life where you want to make changes that don't involve the direct give and take of specific things, people, time, or places, there exists fantastic freedom for creativity and abundance because you're immediately freeing yourself from all your other beliefs that would have otherwise been invoked. If you want love, happiness, health, or wealth, create it first in your mind. Imagine, as vividly as you possibly can, your life as if you've already received whatever you want. Visualize sights, sounds, sensations, and most importantly, the emotions you expect to feel. Here's a fun end result to imagine: the stunned and happy reactions of others. Or imagine helping people who want to achieve as you have. It's *not important* that you first imagine why others are reacting happily or exactly what kind of help you will be giving. By not insisting on those details, you let the Universe figure them out for you, in the fastest, most harmonious way possible.

Infinite Possibilities

I often hear people say that beliefs are hard to deal with because they're so loaded with mystery and because they're presumably buried deep inside the psyche. Of course, these are simply beliefs themselves, but even if they are possibly your own, don't let them stop you from doing what you can. Don't think you have to first pinpoint or unwind all your beliefs before you can begin making any progress. Working with your beliefs need not be an "all or nothing" endeavor. Every journey begins with a first step, and working with your beliefs follows the same principle. Do what you can, do what you're comfortable with, and follow your feelings and impulses, and as you progress you'll elevate yourself to higher and higher levels of understanding, giving yourself ever-new vistas of awareness. You'll begin to see things that were not visible before you started, and you'll be empowered by your progress and momentum.

> **Enjoying your life today, by living your dreams
> to the degree you presently can, is perhaps one
> of the most powerful things you can do
> toward expanding your belief system.**

Remember, we're all made of the same stuff, so what one person has done, all may do. It's so simple; it's so obvious. It's just a matter of the thoughts you choose to think. We all write our own book of rules, where all our "shoulds" and "should nots" are named, but there's another book, the Book of Infinite Possibilities, that you've barely started. And the ideal way to rifle through its pages begins with aligning your beliefs with the life of your dreams.

Your thoughts provide the creative spark that sets all things, including time and space, into motion, and it's your beliefs that tell you how and what to think. Apart from a very, very few shared illusions, we're all bound by a different set of "rules" that govern the most profound aspects of our lives: our beliefs. Yet in time and space, we can believe whatever we like, for any reason we like, and as we believe, so will it be. Dwell on these ideas. Think about them inside and out. Question everything that doesn't make sense until it *does* make sense, because it will. Strive to understand, in your own way, that there are certain knowable truths about our reality—truths that clearly reveal your power. Seek and you shall find, knock and it shall be opened unto you, *believe* and thy will be done.

3

Blessed Emotions

So what is it that you want most? A home in the country? What do you want with all your heart and soul? The love of your life? What would you give anything to have: More friends? More laughter? More time?

Actually, I think we have a lot in common, because the thing you want most is also the thing I want most: to be happy. And the good news, as you already know, is that *happiness is an inside job*! And how you can "apply" for that "job" is the basis for much of this chapter.

Before we go too far, I'd like to make a distinction between our emotions and our intuitive feelings, the latter of which get special attention with its own chapter in this book, "Gifts from Heaven" (chapter 5). For now, suffice it to say that when I speak of our emotions, such as happiness, sadness, anger, or depression, I am referring to the *byproducts* of our experiences in time and space, as filtered through our beliefs. Feelings, on the other hand, spring from the vastness of our present spiritual selves, typically appearing as insights, bursts of comprehension, hunches, instincts, and impulses to help us find our way, make decisions, or chart a new course.

But what is happiness? It's the emotion we spontaneously experience whenever we think the circumstances of our life are favorable, in harmony, and pleasing to us. *Hmmm* ... "when ever we *think* the circumstances of our life are favorable." This is *really* great news because it means that we decide when we'll feel happy based on our *perception* of the circumstances in our lives. And since we know that the circumstances of time and space are just a reflection of our thoughts in time and space, we also know that we can change the circumstances we don't like by working on our thoughts and beliefs.

Perception is our view of the world and of ourselves *through our beliefs*.

The short-term fix that will bring about happiness is to change our *perception* of circumstances that seem unpleasant; the long-term fix is to begin the work of aligning our thoughts and beliefs with all we want the future to hold so that we can *change* those circumstances. Both are viable options, but because we've already talked at length about how to affect change in the future by working with our thoughts and beliefs, this chapter will be more about our emotions in the present or, better still, our perception of the circumstances that now surround us.

In the Eye of the Beholder

Perception is our view of the world and of ourselves *through our beliefs*. I'll give you a personal example: When my brother, mother, and I first started TUT (Totally Unique T-shirts), the business that preceded my writing and speaking career, it was really slow going. "World headquarters" was crammed into my tiny Orlando apartment, and I remember one beautiful workday in the spring of that year when I decided to give myself a little break. I went to my apartment's community swimming pool to relax and soak up the sun. Up until that time, I'd worked for P.W., so I thought I could now enjoy some of the slow time that you sometimes encounter when starting a new business. Unfortunately, my beliefs about working hard, sacrificing, and struggling as necessary hardships for starting my own business left me feeling incredibly guilty, lazy, and unhappy. My morning by the pool was pretty miserable.

The emotion of happiness, which is what we're *all* really after, is a product of our perception, like all our emotions, and our perceptions are a product of our beliefs.

Had I thought to change my perceptions that morning, I could have seen my time spent by the pool as *evidence* that I was on the right path toward making my dreams come true. I could have understood that I did deserve to enjoy life as I pleased. And then, from that perspective, I could have really enjoyed the spring air and the cool water, listening to the birds and fully appreciating the paradise I lived in. But instead, I derided myself for not working harder, and I worried that I was being negligent in my responsibilities.

Fortunately, I've remembered that morning well and have often looked back at the lesson learned, because within just two short years, TUT began breaking the million-dollar mark in annual sales. Looking back, I now realize that if on that spring morning I had any idea of just how well our company would soon be doing and just how effective my efforts were, I'd have wholeheartedly enjoyed myself. These days, whenever I feel beset with guilt or doubt about what I'm doing or whether I'm working hard enough, I examine my *beliefs*, change my perception, and think to myself, "Oh, Mike, if you only knew how well you're going to be doing in the near future, you'd really just relax and enjoy today for all that it already is."

So the emotion of happiness, which is what we're *all* really after, is a product of our perception, like all our emotions, and our perceptions are a product of our beliefs. Do you want to change how you see something? Just look at your beliefs. And in instances like this, finding your beliefs is relatively easy because you already have a clear starting point—*the unpleasant emotions you're feeling.*

In this way, emotions (particularly happiness) are not only some-thing to strive toward but they're also powerful indicators pointing at beliefs that are holding us back from seeing things in a new light. They tell us exactly where our thinking lies and *thus where our beliefs lie*. And whenever they're unpleasant, they serve as a reminder that our present perception is not based on truth but on misinterpreta-tions of truth.

Joy Is Only a Thought Away

I was recently reminded of how powerful our beliefs are in forming our perceptions, and thus in determining how we feel, when my relationship with a girlfriend ended. It was extremely painful for me during the first week, complete with that mild feeling of nausea and the literal pain of a broken heart. But during that week, there were also spells of uncertainty with regard to our dating status, at least in my mind, when all of a sudden I believed (perceived) that things between us were on the mend.

Much to my surprise, during the moments of believing that things were on the mend, my painful emotions and their related physical symptoms *completely vanished* in a split second! In fact, during those moments, which never lasted more than half a day, I remember wondering how it was even possible that I could have been so absolutely devastated by the breakup. Then, without warn-ing, a new conversation or insight of my own would indicate that the relationship was in fact over and throw me back into black despair. *So even during those brief reprieves while thinking I was again on top of the world, I was still blind to the beliefs that hinged my happiness and self-love on another person.* This flip-flopping happened several times in the week and always with the same observations on my part. If I hadn't experienced this for myself, I don't think I could have easily believed the *instantaneous* power that my beliefs had on my perceptions of myself and, consequently, on the way I felt emotionally.

Now when I'm in a low spell, I think back to that realization and remember that anything unpleasant I'm feeling is based on a poor perception/belief of my situation. Knowing how quickly I can begin feeling better, I immediately begin thinking more enlightened thoughts that expand the boundaries of my beliefs and perceptions. I start expecting to feel better and then I do feel better. Just as I witnessed the profound power my beliefs had on my happiness, I realized that our beliefs can do this with any and all our emotions. We're literally only ever *just a thought away* from allowing ourselves to possess new beliefs that can fill us with unspeakable joy, profound happiness, and a complete sense of well being, right now.

What if today someone came to you—someone like the "God" most people believe in—and definitively told you that in the immediate future all your dreams would manifest? The psychological and physical changes you would go through are more than you can even comprehend. You'd be elated, confident, relieved, excited, happy, accepting of the world, *and so much more*. You'd breeze through the rest of today no matter what surprises it might hold. Nothing could faze you. You'd be indomitable, unstoppable, and walking on air. So how about it? Right now, why don't you tell yourself that all your dreams will soon manifest? What would it take? You hold the key—the world is your oyster—and you have been given the freedom to think as you choose and to thereby create whatever you can imagine.

Our emotions color our every experience; without them, what would matter? *Nothing!* If it weren't for emotions, what would we pursue? What would motivate us? What would we care about? Nothing. Our emotions are rich with rewards and lessons, and the good ones are worth slogging through the bad ones to receive those benefits.

Emotions give our lives meaning and reason, and the unpleasant ones serve us by hinting at how we can get back on track with life's truths. They spark our desires for a better life, and they inspire us to take on challenges—not challenges that will squash us but challenges that will enlighten us.

Challenges—*La Pièce de Résistance*

It's in our human nature to love challenges because we know deep down that every challenge is surmountable; that we are special, destined to prevail; that we cannot fail; and that in the end we'll reign triumphant, emotionally fulfilled, and wealthier for the wisdom imparted by the emotions that keep us on track. Facing challenges doesn't have to be an unhappy affair, especially when you realize that your challenges are "gifts" that will bring you greater understanding and a deeper happiness than you can now imagine.

Spiritually speaking, no matter who you are, where you are, or what your issues are, given the infinite number of adventures we can choose from, you will always—eternally—"end up" on top. Besides, how adventurous would life be if we were "challenge free"—if we all had perfect bodies, perfect self-esteem, and lived perfect, cushy little lives? Blahhh! But what if, painful as they may temporarily be, we could litter "the course" with obstacles *on the sole condition that they could all be overcome*? And what if we knew that the playing field held the potential for the realization of our greatest hopes and dreams, and that *no single peril we might face would be insurmountable*? Pretty cool concept, isn't it? But it's definitely *not* for every celestial couch potato. This is a concept suited only to adventurers willing to be rocked and taught by their emotions. It's an adventure *perfect for you*, eh?

**Emotions give our lives meaning and reason,
and the unpleasant ones serve us by hinting at how
we can get back on track with life's truths.**

The very sway of our emotions reveals a path to a new kind of enlightenment—a gateway of wisdom and peace unknown before time and space warped into being. Here your emotions appear as signposts to a promised land, and what feels right and pleasing beckons us further. Meanwhile, emotions that are unpleasant or disconcerting can serve to open our hearts to deeper understanding. Together, your emotions join the choir of your inner voices, speaking to you by way of your feelings and impulses and nudging you onward through your self-made obstacle course of matter and events.

People manifest their thoughts; there's little accomplishment there. But as our thoughts propel us through life, so do they send us through a kaleidoscope of emotions, each adding a precious jewel to our crowns of compassion and understanding. That's why *it's the journey and not the destination* that matters so much in time and space, for it's during the journey that emotions color our experiences while providing feedback and insight into our beliefs. Our emotions appear as the psychological reaction to the objects and events that we've "thought" to life, with an intensity based entirely on our ability to understand these same objects and events. The less understanding we possess, the more discomfort—even pain—we'll feel. The *more* understanding we possess, the more joy and acceptance we'll feel. If acknowledged and allowed, unpleasant emotions provide a natural therapy, administered in just the right dose at just the right time. These emotions are so effective that their presence alone is often enough to rectify misunderstandings. We can easily witness this in the sobbing child who spontaneously bursts into laughter even before her tears have dried.

But your emotions needn't bring you to tears for you to benefit and learn from them. They're like a river that runs through you constantly, carrying a wealth that needs only your recognition to be spent. They're a resource that can enable you, at any time, to find where your thinking is, deduce what your beliefs are, and understand what kind of life you're in the process of creating.

Your challenges are "gifts" that will bring you greater understanding and a deeper happiness than you can now imagine.

I'd like to spend some time now talking about some of the more common emotions we have, sharing with you how and why they appear in our lives and what their presence often means. First among these emotions, of course, is love.

Love

I believe there are two kinds of love: the one that people talk about when they describe falling in love and the kind that God, or the Universe, possesses for us. These two kinds of love are actually so different that there should really be a whole new word to describe the kind that the Universe exudes. But since there's no such word, I'll call it "Infinite Love."

Infinite (Unconditional) Love

"In the beginning," the spark that was necessary for time and space to explode into existence was a profoundly huge wish or desire, made or felt by Divine Intelligence. In the twinkling of an eye, what hadn't existed before suddenly sprang to life, and the heavens and Earth were born. Now, by simple deduction, whatever this Divine Intelligence was back then, it had to be of good intent, because evil always inevitably self-destructs. And this Divine Intelligence had to be all-powerful, which is evident simply in that this vast, complex, mind-boggling world exists at all. And this Divine Intelligence had to be the one and only, because everything, everywhere can *always* be broken down or traced back to a single source. And finally, this essence had to be all-loving because creation and growth are so dependent on it (and have been for billions of years). Besides, as I asked earlier, without love, why bother creating?

When considering the magnitude of the Universe and the perfection, balance, and harmony that exists in nature, we're obviously dealing with a creator made wholly of Infinite Love. There could be no room in such an awareness for imperfection or any other sense awareness other than love. In the beginning, there was only this awareness, and this awareness could only comprehend Infinite

Love. Thus, its creations and all that comes from it could only ever be of Infinite Love.

Without love, why bother creating?

Infinite Love is everywhere, always. It has no antonym. It *is* time, space, and matter. It *is* thought, awareness, and energy. It's the present moment and every form of consciousness it contains. It's the desire and fulfillment of every dream ever dreamt, the spirit of life in an endless dance of joyful becoming. This love, therefore, can't be escaped, even if you wanted to escape it; it's absolute. Right now, no matter who you are, it holds you in the palm of its hand—a hand big enough to hold, keep, and *understand* the most misguided and vile of all people. This kind of Infinite Love is not an emotional love; it's not contingent on time, space, or matter; thoughts, beliefs, or perceptions. Yet if it's not an emotional love, why am I mentioning it here? Because it's your heritage—it's what you are made of—and *it's your destination*. It's always there to be drawn upon for comfort and support, but all too often we're oblivious to its ever-present existence, which is invisible until you look for it.

My reasoning may seem pretty naive, but sometimes the answers we seek are simple. And for the pockets in the world where you don't see evidence of this Infinite Love, perhaps it's because we can't see all things from the extremely limited vantage point offered by our physical senses alone. Still, we can at least grasp that in time and space there is far more happening than meets the eye. And for the mind-numbing abundance, perfection, and harmony that we do see everywhere that makes life on our planet possible, we can safely and conservatively conclude that there is indeed a greater good that belies all things.

Human Love

The human kind of love *is* beautiful, but it's almost always emotion-based, which means that it's conditional—based on beliefs and perceptions—so it becomes something that can be given and taken. Unfortunately, it's often knotted with conflicts, expectations, and hopes. It's often transient, felt only when circumstances fit into a predefined mold or when certain personal rules are met, contingent upon approval, respect, reciprocation, or friendship. It's rarely, *if ever*, truly unconditional.

> **Love only hurts when you have a belief**
> **that has provided you with a limited perspective**
> **of yourself and your reality.**

Human love has become like this because we perceive our illusions to be more real than the reality from which they emerge, so our love is based on the things and circumstances of time and space rather than the spirit that moves them. By looking to spirit first, however, we can see and tap into a love that is forever, compassionate, inspiring, forgiving, unyielding, *truly* unconditional, and most certainly *not* emotion-based.

The upside to human love, besides its obvious beauty, is that it has a lot to teach, and when it hurts it means you really have some valuable lessons to learn. Love only hurts when you have a belief that has provided you with a limited perspective of yourself and your reality. And very likely, this has been a false perception that has always existed in your life but was masked by various circumstances, including, most recently, the relationship you were in before it began "hurting."

But painful challenges in life don't arise haphazardly; they arrive when you're ready for them. So don't look at the pain as something attributable to misfortune, but rather as an indication that it's time to grow and move on to higher understandings of yourself and your life. Use the pain to pinpoint what your limiting beliefs are. In this way the gift is your invitation to erase the pain by seeking and finding greater truths about your reality, including that of your eternal magnificence, thereby insulating you from any misunderstandings and future possibilities of feeling pain for the same reasons.

Do you feel rejected and unworthy of love? How so, considering you've been bathed in it since birth as a child of the Universe, one with the Divine yourself. Do you feel like you have to start over in life when a relationship goes awry? There's nothing wrong with starting over. We all have to do it every day, *even when we're in a relationship*. People are always changing and evolving, and any given relationship is not the same today as it was just a year or even a month ago. Do you feel like you're facing the world alone? How could you when there are billions of others, here and now, having the same adventures as you, not to mention an entire Universe that you are intimately a part of? Pain is par for the course when there are misunderstandings, but it gives birth to new insights. Allowing it into your life is just as important as allowing it to move on. And when pain does show up, even if you don't yet feel enlightened for your suffering, you will be further along than you realize. You'll be better prepared for even greater happiness in the future, and you'll have closed a gap to understanding the mysteries of your heart.

Pain is par for the course when there are misunderstandings, but it gives birth to new insights. Allowing it into your life is just as important as allowing it to move on.

Hate

Hate is love in retreat, which means that had love not been present in the first place, there could be no hate. Hate among strangers isn't hate; it's either fear or anger. Hate among former friends, however, is the reflection of an emotional love that had conditions, and most likely the condition not met was the love's return. Remember that we're talking about perceptions here, and *perceiving* that love is not returned doesn't necessarily mean that it's not.

For hate to exist, there must be some rule or condition you held or believed that was not met. By understanding the pain you feel from your hate, you can follow it to the cause of your misperceptions. Did you feel that your happiness depended on someone else? If so, remember that happiness is the product of perception, and *you alone* control your perceptions. Did you feel violated? Violations are like challenges: you experience them only when your thinking or misunderstandings have drawn you to a place where higher learning can take place. Those thoughts, coupled with all your other thoughts, have crafted the perfect circumstances for your training. And just because you can't see the merit in the possibly cruel circumstances you've faced doesn't mean that your own inner objectives haven't been met or that you didn't seek out the lesson. It's not easy to see the perfection when we feel violated, but by understanding that there are no accidents and no coincidences (or, as I asked a religious friend so he could understand it in his terms, "Do you think God makes mistakes?"), we begin to grasp that everything always happens for reasons—reasons that we are intimately tied to—and accepting this helps heal the pain.

Hate is love in retreat.

Fear

Fear is a scary emotion, but don't just feel it—use it! Every unpleasant emotion of yours screams out that you have limiting beliefs or a false understanding, and fear is no different. Let me relate a personal fear-based experience I used to have.

In my life, I've flown hundreds of thousands of miles on every rickety airline and type of aircraft imaginable. Yet about fifteen years ago, when flying across the United States, I looked down at the Earth from my window seat about seven miles high and suddenly felt a terror I'd never known before. And I do mean terror. It was as if every cell in my body was vibrating fear—a horrible fear, a fear that you'd do almost anything to avoid. This fear seemingly came from nowhere and it tore through me. I'd never even been remotely scared of heights before, so I was shocked to be having these feelings.

Well, that terror sporadically appeared on almost all my flights over the next seven or eight years, and because it seemed so irrational to me, I couldn't pin down the limiting beliefs or mis-understandings that gave it occasion to arise. Instead, every time it happened (and in between flights), I just blasted myself with countless reasons (beliefs) why I shouldn't be afraid, includ-ing flight safety statistics, the fact that as a spiritual being I'm indestructible, that so-called accidents (like coincidences) never happen, that death is only an illusion—things like that—and finally, having willfully and regularly immersed myself into seeing things from a new perspective, *and forcing myself to continue fly-ing when I had the option*, the terror gradually subsided. It's like the fear existed in one room of many in the mansion of my mind, and I learned where that room was and developed the ability to avoid it. And while I still don't know how that room got there, I do know that I'm better off for having moved through it, and that because of it, I was able to ingrain into my being greater truths about myself and the world I live in that were quite obviously lacking from my repertoire.

Of course, not all fears are so obvious. The fear of failure, dis-appointment, being hurt, or not being approved of, for example, are all virtually invisible fears until you're tested. Then, wham! You know something's going on! But again, once you're tested, it means it's time to grow, which can only happen by facing and dealing with your fears and, when possible, following them to the limiting beliefs that have created the false perceptions. As I did with my fear of flying, I use my Bulldoze and Liquefy approach to deal with my limiting beliefs, supplanting the invisible beliefs that gave rise to fear by understanding *and acting* on other truths about my con-dition and my reality. Incidentally, I never did figure out what my limiting beliefs were that created my fear of flying, *which illustrates that uncovering the culprit isn't even necessary* when it comes to moving forward and beyond it.

Sadness and Depression

The best thing I've ever read about depression came from one of Jane Roberts's Seth books: very simply, depression is the result of feeling powerless—powerless to change your circumstances, and feeling trapped by your life. If this is where you are, facing it or admitting it is the first step. Then begin realizing that you are, of course, powerful. You've just lost some momentum. It's like riding a bike; you've got to keep moving in order to stay balanced. I know that's easier said than done, particularly under stressful or challenging circumstances, so the best advice I can give is to begin taking baby steps—*forcing* change in the areas of your life that trouble you most. If you're lonely, go to the mall (or anywhere), and smile and look for friendly faces. You don't have to talk to anyone, but go—get moving.

If you're sad about something, after the initial healing that may require some alone time, start encouraging yourself to focus on other things: go to new places, try new things, get on your bike and ride. And while this may not be easy at first, enduring the sadness or pain you may feel isn't any easier. Only by doing something about it will you enable the emotions to subside. *Always do what you can.* You might not meet someone at the mall, but on your way you might see a billboard advertising an event that interests you (this is an example of life's magical serendipities that can only be encountered by taking action). By keeping yourself busy, maybe by resuming an old friendship or taking up an old sport or game you used to enjoy, you can then branch out to find new friendships and experiences that you can't even imagine now. Best of all, when you do what you can, you make yourself far more available to all your other wonderful thoughts that are seeking to burst into your life as new manifestations. And these thoughts simply can't do this if you are unreachable—at home waiting for a miracle.

Anger

Anger is similar to depression in that it results from a perceived loss of power or control felt over a period of time. Yet instead of, or in addition to, being overcome with a passive sense of depression, and instead of constructively dealing with these perceptions as they arise, the situation is allowed to simmer until it is ultimately attacked with rage. Of course, since you're the one going into a rage, you're the one who will suffer its consequences in the form of disturbing your own health, increasing the friction or stress in your relationships, and providing no solution to the original disturbance. The sad irony with anger is that it's always expressed in an attempt to correct or rectify a situation, yet its expression does the exact opposite.

Anger worsens any situation for you, whomever you're angry with, and the relationship between you. And because anger is destructive, it's especially important that it be addressed, not suppressed. Suppressed anger will only reappear, amplified each time it does due to its prior suppression. Alternatively, by feeling your way through your anger, you can begin to understand it. If it's another person you're angry with and avoiding her isn't an option, then perhaps begin by understanding that this person is simply doing her own best, however poor you might judge her best to be. It's just where that person is in her own spiritual evolution.

Realize that you are the source of your anger, not someone else or the events of your life. They just are what they are until you come along and pass judgment based on your beliefs; that's when emotions are ignited. Without you in the picture, there wouldn't be any anger— at least not *your* anger. And while you may feel justified with how you feel, how much good will that do you if you are still left with the anger? Instead, work with your thoughts, beliefs, and perceptions to avoid its expression and, just as importantly, its suppression.

Grief

Grief is perhaps the darkest of feelings and usually sparked by a loss, perhaps due to a death. This emotion robs you of your will to live, yet it's an emotion that every life faces and that everyone must overcome. Time is the best remedy for grief, and allowing yourself to feel it is part of the healing. Afterwards, however, there needs to be a concerted effort to get back into the swing of things.

Grief, like all unpleasant emotions, also arises out of limiting beliefs that tell you your loss is permanent and forever. But as an eternal, spiritual being, you should be able to grasp that no loss is ever permanent, that there are no final good-byes, and that there are no irreconcilable separations; these are all illusions. You will be together with your loved ones again, and it will be soon. In the meantime, you still have the gift of life—that priceless opportunity to live, love, and laugh. It's still your turn in time and space, and the band is still playing. The fact that you were "left behind" unquestionably means you still have some living to do.

My uncle used to say, "Things are never as black as they seem," and while the blackness may seem absolutely impenetrable at times, it will later seem impossible that you ever saw things as dire as you did. We've all been there, and if that's where you find yourself one day, just hang on; it will pass.

Guilt

Guilt, like humanity's definition of sin, should serve only to teach, not to punish. Learning, not to be perfect, is why we're here, and no transgression of yours can ever take away from your divinity, nor has it—no matter what you've done. And nothing you've ever done can keep the Infinite Love of the Universe from shining on you. When there's guilt, let it emblazon the lesson learned in your memory so that the mistake will never again be repeated. But just as importantly, keep looking forward with hope and optimism.

Joy and Happiness

Thankfully, not all emotions are unpleasant. Joy and happiness are the emotions that signal your progress through prior lessons that have brought you to a place of peace and acceptance and an inner spiritual pleasure about your affairs. And whether or not it's apparent, these are the fruits of earlier pains, challenges, and obstacles faced and conquered. For instance, you might think vacationing in Hawaii is the ultimate holiday and that it brings you happiness; you might even think that it's because of the beautiful scenery, the laid-back atmosphere, and the perfect weather. But what you're really feeling is the accomplishment of having persevered, persisted, and faced earlier life challenges—some even many years ago—that have brought you to a point in time where you could choose to enjoy an idyllic holiday destination. Because you dealt with challenges and fears you've long forgotten, you were able to grow and gain momentum in the pursuit of living the life of your dreams.

Just ask anyone who lives in Hawaii. They'll tell you, "It's just a place," albeit a beautiful place. But joy and happiness don't come from a place; they come from inside. And that's where they come from when you've gained a mastery over your perceptions.

Panning for Gold

Your emotions are jewels that each have its own lesson to impart, and when dealt with, their teachings will reveal the beliefs behind the illusions you've created. Dealing with them first means feeling them. And only by feeling them can you begin to understand their presence in your life and the wisdom they offer. If you're experiencing emotions that hurt or distract you, get to their source, their root—to the beliefs that gave them rise—and begin understanding those things that you currently misunderstand. Like pulling weeds in the garden, you don't just shear them off at the top unless you want them to come back. You go to their roots and completely dispose of them.

By suppressing your emotions, they build up like water behind a dam, because thoughts, once born, seek their own time and space expression. If they are repeatedly unexpressed, they'll finally explode into your life with such a pent-up force that their sudden presence will exceed the balance necessary to view your life in the proper perspective. They'll overwhelm you with such a distorted view of your "reality" that your subsequent reactions may also be wildly out of proportion.

Suppressing your emotions is like ignoring the smell of smoke in your home: you're avoiding the recognition that there are underlying beliefs of yours that are their cause. Acknowledge your unpleasant feelings—you're their source, and only you can release or replace them once their presence is understood. You can change how you feel, but to do this you must begin with yourself. Take action, do something, and remember that you are living in a perfect and fair world—one that throws you a hook only when you're ready to swing, understand, grow, and be happier than ever before.

Just as important as not suppressing your emotions is not allowing yourself to wallow in them. Their natural state is flowing; they come and go like tides in the sea. Allow them to run their course, and you'll find they lend a new perspective to the life you lead, administering their own remedies and insights in the perfect doses.

**Acknowledge your unpleasant feelings—you're
their source, and only you can release or replace them
once their presence is understood.**

Having unpleasant emotions doesn't necessarily mean that you must suddenly begin exploring the depths of your beliefs. In fact, unless they're really crushing you, just feeling them often provides a sort of therapy. But *feeling* is wildly different from wallowing. When you wallow in your emotions, you empower them; you draw to yourself more of the same. Sadness breeds sadness, not just among groups of people but within your own mind—just as happiness breeds happiness.

Like Begets Like

Your thoughts not only become or attract things but they also draw to themselves similar thoughts—more of whatever it is you're *thinking* or, in the case of emotions, whatever it is you're *feeling*. I believe this is how I've been able to deduce so many truths about time and space. Because I dwell on these things, by thinking and even questioning thoughts of "truth," I actually draw to myself such thoughts and answers. Perhaps you've heard of spontaneous illumination? It's the same thing—a phenomenon where, for no apparent reason and without any outside stimuli, you suddenly have answers and insights to questions or dilemmas that were not within your grasp just a moment before.

Another and more startling way that your thoughts or emotions perpetuate themselves is tied back to the *thoughts become things* principle. Thoughts of sadness or happiness strive to become things, but they're very tricky. While emotions, such as depression or joy, cannot become a physical thing, their expression on this "plane of manifestation" *can* be achieved when *events and circumstances* in your life are literally rearranged (just as they are when thoughts manifest as tangible things) in such a way that your reaction to the new circumstances will manifest those emotions all over again. For instance, I went through a period where I decided to visualize being congratulated. I vividly saw in my mind's eye associates, neighbors, and friends all giving me great praise, handshakes, compliments, and pats on the back, but I deliberately did not pick any event that would generate the congratulations. Instead, I just imagined the emotions generated by having these sentiments addressed to me.

In the following months and year after my experiments of imaging being congratulated, TUT's sales went through the roof, breaking records. I bought a large new home; I adopted my first dog; and a host of other achievements came my way. Congratulations were unending. Of course, I was also doing many other things at the time that helped contribute to those successes, but the point is, by dwelling, or wallowing, on certain emotions, happy or sad, those thoughts will literally draw *circumstances and events* into your life, further perpetuating those very emotions.

Another example of this is the downward spiral that we hear of people falling into, where their thoughts and emotions, bolstered by every misfortune, build incredible momentum, creating more negative thoughts and emotions and more misfortune. Their lives become "runaway trains." But the good news—the great news—is that upward spirals are even more common, and are far more in keeping with our naturally optimistic natures, and they happen all the time. Wonderful thoughts and emotions beget wonderful manifestations and circumstances, which beget more wonderful thoughts and emotions, and so on. And it only takes a few thoughts and emotions to get them started.

Another Advanced Visualization Tip

This is so important: let me clarify and again suggest that when you visualize, from time to time just visualize positive, happy emotions without thinking of any objects or events. I sometimes see myself walking quickly through my house with my arms pumping over my head, whooping and hollering because of some (undefined) great news I'd just received, or running out my front door and jumping for joy. (Sometimes I actually do these things!) I imagine driving down the interstate that runs through Orlando, listening to some really loud, happy music, yelling "YEE-HAAAA!" at the top of my lungs, barely able to contain the joy I'm feeling, while still imagining friends and neighbors calling me with congratulations for some unknown victory or accomplishment.

These kinds of visualizations are actually fun, and you can let yourself get totally carried away. The magic you invoke will literally

brace and understand your emotions, especially the unhappy
~~nd~~ appreciate their meaning—even their beauty—in your life.
~~rom~~ the journey, you can come to know yourself, your divinity,
~~:~~ awesome power you wield—a power so great that all dreams
~~:~~ forever possible, wherever you may find yourself today.

rearrange the "furniture" of your life so that such feelings can be
made manifest.

You Are Not What You Feel

Another thought for dealing with your emotions, particularly your
unpleasant ones, is to not let them define you. For instance, after
the breakup of my relationship, I was faced with a lot of unhappy
emotions. The emotions were sad, which led to feelings that I had
failed, and then I began thinking I was an unlikable guy, unworthy
of love based on my character and personality, and I kept focusing
on my every weakness. The emotions had me labeling, defining,
and limiting myself; I was becoming more and more blind to any
of my character strengths and unappreciative of my own unique
personality.

Left unchecked, I could have gotten completely carried away in
my own downward spiral. Instead, though, I remembered that those
kinds of emotions only pointed to specific perceptions and limiting
beliefs, *not to who I am*. I began using them as the tools they can be,
without getting carried away with defining who and what I am, and
I began exploring my beliefs. I also reminded myself that I am a
thought machine, that my thoughts paint the circumstances that lie
in my future, and that I alone am the programmer of everything I
may choose to think.

Emotions don't define us; they simply point to our perceptions
and beliefs at any given moment. They're like barometers that measure our understandings of ourselves and our lives, but they are not
who we are. Let yours point the way to patterns in your thoughts
and beliefs.

What You Really Want

Whenever we think we want new "things" in our lives, what we're
really after are the feelings we think these "things" will bring us. But

of course it's not "things" that bring us feelings; it's the journey they inspire and the accomplishments they signify. That's undoubtedly why there are so many unhappy lottery winners who at first thought their dreams had come true but then found themselves miserably unhappy and eventually broke. I look at it like this: we all want to be in the "winner's circle" of life, so to speak, because generally people in a winner's circle are people who have persevered and achieved. But being in the winner's circle, by its very definition, requires facing challenges and "winning," not in the sense of being better than others, but by reaching the very bars you've set for yourself earlier. Then the greatest of all rewards will be the happiness you feel for having made the pilgrimage, for prevailing in spite of your fears and doubts. Being happy comes from doing what you love, doing it well, and facing your challenges along the way. It's as if life rewards you with success at work, in your relationships, and in other material and *nonmaterial* ways. To want the rewards, however, without the growing; to arrive at the destination without the journey; or to dream of being in the winner's circle without "running the race" points to huge life misunderstandings, particularly with regard to the nature of challenges, dreams, and happiness.

The Fast Track

Interestingly, we're actually inspired by the way we want to feel, compared to how we now feel, so it shouldn't be forgotten that how you *now* feel is a perception. Of course, there's no dream that's unattainable and there is nothing you can't do, but if we place our attention on the perception of where we are now, giving ourselves credit for having made it this far and loving ourselves as we are, then with the happiness that this frame of mind will yield, going anywhere else our dreams might lead becomes even easier. After all, who do you think could achieve more: someone who starts out happy or someone who is motivated by unhappiness?

We're all different, and sometimes dis
motivator, but I think we all know that peop
go further in their lives—and faster—than
If you're happy, you feel less stress to *have*
doesn't mean that you shouldn't or that y
does mean you'll worry less; you won't fee
world on your shoulders; and you won't
lies a deal away, a contract away, a day a
person away.

Jewels in Your Crown of Ur

There's little we could ever achieve, no
times, that compares to the simple fact
Right now we are alive in time and spa
to think as we please. Right now it's c
are millions of people in the world who
be in your shoes, have your life, and
fact, all that you now have is far mo
dream of having. You're blessed. I'm b
to lose this perspective and find ou
unhappy. By catching yourself when
use those emotions to understand v
balance and, most importantly, which
ing you from the truth, thereby enab
move your miraculous, amazing life
pleases you.

Emotions are actually the reward c
giving depth and meaning to every
show themselves when our illusions
levels, thereby hinting at the beliefs th
ence in our lives. They're the unexpe
the jungles of time and space, and th
passion unattainable by intellect alon

4

Life Is Waiting for You

*P*eople often say that the only constant in life is change, but I think there's another way to look at life—a better way. Life never changes; it's perfect and finished. Life is like the big silver screen that movies are shown on, never changing even while the pictures on it do. It's just that here, in time and space, we are the projectors shining our thoughts onto the screen of life; it's we who change constantly, not life. Life itself is very predictable when you stop looking at the effects of your creations and start looking at the underlying steadfast principles involved.

Let me elaborate a little more on the constructs of this time and space theater we're all performing in. Doesn't it make sense that there must be certain inviolate principles? If all of a sudden cows could fly, oceans could disappear, cities be moved, or material things occasionally flickered in and out of existence, there'd be nothing to depend on. How could you have a reality in which the rules, or the props, constantly fluxed without your involvement? Living in time and space would be impossible without certain inviolate principles. This is especially true when you believe that one of the fundamental reasons we're here is to learn of our absolute power to shape the lives we lead.

If you understand then that "life" is constant, you must also believe in the need for certain absolute, unchanging principles that make this possible (what I previously referred to as the Truths of

Being), and that there also must not be *any* forces outside of ourselves that could manipulate the results of our own thoughts, beliefs, and intents. If there were such outside forces ("non-us" forces) that influenced the direction of our lives or the things we manifest—be they angels, gods, or lucky stars—then, again, it couldn't be said that we've been given dominion over all things. Instead, it would be said that we've been given dominion over *most* things; or only on certain occasions; or based on some other criteria, circumstances, or judgments that are not our own. Without unchanging principles, it also couldn't be said "Believe and all things are possible." Instead, caveats would have to be added, such as, hypothetically, "as long as it's Friday, Saturn is rising, or Gabrielle is nearby."

If we make our own reality, then we make our own reality, and it's not a part-time thing based on any conditions or variables *whatsoever*. Only with perfect, flawless consistency can life, like a mirror, accurately show us what we're "putting out" there. And the implications are staggering, because this means that once we understand these simple principles and build our lives upon the rock of their truth, the manifestation of our dreams is utterly inescapable.

This is what I mean when I say "Life is waiting for you." Your life, for the reasons just given, is a *blank canvas* with far more room for creativity and expression than we've ever suspected. We tend to think in generalities when it comes to defining life, but there really is no such thing as life "in general." You have your life, I have my life, and there are billions of other adventurers with their own lives, but there is no life "in general." Our lives are far more personal, precious, and unique than we've been taught, and this is because they are far more *a product of how and what we think* than they are of evolution or destiny.

It's as if we all think we're sitting in the same movie theater—the theater of life—and we think we're all watching the same show, just with different perspectives, but actually it's far more accurate to think that we all sit alone in our own movie theaters. Apart from life's unchanging principles, we all live by different rules and truths based upon different beliefs. (I hope you're following me, because with this perspective you'll realize that whatever aspects you've ascribed to life "in general" really apply only to *your* life. Your life is just an externalized reflection of all you think, believe, and anticipate.)

There is no "life" without you—only an inert potential that needs you to give it meaning, shape, and purpose. Life is waiting for you to *live* it—*your way*. "Live" is a verb; it means to take action, and that's the point. Life is waiting for you to *take action*, to exercise your free will, to choose your path by using its principles to invoke the magic behind creation in order to live the life you've always dreamed you could live. *This is why you're here!*

Life's Ultimate Dance

By deliberately taking action, by physically moving with and toward your dreams, you set the entire Universe into motion. *Action is the key*. It is the demonstration of expectation, sending shock waves into the unseen of your intent. Through it, you provide the spark and the Universe lights the fire. It's as if we sit at the control panels of our life (like a captain might stand at the helm of some vastly complex sailing vessel of the future) and simply give directions while countless crew members, machines, and computers fly into action at our behest. The only difference is that our own personal lives and the commands we issue are infinitely more intricate and complicated than this vessel, and instead of a fallible crew, machines, and computers, *we have at our disposal an infallible, loving Universe—an extension of yourself—armed with inviolate principles.*

Do you find this hard to believe? Here are some undeniable examples of your own relationship with the Universe in action,* in life's ultimate dance, during which you effortlessly draw upon it to

---

*I remember reading two or three of these examples in a Seth Book by Jane Roberts more than twenty years ago. They are so stunningly obvious and so clearly make their point that I wanted to share them here.

finish what you've started and what you've commanded it to do: You start sentences that you don't even know how you'll finish, but you always do finish them and they make perfect sense. *Where do these sentences come from?* You perform profoundly complex muscle movements every time you do the simplest of physical activities, yet you haven't a clue how you do what you do—*and who does?* You open any book—this book even—and you see on each page black squiggles representing information that does not exist on those pages, *but it exists somewhere.*

Intent, or thought without action, is *not* enough.

In each of these examples, you set into motion, by your intent and *subsequent actions*, the magic of the Universe. Intent, or thought without action, is *not* enough. But as you open your mouth to speak, as you put forth your leg to walk, as you pry open the pages of any book to read, these *physical gestures* overwhelmingly imply that you *believe* your intent will be matched with results. All this adds to the energy of your initial thought sufficiently enough that a tipping point is reached; critical mass is achieved, allowing the Universe to grab the baton and take over, *all for the seemingly feeble actions we initiate.* You don't even have to know *how* to complete the processes started, yet starting the process clearly demonstrates a belief that it will somehow be completed. The original intent (vision, desire, dream), bolstered by the expectation and empowered because of the action that follows, is sufficient to cause the necessary articulation, muscle movements, and idea formulations invoked by life's magic via the *thoughts become things* principle for there to be the corresponding manifestation.

Do you want to argue that it's your subconscious mind that finishes your sentences and makes your heart beat? Even if you believed this, what or where is your subconscious mind, anyway? It most certainly is not *physically* located in your brain. It springs from your spiritual self, which, again, brings us back to thought being the spark that triggers principles in the unseen, igniting a seemingly magical process for every manifestation we witness. And what stirs up this magic the most is us dancing the ultimate dance, *physically moving with our dreams* by demonstrating an unquestionable belief in the processes we have unwittingly started.

The actions we take or don't take reveal the thoughts of ours that are believed-in the most or the least. And understanding this, we immediately begin to see how important taking action is to the fruition of our dreams upon the blank canvas of our lives. *This is not so much because of what we may accomplish for the meager steps taken, but by simply taking these steps, we demonstrate where our true beliefs lie and where our thinking is, thereby engaging the magic of life to finish what we have begun.*

Let's look closer.

Action: Our Beliefs in Motion

Setting Divine Intelligence, or the Universe, into motion begins with the thoughts you choose to think, and those, of course, most often stem from your beliefs. However, we're physical creatures, and getting anything done requires movement and action; otherwise we'd remain in bed dreaming or at our computers surfing. So let's look at this movement of our actions and deeds to see what they mean and find out what they can do for us.

Graceful or fluid action, whether in dancing, athletics, or as one simply moves through life, has sometimes been described as poetry in motion, but really, our actions are our *beliefs in motion*, linking the present we know to the future we expect in time and space. They are the physical extensions of our beliefs, often appearing as reactions to the world around us. For example, if you believe that you're about to be devoured by a charging lion, *you run!* Or if you believe your fellow adventurers are kind and wonderful, you greet them with open arms. And if you believe that you create your own reality, you accept responsibility for all that has ever happened in your life, while behaving responsibly each and every day with this belief in mind. Generally, we *automatically* act in line with our beliefs.

Sometimes when people hear me explain the *thoughts become things* principle, they want to correct me by adding that you must also have the conviction of your dreams to follow up and *act*. But to me that goes without saying, because you cannot help but *act* with your true beliefs about life; it's virtually impossible. Let me ask you this: If you knew with certainty, with all your heart and soul, that all you had to do to write an internationally bestselling novel was to put pen to paper and the entire work would gush from you in perfect form, would you do it? You bet you would! You couldn't help yourself. But if you didn't believe it, if you thought it was very difficult, if you thought your chances of being discovered were slim to none, would you then put pen to paper? No, unless you really forced yourself to.

Thoughts *do* become things, but because not everything you think can instantly spring into time and space, only those thoughts that are aligned with your beliefs and are felt intensely, to the degree that they automatically throw you into action, can appear. *Thoughts become things*; this needs no modification, though if anything should be added to those three magic words it would be to work on your beliefs, which are generally the root cause of all we do and don't do.

**Our actions are our *beliefs in motion*,
linking the present we know to the future
we expect in time and space.**

Of course, this is the *action* section of this book, so it may seem that with all this talk about beliefs I've strayed off course. Yet in a moment, once I've said all that I have to say about how our actions mirror our beliefs, I'll talk about how we can do some "reverse engineering," using our actions to change our beliefs.

Actions Speak (About Your Beliefs) Louder Than Words

We can learn about our beliefs from observing and understanding our normal, everyday behavior. Once you understand the motivation behind the things you catch yourself doing (or not doing), you can then automatically see straight through to the beliefs that have possessed you. This is all the more important when you realize that not only do your actions and inactions extend from your beliefs, *but they also support and reinforce those very beliefs*; thus, a cycle of manifestation is born. If the beliefs serve you, it's great, but it's a big problem when they don't.

To give you some examples, realize that even placing one foot in front of the other as you walk down the street reflects *and reinforces* your beliefs in your own muscular strength, health, and coordination and in gravity, to name just a few. Or if you think you're overweight, by shopping for low-calorie foods you both reveal *and reinforce* this belief. If you haven't surrounded yourself with material abundance yet, it's possible that by simply playing the lottery, the purchase of your ticket *may* reflect and reinforce your sensed lack of power to otherwise change your financial condition. This doesn't mean you shouldn't ever buy low-calorie foods or lottery tickets, as there may be a number of great reasons why you should do both, but these small examples clearly show how your actions point directly to your beliefs, *serving to reinforce them as further evidence of your present state of affairs*.

The message your "inner witness," or your observing self, receives is that you buy low-calorie foods because you *are* overweight. "Aha," it notes, "I'm overweight!" And as all beliefs do, this one will begin generating the accompanying mental imagery, which in turn draws you silently into a physical reality that mirrors the reality you believe in. Effortlessly, and without notice, you'll eat more than necessary, you'll exercise less, and you'll be disposed to the wrong foods at the wrong time, and your metabolism may even slow, not as a result of body chemistry (although this too will be affected) but because you *believe* you are overweight. Change the belief and your diet, *life circumstances* and buying priorities will effortlessly change too, as will all things you associate with your weight.

Now, you're probably thinking, "If I'm overweight, or if I'm not surrounded by wealth and abundance yet, how can I start believing and then acting like I'm not overweight or pretending that I'm not just barely getting by financially? Isn't it a bit crazy to start eating fat-filled foods or avoiding the lottery in my situation?"

Let me answer that in two parts. First, you can start changing your behavior incrementally by occasionally splurging or acting *as if* (more on that later), and second, and most important, you must begin realizing that your present conditions have nothing to do with what you eat today or with the lottery. Your situation arose only after you began believing that you were overweight or, maybe better, as you gradually and incrementally began believing that you were overweight. If you're not yet surrounded by wealth, your present situation arose when you stopped seeing that the world was pressing out its abundance to you, or perhaps because you never learned of this truth.

Chocolate alone doesn't make anyone overweight any more than not playing the lottery deprives people of abundance. *The real error in our thinking has been that we think we must react to the physical, instead of the spiritual, side of life.* When you understand fully that your present conditions sprang from your thoughts and beliefs, you'll also realize that that's where you need to initiate any offsetting changes.

**The real error in our thinking has been that
we think we must react to the physical,
instead of the spiritual, side of life.**

I know this can seem a bit tricky—learning to *behave* according to your dream, your inner vision, especially when you've relied, perhaps exclusively, upon your physical senses to decide how you will act or behave up to this point. It's been even trickier because our entire planetary culture, so far, has conditioned us to look outside ourselves for direction, meaning, and "proper" behavior. But dancing with your dreams and not the illusions around you (obviously only to the degree you can manage this) is precisely how to bring those dreams about, which is exactly the opposite of how it may appear. It takes practice to think in these terms, but the payoff is well worth it. The physical world is simply a mirror of your own beliefs and thoughts, which means that if there are any appearances you'd like to change, you must first go within.

Reverse Engineering

Hopefully I've made it clear that our actions are part and parcel of our beliefs, so now let me try a little reverse logic. If we can say that our actions are simply an extension of our beliefs, then obviously you can begin changing how you behave by first changing what you believe. Yet if they're one and the same, couldn't we begin changing our beliefs by first changing our actions? This line of thinking should be especially plausible considering that in the deepest sense, with time being relative—or an illusion—all things are actually happening simultaneously.

We *can* begin changing our beliefs by first changing our behaviors. And given how challenging it can sometimes be to decipher our beliefs, with lines blurred between where one ends and the next begins, or when we struggle to differentiate between "reality" and what we think we believe about it, it makes a lot of sense to use this approach. With a simple awareness of the beliefs you'd like to possess or the end results you'd like to achieve, you simply start working on some of the things you *do* throughout each day.

This means initiating actions that are presumably just "outside" your current set of beliefs, by performing some token deed or deeds, on a regular basis, *that don't make sense* in the context of your normal life or normal surroundings but that *are* in line with the life you'd like to lead. These new actions then imply the existence of a corresponding *new* belief, and when they're consistently repeated, the new belief has to emerge.

When you act in new ways, anticipation of the unexpected is aroused and previously closed doors to fulfillment begin swinging open.

By acting out of the norm, it's as if we temporarily suspend the old beliefs that would have normally prevented us from behaving in this new way, and this suspension works magic! When acting *outside your norm*, in line with the new beliefs you wish to possess, old limiting beliefs, *even unidentified beliefs* (as shown earlier with my fear of flying), begin dissolving. They have to, because obviously they no longer make much sense in view of your new actions and behaviors. And while these energies set into motion are outside our normal awareness, proof of their existence is everywhere around us. By simply acting in some new ways, with small deviations from the life we normally lead, we actually tap into and harness the power of the Universe and our thoughts.

So your actions, in addition to pointing to your existing beliefs, can be used to form and install new ones. In an instant, you can begin changing some of your behaviors, which in turn will start affecting all the rules you've ever made up, including the ties that may have bound you to anything unpleasant.

To put it plainly, you can decide in a flash to turn left instead of right or to laugh instead of cry, and on a bigger scale, you can decide to behave as if some or all your dreams have *already* manifested. These kinds of actions send a signal to your inner witness that tells it that your *reality* is no longer what it used to be. And by repeatedly catching your inner witness off guard, it'll find that it can no longer slumber through the predictable routine patterns it's become accustomed to, nor can it count on the old beliefs it has

rearrange the "furniture" of your life so that such feelings can be made manifest.

You Are Not What You Feel

Another thought for dealing with your emotions, particularly your unpleasant ones, is to not let them define you. For instance, after the breakup of my relationship, I was faced with a lot of unhappy emotions. The emotions were sad, which led to feelings that I had failed, and then I began thinking I was an unlikable guy, unworthy of love based on my character and personality, and I kept focusing on my every weakness. The emotions had me labeling, defining, and limiting myself; I was becoming more and more blind to any of my character strengths and unappreciative of my own unique personality.

Left unchecked, I could have gotten completely carried away in my own downward spiral. Instead, though, I remembered that those kinds of emotions only pointed to specific perceptions and limiting beliefs, *not to who I am*. I began using them as the tools they can be, without getting carried away with defining who and what I am, and I began exploring my beliefs. I also reminded myself that I am a thought machine, that my thoughts paint the circumstances that lie in my future, and that I alone am the programmer of everything I may choose to think.

Emotions don't define us; they simply point to our perceptions and beliefs at any given moment. They're like barometers that measure our understandings of ourselves and our lives, but they are not *who* we are. Let yours point the way to patterns in your thoughts and beliefs.

What You Really Want

Whenever we think we want new "things" in our lives, what we're really after are the feelings we think these "things" will bring us. But of course it's not "things" that bring us feelings; it's the journey they inspire and the accomplishments they signify. That's undoubtedly why there are so many unhappy lottery winners who at first thought their dreams had come true but then found themselves miserably unhappy and eventually broke. I look at it like this: we all want to be in the "winner's circle" of life, so to speak, because generally people in a winner's circle are people who have persevered and achieved. But being in the winner's circle, by its very definition, requires facing challenges and "winning," not in the sense of being better than others, but by reaching the very bars you've set for yourself earlier. Then the greatest of all rewards will be the happiness you feel for having made the pilgrimage, for prevailing in spite of your fears and doubts. Being happy comes from doing what you love, doing it well, and facing your challenges along the way. It's as if life rewards you with success at work, in your relationships, and in other material and *nonmaterial* ways. To want the rewards, however, without the growing; to arrive at the destination without the journey; or to dream of being in the winner's circle without "running the race" points to huge life misunderstandings, particularly with regard to the nature of challenges, dreams, and happiness.

The Fast Track

Interestingly, we're actually inspired by the way we want to feel, compared to how we now feel, so it shouldn't be forgotten that how you *now* feel is a perception. Of course, there's no dream that's unattainable and there is nothing you can't do, but if we place our attention on the perception of where we are now, giving ourselves credit for having made it this far and loving ourselves as we are, then with the happiness that this frame of mind will yield, going anywhere else our dreams might lead becomes even easier. After all, who do you think could achieve more: someone who starts out happy or someone who is motivated by unhappiness?

We're all different, and sometimes discontent can be a great motivator, but I think we all know that people who are happy often go further in their lives—and faster—than those who are unhappy. If you're happy, you feel less stress to *have to* change your life. That doesn't mean that you shouldn't or that you won't change, but it *does* mean you'll worry less; you won't feel like you're carrying the world on your shoulders; and you won't feel like your happiness lies a deal away, a contract away, a day away, a dream away, or a person away.

Jewels in Your Crown of Understanding

There's little we could ever achieve, now or in ten thousand lifetimes, that compares to the simple fact that right now we "are." Right now we are alive in time and space. Right now we are free to think as we please. Right now it's our turn in the sun. There are millions of people in the world who'd give almost anything to be in your shoes, have your life, and have your perspectives. In fact, all that you now have is far more than many could even dream of having. You're blessed. I'm blessed. And yet it's so easy to lose this perspective and find ourselves unappreciative and unhappy. By catching yourself when you feel like this, you can use those emotions to understand why your perception is off balance and, most importantly, which beliefs of yours are keeping you from the truth, thereby enabling yourself to deliberately move your miraculous, amazing life forward in a direction that pleases you.

Emotions are actually the reward of any time and space journey, giving depth and meaning to every experience. Left alone, they show themselves when our illusions are at their most captivating levels, thereby hinting at the beliefs that then hold the greatest influence in our lives. They're the unexpected prizes of an odyssey into the jungles of time and space, and their yield is a wisdom and compassion unattainable by intellect alone.

Embrace and understand your emotions, especially the unhappy ones, and appreciate their meaning—even their beauty—in your life. Then, from the journey, you can come to know yourself, your divinity, and the awesome power you wield—a power so great that all dreams remain forever possible, wherever you may find yourself today.

relied upon to form its reality. When you act in new ways, anticipation of the unexpected is aroused and previously closed doors to fulfillment begin swinging open.

It works like this because our focus in life is currently skewed by the effects of time and space and our place in it, which means that our beliefs are then perpetually developed and refined *as we witness* our life's physical progress. Our every action is recorded in its finest detail and assimilated through the layers of our beliefs. Your behavior, like your thoughts, especially when repeated, is recorded, and these recordings then prove and reinforce the belief you hold that says "That's the way life is." If, however, despite contradictory circumstances that surround you, you can gather the courage to act even a little out of step with your old beliefs—as if to say "That's not the way it's going to continue"—it will be recorded, documented, and carry a message that states "From now on things are going to be different!"

Acting *As If:* Seeding New Beliefs

To give you some examples of actions you can take to help suspend an old belief and install a new one, I'll start with something I've always done whenever I had money worries (meaning I was afraid my supply was drying up).

Overcoming Poverty Consciousness

Whenever I've encountered the illusion that I would soon be out of money, I immediately started giving more money to charities. In addition to everything else I've talked about so far, I'd write a check weekly to a new charity. The check was nothing remotely extravagant but large enough to give me pause to suspend the belief that I did not have a ready source of predictable income or revenue. And here's the point: When I've been concerned about money, it was never easy to cut those checks, which told me that I was definitely going against the grain of my old, limiting beliefs. I'd want to rationalize and say to myself, "Oh, I'll send them something next week," or I would question whether or not I'd already sent them something recently, but I made myself do it. Once I set myself into motion, to the best of my ability, I'd begin feeling a sense of gratitude that I was in a position to help others, and a sense of knowing that my coffers would be replenished by the Universe (i.e., the principles that would be triggered by my demonstration)— and they *always* were.

Another example of what you might do to eliminate poverty consciousness is adding just a couple of dollars to the "minimum payments" you make each month on your revolving credit card bills or mortgage—*as if* you now had more money than in prior months when you could pay only the minimum.

Using this understanding of how your actions can send a clear signal to your belief system, you can gradually chip away at your old, limiting beliefs. Of course, one of the keys here is sticking with it and repeating such actions on a regular basis, without regard to the old life that still surrounds you, as well as simultaneously visualizing and becoming aware of your beliefs.

Overcoming Illness

If someone were ill and bedridden for months, longing to resume his morning walks outdoors, instead of just waiting to feel better, he might first begin listening to the weather service every morning. He would then know whether or not he would get rained on and therefore how to dress, *acting as if* he were going for a walk that very morning. He might also start setting his alarm in the morning for the time he would need to wake up—*as if* he knew he was going for a walk. If he could at least get out of bed, he could lay out his walking clothes each night *as if* he knew he was going for a walk the next morning. And each morning, if and when possible, he could start dressing for the walk *as if* he were capable of going outdoors. Once his health began improving to the point where he could get out of bed, he could at least begin walking around the house *as if* he were just getting loosened up for the walk outside. Of course, also visualizing these walks would be a powerful aid to his recovery as well.

All these actions would temporarily suspend his belief that he was ill and bedridden, and coupled with the desire to change the situation, his physical condition (which is intimately connected to the matrix of his new and evolving beliefs) would similarly respond. New messages would be received and stored by his inner witness—"prepare all systems for a walk"—and the old beliefs would begin being eroded. Optimism would be generated, new thoughts would be thought, and the healing process would be accelerated.

Of course, all these actions would supplement the customary actions one performs when he or she wants to recover from health challenges, such as consulting with physicians, eating properly, and so on.

Finding Employment

If someone were without a job, she could start behaving *as if* she were already employed. She could set her alarm clock each night, and she could make sure her wardrobe was up to par. If she couldn't afford all the clothes she'd need, she could make an effort to go window-shopping for whatever she'd buy *as if* she could afford it; she could also try on a few suits. She could even leave for work on the occasional morning *as if* she had the job of her dreams. She wouldn't have to spend the day away from home—just enough time to go through her morning "get ready for work" procedures. Perhaps the outing could involve a visit downtown (if that's where she wanted to work) or a drive to different prospective employers' buildings—*as if* she already worked there. She could meet a friend and have coffee, lunch, or dinner wherever people employed in her field go to have coffee, lunch, or dinner. And again, all these actions would supplement the customary actions people perform when they want such a life change, such as preparing a new resume, contacting employment agencies, reading "Help Wanted" ads, and so on. But she'd also be acting the part, on occasion, of someone employed in the manner she wished to be employed—*as if* she were already employed.

Traveling Internationally

If you dream of traveling internationally one day, get a passport today, call travel agents, surf the internet, price trips, and read up on the places you want to go, and do these things *as if* you were scheduled to go wherever it is you dream of going, even if—*especially if*—these actions go against the grain of your existing beliefs.

Creating Romance

If you want a significant someone in your life, start looking for the kind of gifts you'd buy for him or her, set aside time in your calendar for weekends away, call for brochures of places you'd like to visit with that person, and become aware of things you could do as a couple, like theater schedules and concert dates. Don't just prepare; act *as if* you already have a romance. I've even gone so far as buying concert tickets, one for me and one for my date, without even knowing anyone I could invite to join me. Or you could make other small purchases, like a tie or a teddy bear, *as if* you already have someone to give it to.

A New Car

If you're dreaming of owning a particular car, go to the car dealership that sells it and test-drive it, or call people in the classified ads and ask them about their cars. Find out the trade-in value of your present car. Finally, call an insurance company to get a quote on your new rates—all *as if* you have your new car.

Prosperity Consciousness

In addition to many of the examples above that equally apply here, if you dream of living the champagne-and-caviar lifestyle, buy the shoes! Price the villa in Saint-Tropez, call the country club, form your own charitable foundation, or open an online investment account—*as if* you were about to drop a load of money into it. Window shop, order catalogues from the stores you'll shop from, and ask your credit card company to raise your spending limits. Plan a celebration party, create the invitation list, and pick the location, and do all these things *as if* you already live in abundance.

Other Handy Miracles

If you want your health to improve, do something—anything—that only a healthy person would do. Or if you want to lose weight, then for a day, eat whatever you think only thin people would eat, ideally in the same proportions they would choose! If you want more friends, start planning the kind of things you'd do with more friends, and when you make inquiries about events or programs you'd like to attend with your friends, always speak in terms of "we."

If you want a busy social calendar, go and get a social calendar. If you want to overcome your fear of flying, call an airline and enroll in its frequent-flyer program (it's usually free). If you want to publish your writings, get them copyrighted and start doing whatever it is you think authors do. If you want to be famous, practice signing autographs. If you want to help others, begin at home. If you want to quit smoking, start by cleaning and putting away your ashtrays. If you want to double your sales, pick the reward you're going to give yourself once you succeed, shop for that reward, and learn all about its every detail (you don't have to buy it . . . yet). If you want to hobnob with someone special or with a particular group of people, begin writing their names in your date book for lunch or for weekend trips. If you want to start your own company, jot down some of your corporate goals and write a mission statement.

These kinds of actions are fun and easy, and you don't even have to spend money doing them. You just need to be a little creative. Let there be no limit to your ingenuity.

And always, as I said in the previous chapters, *just do what you can*! Don't wait for the dam to burst before living the life of your dreams; begin living them now *to any extent you can*. If you dream of having big money to spend on extravagances one day, then start buying little extravagances that you can already afford today. If you want to travel far and wide, start now by traveling as far as you can. And finally, as already mentioned, let all your new behaviors supplement, not replace, the many traditional things you could also be doing to bring about change in your life.

In most of these examples, notice that the actions were all actions that would normally be taken only *after* the person's dreams were attained; they weren't just preparatory steps in line with the goal's achievement. Not that there's anything wrong with preparing; these too are important actions to take, and they speak of your confidence in and expectation of moving forward. But actions that presuppose that your dream has *already* come true are even more powerful than those that prepare for your dreams to come true.

By behaving *as if* your dream has already come true, you powerfully impact your thought processes and ultimately your belief system. Whatever it is you want today, to the degree that it's possible and feasible, act *as if* it's already in your life.

Pretending Is Powerful

I remember preparing to run a marathon—26.2 miles—a number of years ago, and though I trained well for it, I was really scared that

I'd hit the proverbial "wall," that I'd get cramps, or that, for some reason, I just wouldn't be able to finish. I was so scared that a week before the run I couldn't even keep some of my meals down. Big problem.

So as an act of faith, I started thinking of something I'd do only if I had *already* successfully run the marathon, and what I decided was to write a letter to my grandmother in New York, *as if* the marathon had already come and gone and I had happily completed it. I wrote her a couple of pages, excitedly telling her how easy it had been and even making fun of myself for having worried so much the week before the race. I kept this letter with me all week, because, of course, I didn't really write it with the intention of mailing it. I wrote it for myself, and I read it to myself from time to time throughout the week whenever I felt nervous or overwhelmed. And come race day, I ran 8.5-minute miles the whole way—no wall, no cramps, no problem whatsoever, just like I'd written to my grandmother. This is also an obvious example of how I coupled my normal, conventional training with my spiritually motivated act of faith.

Too often I encounter people in my audiences who somehow seem to think that because they suddenly grasp deeper spiritual truths, they no longer have to go out and engage life by taking action. Just as it would have been rather ridiculous for me to forgo my physical training because I wrote my grandmother this letter, it is equally ridiculous for them to think they can perhaps live in abundance, find their "soul mate," improve their health, or even simply live happily without taking regular, consistent physical action in those directions. Of course, knowing the truth about our reality does mean you can have *far more* and get it *wildly faster* while physically doing *much less*. But knowing the truth is not an invitation to withdraw from life so that the Universe can live your life for you, *especially* not when you wish to bring about major life changes.

To supplement the more traditional, physical actions you take as you move toward your dream, you, too, can write an old friend, an anticipated new friend, or a relative a long letter, telling in great detail of your latest adventures, conquests, and accomplishments *as if* you've just completed whatever it is you still want to do. And you don't have to mail it; just keep it around and read it to yourself from time to time.

Here's another idea: write yourself a letter, *as if* you were someone else sending you praise, inquiries, offers, or business proposals that are all in line with your dreams. For example, if you wanted to land a certain job, you could write yourself a letter *as if* you were the head of that company's human resources department, extending yourself an offer to work for the company at an awesome salary. Or the letter could come from an agent, a publisher, a romantic interest—whomever you'd really like to receive these kinds of letters from. These are the letters you will read back to yourself later so that you can get into the *feeling* of what it would be like to really receive one.

Another playful thing you can do is go on lavish shopping sprees through expensive mail order catalogues and write down the items and prices of everything you'd like to buy *as if* you had more than enough money to purchase them. Total your order and say out loud, "That's all?" and then go back through the pages to see if you missed anything else you'd like. You could also call stores with picky but polite questions about a particular item you want—something that you're not able or ready to buy but that you dream of having. Call *as if* you were about to make the purchase, making certain that the item is just right for you.

To help myself think of some new actions, I make a list of whatever dreams I have, and under each dream I write down simple, inexpensive acts of faith that I can start doing right now. These are things that I'd normally do *only after* I've achieved whatever it is I want to achieve, and I begin doing them as often as I can. I try to do at least one of these things every day or at least several things each week. Try it and you'll see. It's actually fun, but if you don't make the initial list ahead of time, it's harder to think of how to go out of your way each day to do these things. You can repeat any of these actions as often as you like, but mixing them up helps keep them fresh and believable. The possibilities are endless, and once you get going, keep going. Do new things and repeat your favorites.

It should go without saying that it's not enough to do one thing, write one letter, or make one purchase and then wait. You must be *consistently* active, repeatedly behaving as if your dream is *already* a reality. You wouldn't work out at a gym once and call it exercising; you'd go regularly. And always—this is important, which is why I keep repeating it—imagine that you're doing what you're doing because your dream has *already* arrived, not because you want it to arrive and you think these steps will help. Don't think of these actions as preparation for your dream, but experience them as *living* your dream.

When performing your acts of faith, really get into it. At first it may seem awkward or even ridiculous, but neither of those feelings will diminish the message you send within. Do your best to play the part as though you were auditioning for a role in a movie; think of every consideration that would make the situation and your part seem more "real." And while you'd want it to appear real to any bystanders, it's most important that it feels *real to you*! Keep with it as best you can, and as the changes begin to manifest around you, remain alert. Just because the results may be suddenly successful, make sure that their foundation is just as solid as your old way of life was. Don't let jubilation dampen your drive for consistency. Keep with it until every area of your life matches your inner dream-world, and let the exercises of visualizing and acting be ongoing and intertwined with your many other habits and routines.

This acting, or pretending, *is* game playing, but it's no less significant than the acting and roleplaying you already do based on your existing beliefs. Watch yourself and you'll see by your "involuntary" actions what your beliefs are. For instance, if you find yourself saving or preparing for a rainy day, what does that say about your belief in the "weather" ahead and your ability to handle it? This doesn't mean you shouldn't be prudent, but it does mean you can start identifying your hindering beliefs and begin eroding them with token acts of faith (while continuing to be prudent). Or if lately you find yourself reading up more and more on "challenges" shared by people like you, maybe it's time you changed your focus to the successes shared by people like you—*if there really are "people like you."*

After one talk I gave, an older man came up and told me that the U.S. military has some beliefs similar to mine. He explained that whenever a serviceman went to his superior and began asking about retirement, that person would be helped to retire as soon as possible, because his action alone—inquiring about retirement—meant that his heart was no longer behind his military service. What we do says a lot about our so-called invisible beliefs, especially when we can catch ourselves preparing for certain future outcomes.

You must be *consistently* active, repeatedly behaving as if your dream is *already* a reality.

The Power of Your Words

There's another type of action that some books address in their entirety, and it is *your word.* Your word is thought crystallized, taken to another level in specificity and clarity. You may think sixty thousand thoughts each day, but the number of words you speak pales in comparison. And your words often reflect the thoughts that you most intensely believe in. You may think thoughts of abundance—lots of thoughts of abundance—but if you also have dominant beliefs in scarcity, you'll likely hear yourself say things like "Good-paying jobs are hard to find." The beliefs of yours that are the strongest will ultimately muster up the most powerful thoughts you think, determine the words you speak, and eventually manifest the life you lead.

It's as if your words are the thoughts you've selectively brought down to Earth to show the light of day, based upon the beliefs that gave them rise, so they lead the pack of your other as-yet-unmanifested thoughts.

Your words, like the actions they are, can be broken down into two types: those you speak somewhat spontaneously in conversations—the words that mirror your beliefs—and those you deliberately choose, such as affirmations or mantras, that can begin installing new beliefs.

**Your word is thought crystallized,
taken to another level in specificity and clarity.**

Exposing Your Beliefs

The first type—words spoken spontaneously—provides an excellent roadmap to your beliefs, which is why I always strive to pay close attention to everything I say. When we listen to ourselves as we converse with others, we can catch ourselves espousing our beliefs, as was true about observing our actions. For this reason, it could be said that our words are simply our thoughts that will become things the soonest. But by following those words back to the beliefs they were drawn from, we can begin identifying which ones either support or deny our dreams.

Creating New Possibilities

The second type—words that you deliberately choose, such as affirmations—can be an amazing tool for installing new beliefs and attracting new thoughts and ideas that are in line with your dreams. Affirmations are not only helpful in installing new beliefs, but like our *acts of faith*, they can also help us make strides in eroding invisible, limiting ones. In case affirmations, which are sometimes also called mantras, are new to you, they're simply short, empowering statements that you repeatedly say to yourself. An example would be a statement such as "I am surrounded by wealth and abundance," or instead of "wealth and abundance," you might choose "friends and laughter"—anything at all that you want to be surrounded by (stated *as if* they *already* surround you). There's no format and there are no magic patterns; it's just a short phrase or two (or three) that you repeat again and again, usually out loud but sometimes silently.

Using affirmations and mantras is actually a simple form of self-hypnosis, because by repeatedly saying and *feeling* what you want to experience emotionally—*as if* you were already there (as opposed to repeatedly stating your desires, such as "I want xyz, I want xyz, I want xyz..."), you create an energy that gives them and their related thoughts more permanence and credibility in your own mind. And I hope you noticed that I did just use the word "feeling," because without *feeling* the things you're saying, there's little point in saying them. There must be emotion, or these words and their related thoughts won't be able to compete with all your other thoughts vying for your emotional support, be it through fear or happiness. By feeling the emotion of the words you speak, you magnify the power of the thoughts behind them and you intensify the beliefs you want to embrace. Really get into the words you choose, and listen to yourself as if you were listening to some higher authority telling you about the way your life already is.

I've never been very consistent with using affirmations myself, but sometimes I go through spells when I'll use them a lot. I think that one of the tricks with using them is mixing them up and not being too methodical—not using the same ones again and again—because they lose their freshness with too much use and the words begin to sound hollow.

Along these same lines, something that's always helped me in choosing affirmations is to use language that has personal meaning to me. For instance, when we first started TUT, I lived for over a year without a paycheck, and my spending habits were generally very, very frugal. But when we first started getting some consistently large orders, I noticed that when I had personal spending decisions to make, ranging from groceries to vacations, I started to hear myself thinking and saying, "It's okay; the money's coming in now." I hadn't formulated those words to be meaningful, but I heard myself thinking them involuntarily and they gave me comfort. They were naturally chosen, and they signified that I believed I was achieving a certain financial freedom. So in subsequent times, whenever business slowed or cash was tight, I recalled my prior little mantra and would start *deliberately* saying to myself, "It's okay; the money's coming in now" over and over again.

Whenever we want something—an event or a thing—to come into our lives, it's obviously because that event or thing is not currently in our lives, and the trick is that we must begin thinking and acting as if it is already there. We must talk as if it's already there, and while saying such things seems a bit crazy, that's the way it works. That's the key to living your dreams: you must live them first, at least in your thoughts, in order to manifest them.

**Words are simply our thoughts that
will become things the soonest.**

When I go jogging, I often begin a mantra (usually spoken in a whisper) that affirms my body's health, and I use each step to create a beat or cadence to my running. I say something like "My heart is perfect and healthy." Then I'll say, "My lungs are perfect and healthy," then my kidneys, and then my skin, my eyes, my blood—everything I can think of.

Other times, when I'm jogging or driving, I'll verbally give thanks: thanks for my life, for my dogs, for my perspectives, for my wealth, for my peace of mind, for my divinity, for my car, for my family and friends, and, just as often, *for things that I do not yet materially have*, as if *I already have them*.

Why Gratitude Rocks

When you think or speak thoughts of thanks, what you're really doing is *thinking thoughts of having received* or of having been blessed (however you want to name it). Remember what happens when you think thoughts—any thoughts? *They become things* in your life. This means that when you think thoughts of *having received*, those thoughts seek to come back to you experientially (manifesting in time and space). And they can only do this by *crafting circumstances* in which you will physically receive whatever you were giving thanks for so that you can then experience that gratitude you "previously" sent out.

As always, *it's the feeling* you put out that matters the most. In fact, you don't even have to be thankful for anything in particular when you send out gratitude as long as you send out the feeling "I have received." In response, the Universe (your Greater Self, *your thoughts*) will give you reason to experientially feel the gratitude you first put out, crafting occurrences and surprises *that you may have never even thought about* but that were exactly the kinds of things that would manifest the feeling that you *did* think about!

This is why gratitude works in bringing about fantastic change. Contrary to popular belief, it's not because the Universe is happy to hear you're grateful and will therefore send you more; there's no such judgment system. In fact, there *couldn't be* without it interfering with your ability to create or without it limiting you and the infallible principle *thoughts become things*! It works because of the thoughts and feelings it generates, which can only be made physical by becoming the appropriate things and events of your life.

Now, if you think that giving out gratitude in order to receive something back is very self-serving and therefore undignified (just wanting and receiving more), it's not. That's just a limiting belief. The truth is that there is enough for everyone, and your receiving your heart's desires does not mean others are going without theirs. Plus, how can you give to others until you have first received? And how could anything manufactured of thought be limited?

Give thanks and praise to life, its grace, and its unfailing principles for having *already* manifested your dreams.

Gratitude is powerful and it *does* work magic, so it's great to work it into your affirmations whenever you can. Give thanks and praise to life, its grace, and its unfailing principles for having *already* manifested your dreams; say things like "Thanks for surrounding me with health, wealth, friends, and laughter! Thank you, thank you, thank you!" and really feel it.

Life is waiting for you—waiting for you to give it direction, give it meaning, and provide just a spark. When acting in line with your dreams, you invoke life's inviolate principles, you set into motion an array of unseen forces, and you unleash the magic behind the illusions of time and space. It's the same magic that helps you finish a sentence before you even know how it'll end, knows just how fast to beat your heart, and spins your dreams each and every night. It's also the magic that sweeps birds into formation, sends bears into hibernation and bees after honey, and pushes up trees and all things green. This is the magic *you* invoke when you act with certainty and the magic that makes dreams come true; all that's needed to get the ball rolling is for you to aim and throw. And like a boomerang, your intentions—supported by your thoughts, deeds, and words—will indeed return to you, manifested within time and space.

We're all sorcerers. We're all magicians. And we can each invoke this magic to live the life of our dreams. Indeed, it's our greatest birthright.

5

Gifts from Heaven

*W*e've talked about thoughts, we've talked about beliefs, and we've talked about emotions and actions, but which comes first? Where does the cycle begin? What inspires our thoughts, which then become things that give rise to our emotions—emotions from which we pass judgment, formulate beliefs, and then base our subsequent thoughts, feelings, and actions upon? Where does the chain start?

In chapter 3, "Blessed Emotions," I said that in the beginning, what was necessary for time and space to explode into existence was a profoundly huge wish or desire made or felt by God (Divine Intelligence), and therein lies the answer: desire comes first; it precedes time and space, and it's what we were born of. And now we are inside this wish—divine ourselves, creators ourselves—here to take this dream to another level with our own inborn desires. And we can do this because we've been endowed with free will and the power to think our own thoughts.

The Dream Is Alive and Well

Some of our desires and dreams are inborn, while others we create or formulate during our journeys (which I'll talk about later in this chapter). Those that are inborn, as if implanted in our soul and as much a part of us as our personalities, come from outside our normal

103

awareness. It's been said by many that we're all spiritual beings having a human experience, and it's from the vastness of our present spiritual selves that we receive direction and guidance in the form of our dreams and desires, as well as from our hunches, instincts, and impulses—*it's our feelings* that help us find our way.

These *gifts from heaven*, our intuitive feelings, have more of a celestial origin than, say, our normal thoughts, emotions, and actions, because these are more often byproducts of our experiences in time and space, arising as reactions to the events and circumstances we craft. Conversely, our feelings—and here I mean desires—intuitions, and impulses—not our emotions—come to us by divine means, as if gifts from heaven. Gifts because they originate outside our normal awareness—not from outside ourselves but from within, *independent* of the physical world we live in.

Of course, there's no real separation of our spiritual and physical selves since space and distances are purely illusionary, but because we focus so completely on the reality of "things and such," we've done a poor job of honing our spiritual faculties. By opening our spiritual eyes, however, we begin rubbing shoulders with our higher selves, we create opportunities for greater happiness and fulfillment, and we approach the magical source within us that gives birth to our awareness.

Direct Knowing

Our hunches, impulses, and intuitions are all forms of direct knowing, as is the "spontaneous illumination" I spoke of earlier, and they originate from a deeper place within us—from our higher selves. These bursts of insight sparkle truths about our reality and the dramas we're in the middle of creating. They're available to us as if through our own private window to Divine Mind, and they often appear when we least expect them. By training ourselves to seek them out, however, the wisdom they offer can be added to our own arsenals of truth.

Since we are indeed unlimited spiritual beings, and because space is an illusion, we really are *everywhere* at once. Our awareness extends to and is part of the farthest reaches of space, encompassing every atom and molecule on planet Earth.

Right now as you're reading this, you're literally connected to people living their lives in China, Italy, and Saudi Arabia—to everyone, everywhere, *always*. Some authors and animal behaviorists have scraped the tip of the iceberg by finding just such a connection that is now known (and hotly debated) as the "Hundredth Monkey Effect."* Not only does this connection occur in present time but it also stretches throughout eternity, past and future. We're all there and we're all One, so we have this pipeline—this direct connection with all knowledge and facts—in all times and places, past and future. And with this kind of knowledge, we do indeed already have access to infinite wisdom—unless we think or believe otherwise. If we think we're merely human beings, for example, only capable of knowing what we've been taught or what we've physically experienced, we severely curtail the flow from these fountains of insight.

Our connection to the infinite makes us all psychics to the greatest degree, although some of us can access this information more easily than others. The point here is realizing that your starting point for infinite knowledge and wisdom should begin with knowing that it's all already at your disposal, even though you may have trained yourself into thinking that it's inaccessible. Most of us tend to think (and our society and the evolution of our beliefs has reinforced it) that we must behave as if we know nothing unless we can "prove" it or learn it intellectually, generally from sources outside of ourselves. But the proof lies in your own unending experiences with *direct*

---

*As Wikipedia puts it, the "Hundredth Monkey Effect" is a supposed phenomenon in which a learned behavior spreads instantaneously from one group of monkeys to all related monkeys once a critical number is reached. By generalization it means the instant, paranormal spreading of an idea or ability to the remainder of a population once a certain portion of that population has heard of the new idea or learned the new ability.

knowing—your own personal revelations—during which, from one moment to the next, you went from having a question to inexplicably possessing its answer.

People use their connection to spirit throughout their lives, and you can begin recognizing your experiences with it by simply asking yourself where any of your thoughts, memories, or ideas come from.

Here's a little exercise:

As you read these words, take a deep breath, hold it, and let it out.

Now with your mind still and relaxed, think back to any memory of your childhood that occurred before you were about ten years old.

Got it? Now, where did that memory come from? Surely you don't think it was physically stored in your brain. It was a memory retained by your spiritual essence, and by summoning it with intent and *the belief that you could*, you drew it forth into your present moment.

Now recall a memory that was created yesterday, at any time in the day.

Got it? Now you've brought forth something else. Where did it come from? Only moments ago it was *not* there. And haven't you noticed that when you suddenly start thinking of a distant memory, as you dwell on it, more and more details begin flooding into your awareness?

Now, one more exercise: please recall the mechanics and tools used to raise each block of the great pyramids of Giza.

What happened? You were using your pipeline a moment ago, but now it's dried up. We've been trained to believe that we don't know the answer because we weren't there when the blocks were raised. Yet we *can* intuitively know that our memory is not something that physically resides inside the brain, and we can know that "we are all One." So wouldn't it be true that if another part of us was there, we were there? Moreover, as One with all things, we were there regardless of others being there. In my view, it would be true; it's simply that most of us have not yet learned to exercise the muscle

that gives us such insight. Our disbelief keeps us from creating the intent that would be prerequisite for such illuminations, although this is exactly what happens during countless experiences of both astral projection and remote viewing.

Xenoglossy is a fringe condition describing people who, typically under deep hypnosis, have knowledge of a language they've never learned. Of course, because such stories do not jibe with our culture's present beliefs, they never make headlines. It's rationalized that the hypnotized individual *must have* been exposed to the language at some earlier point in his or her life—end of exploration. It doesn't matter that such stories have reappeared time and again, as do stories, incidentally, of reincarnation memories, ESP, and other paranormal occurrences. And this is exactly why further research into such phenomenona is abandoned—because it just isn't acceptable in our society's belief system to believe that spontaneous enlightenment occurs at all. Our limiting beliefs, as I said in the second chapter, dismiss any evidence of circumstances and events that don't agree with them, and so the subject is dropped. But the truth is, all knowledge and wisdom are immediately accessible to every one of us—they're ours for the taking—once we let up on the beliefs that keep them at bay.

**The proof lies in your own unending experiences with
direct knowing—your own personal revelations—
during which, from one moment to the next,
you went from having a question to
inexplicably possessing its answer.**

The point of mentioning all this isn't to catapult you into knowing *all things* instantaneously or having you speak in tongues, but to help you begin tuning in to your *gifts from heaven*—to enhance your life, bring about change, and live your dreams, which happily, even in our spiritually primitive society, is something most of us already believe is possible.

Creativity: Our Link to Divine Mind

Creative thinking comes from a person's ability to suspend his or her reliance on rational thinking, or the methodical brain, and dip directly into Divine Intelligence. We're all highly creative, actually, yet we often don't allow our own creativity to flow because of the limiting beliefs we possess.

Being creative is like a birthing process, where in the twinkling of an eye what has *never* existed suddenly comes to life—added to Divine Mind, or Divine Intelligence—for all others to reach eternally.

When Mom, my brother Andy, and I were just a few years into the T-shirt business, our sales reps and wholesale customers told us that we needed to add a dolphin design to our repertoire. So we did, and it bombed. We tried again. The second time around the art was gorgeous, but the poem we chose to add to it was pretty pathetic. Andy wrote the first half: "The Deep Blue Sea spoke to me, it was holding back a mystery. A dolphin took me by the hand, it wanted me to understand." But then the rest of the poem really fizzled. We had some deadlines and commitments to make with the new design, and we almost released it with the weak second stanza, but before leaving the office that day, I just felt from the core of my being that this shirt would also bomb if we didn't improve the poem. Not having anyone else to write it, I decided I'd have a go at it. And for reasons I still can't explain, I just knew I could write something better.

Within an hour I was done, and no one was more shocked than I—despite my initial confidence—with how nicely it turned out: "That in this life there's more to behold than bags of money and pots of gold. Believe in yourself and you will see how happy and free you were meant to be." I know it's a little cheesy, but it's also succinct, with a powerful rhyming message. I had known I could do it, but I didn't know how I would pull it off or what the poem would say. Focus, intention, and expectation, *demonstrated by my taking action*—simply putting pencil to paper and "beginning"—drew from Divine Intelligence what is still, to this day, one of the most popular

"thoughts" and T-shirts we've ever offered. Within just a few years, we sold almost one hundred thousand of them, plus coffee mugs, greeting cards, and more, to every corner of the globe. The magic here occurred when I settled on the effects of the end result, not on my brain's ability to deduce and logically formulate the sentences. I knew my intent, believed it was possible, started to physically write, and then, in some magical way, I stepped aside to let the details take care of themselves as I simply held on to the vision (dream) of what I wanted to achieve.

Creativity is just more evidence that we not only exist beyond our physical selves, but that we can draw insights, comprehensions, and solutions from those realms to enhance our time and space adventures.

Channeling and Automatic Writing: Expressing Your Higher Self

Another example of our innate connection to our higher selves is the unending array of channeled work. I'm referring to people who can induce a trance—virtually at will—during which another portion of their being, sometimes even another personality, begins talking through them. Some examples are Jane Roberts, who channeled the Seth material; J. Z. Knight, who channels Ramtha; and Esther Hicks, who channels Abraham. In each of these cases, the dictations for books they've published are in such excellent form that the recorded word appears directly in a bound volume, written in one draft!

Creativity is just more evidence that we not only exist beyond our physical selves, but that we can draw insights, comprehensions, and solutions from those realms to enhance our time and space adventures.

Other people channel by means of what is commonly called automatic writing. *Conversations with God*, by Neale Donald Walsch, and *Jonathan Livingston Seagull*, by Richard Bach, are contemporary examples. The authors claim that they literally felt their pen or pencil begin writing by itself, or that it was as if they were simply taking dictation for a stream of unending words that ran through their minds in perfect order. And again, no significant editing was necessary; the first draft of their books become the final draft. Whether spoken or written, these are both examples of channeled work, of our connection with the infinite, and there's no doubt in my mind that every one of us is capable of such communications.

In fact, I believe we all partake of this kind of communication unceasingly throughout every day of our lives, not necessarily with other personalities but instead with greater portions of ourselves— our intuitions and hunches. And while I don't claim to have ever had any kind of channeled experiences like these people have, I still can't help but marvel at the process of creativity, whether writing, thinking, or calculating, often wondering, "Where does all this stuff (my stream of consciousness) come from?" Given that we're all physical creatures and that *thought* simply *cannot* be a product of the brain (but rather is processed by it), doesn't it make sense that every thought we've ever entertained has been channeled to some degree from our spiritual selves through our physical selves? And while our words are spoken, physically, I'm sure you'll agree that the ideas they convey aren't formulated by our mouths and tongues. Our bodies are just the apparatus that deliver "the goods," which originated from points beyond. We're all channels, and our physical bodies simply translate our spiritual energies out to a physical world, which, again, is made possible because of our divine connection to the infinite.

Now, I want to throw out a little caution when it comes to channeled material. Just because this kind of information comes from outside time and space (which is actually true of all information) doesn't mean that it's always accurate, useful, or even helpful. I've read some channeled material that was very base, degrading, and negative, so each of us must discern the truth for ourselves; we have to be our own guides to what is useful or bunk, and the best way to do this is to follow our own feelings. If any information, channeled or not, including my own words here, rubs you the wrong way or doesn't feel right, then let it go. You have to be your own moderator and filter to all the information that's out there, no matter what its source.

While not all the channeled material out there is necessarily helpful, its occurrence does evidence greater realms beyond time and space, and it demonstrates that knowledge doesn't have to come from time and space events alone, as we've erroneously been taught. We do not have to exclusively use logic to figure out the tasks and challenges before us. By adding to the mix our own hunches, intuitions, creativity, and instincts—our feelings, these gifts from Divine Mind—we can better approach our challenges, calming troubled waters, easing anxious minds, and giving birth to insights and creations that have never before existed. By letting down our guard and using these gifts, we can consider the life before us with a much broader and more complete picture than logic could ever muster up.

Let Your Burning Desire Set the World on Fire

We're not here just to meet our needs so that we can merely survive; the original grand wish that gave birth to time and space was not for us to have some kind of break-even experience; we're here to have fun and be happy, to thrive and grow, and these objectives can only be met by pursuing the unique passions we all individually possess. Too often it's thought that our desires are frivolous and our dreams selfish, yet our planet is an abundant and opulent paradise, and it freely shares its treasures to those who meet it halfway—less than halfway even—with unlimited thinking, great expectations, and the simplest of actions. And the more we allow it to share with us, the more it shares with others, in an unfolding that inevitably and unfailingly far exceeds what was sought by the original dream.

Our desires are gifts, not curses, and they should be honored. They're the spirit of life dancing through us, pointing us in directions that will inspire us and hinting of our true potential. Our dreams, too, are gifts, and they're far more remarkable than is ever appreciated. They're tailor-made for us based equally on what we want and what our soul craves, taking into account all we've ever done, and our leanings, inclinations, aptitudes, outlooks, and strengths, in order to grow and become more. They aren't ours so that they may elude or torment us, but because they're achievable and because we're worthy of them. And even better than the destination they promise is the journey they inspire, through the seas and landscapes of life, making possible endless opportunities for interactions with others, incredible coincidences, and wonderful accidents. But of course, as you already know, there are no coincidences and there are no accidents; these are just occurrences orchestrated by our thoughts—life's magic—as they juggle the players and circumstances of our life to deliver to us the things we have been thinking.

Dreams are selfish only if you believe in scarcity and lack—if you believe that for you to receive something, others must go without. But these kinds of beliefs are impossible when you truly understand that you are a spiritual being and that the props in your life are merely illusions. Your dreams come from the infinite, and only by pursuing them with abandon can you then give to the world all you have to give, remaining true to your own "selfish" desires. Could Thomas Edison, for example, have tended to the downtrodden as Mother Teresa did? Could Albert Einstein have preached salvation as Dr. Martin Luther King Jr. did? Could Abraham Lincoln have built cars like Henry Ford did? You know who these people are because they followed their own unique passions, their own inborn leanings, and their own inner voices. The irony here, though, with regard to the thought that our dreams are selfish, is that the masses—sometimes even for generations—*always* benefit from the individual who insists on marching to the beat of his or her own drummer, or as Richard Bach phrased it in the colossal bestseller *Illusions*, "the divinely selfish soul."

Our dreams and our desires are as unique as our fingerprints, and we're endowed with them based on each of our own unique spiritual quests in life. We have different dreams for a reason: to maximize the chances of us having the kind of adventures and lessons that will enrich us the most. We're not all born wanting to be doctors, we're not all born wanting to be beautiful, and, as hard as this may seem to believe, we're not all born wanting to live easy, cushy lives. No two people want the exact same things. It's like when we're choosing our vacations: some prefer to relax and do very little, while others prefer risks and challenges to varying degrees.

The original grand wish that gave birth to time and space was not for us to have some kind of break-even experience!

Our dreams have veiled, specialized agendas that inspire our journeys and yield what we really came here to get—experience—while revealing our true potential for living the life of our dreams. If written off early in life as frivolous, indulgent, or selfish, or if they're replaced with more idealized, mainstream dreams—dreams that are not really ours but are considered practical, safe, or proven—we only stifle our own growth and happiness.

Sadly, this kind of substitution happens all the time when society—or even our own families—try to point us in the "right" directions, supposedly for our own good. And while their intentions are golden, no one can ever know you like you do. No one else can know what fulfills you or what drives you; no one else can see through your window to the Divine nor hear the instincts and impulses that are whispered in your ear; and no one except you can know what potentials and talents lie dormant inside you. "To thine own self be true," as Shakespeare put it.

Getting Back on Track

If you now find yourself midstream in life, on a journey that's included countless opinions of others and perhaps limiting beliefs of your own, and you believe you're so far off track that you have no idea who the real you is or what your greatest potentials are, then you're probably asking one of the most asked questions of all time: "What should I be doing with my life?" This is not a fun place to be; I've been there. Fortunately, moving on is far easier than it may seem.

Here are a couple of thoughts that'll help get anyone back on track:

1. *Be yourself.* While the following may not thrill you, the fact is, there is no *one* answer to the question of what it is you *should* be doing with your life. Sure, it sounds pat to say that everyone has a special role to play—a special niche to fill that no other could ever fill—but that role or niche comes from *you just being you* and has no relation to what you do for a living any more than what you eat for breakfast or what you wear to bed.

Thinking otherwise implies that there is some profound mission to every life or some deep responsibility to humanity for your presence. But again, both of those are met when you are simply you, regardless of what you decide your career will or won't be. Spiritually, your unique awareness—your mere existence—is one of a kind; *it* is what's important. People tend to think things like "Oh, I must be here to work with my hands, or to teach and heal people, or to write books, or to balance the energy on the planet." But it doesn't matter what "hat" you wear as long as you're *you*. And by being your *real* self—true to yourself—you'll automatically be led by your own natural inclinations and impulses to the roles that will please you most at any given point in your life, thereby enriching the world the most.

2. *Deal with what's already on your plate.* If you're wondering what it is you should be doing with your life, first
realize that wherever you are now has meaning and there's
a reason you're there. That doesn't mean that the reason
is profound, nor does it mean that you must stay where
you are, but because you are there—wherever *there* is—it
needs to be your starting point. And the best news about this
is that it means that wherever you are now is *exactly* where
you should be, so don't look back and second-guess earlier
decisions.

Embrace your current situation for what it is, and for as
long as you remain there, be your best and shine like there's
no tomorrow. Don't fight it, or you'll create such an attachment with your negative thoughts and feelings that you'll
anchor yourself in place! Instead, accept it, go with the flow,
approve of yourself, and understand its worth and value,
and you will rise above anything unpleasant you may now
be facing, releasing yourself from the past and the grip your
resistance has had on your present circumstances. After all, if
you were not where you now are, you wouldn't be asking
the questions and receiving the answers that you are now
asking and receiving.

3. *Follow the fun.* This advice may sound irresponsible to
some, but it's probably the most responsible thing you can
do. Whether or not you feel lost, *always follow the fun.* That
doesn't mean that life should be one nonstop party. Some of
the greatest fun can come from the satisfaction of a job well
done, like being a good parent or spouse, or growing a
flourishing garden. Almost anything can be fun with the
proper perspective.

You know what gives you peace and fulfillment—you
remember the kind of things you liked as a kid—and in this
regard you probably haven't changed much. Think back to
those times. For me it was being in the outdoors, walking

through the woods, paddling a boat, and building things—all of which still thrill me. Scan your life, past and present, and reacquaint yourself with making fun a joy and a priority.

4. *Begin it.* Whatever you decide to do, *begin it.* Even if you're not sure what you should be doing with your life, take baby steps, today, in *any* direction that may possibly resonate with you. Do something. Anything is better than nothing. Move. Take action. Be the spark. Just do what you can. Weave new steps and thoughts into your workdays and throughout your weekends, and inch forward however possible. Be gentle on yourself, forgiving and compassionate, and don't expect overnight enlightenment. It *will* come, and it will light your way; that's inescapable. And you can accelerate its arrival by simply busying yourself in each moment, addressing what's before you and simply expecting it sooner rather than later.

The Hardest Questions

Now, with all this talk of desires, I'm sure you've already thought about desires of yours, or of other people's at least, that are considered—let's just say—unsavory. What about them? Are they gifts from heaven? Should they be pursued?

To begin with, for anything to be unsavory means that someone has passed judgment. So keep in mind that what one person deems to be "bad" could very possibly be deemed "good" by the next. For example, just look at the mixed feelings of people throughout the world with regard to money. To some it's the root of all evil; to others it represents freedom, accomplishment, and security.

But then you might want to ask, "What if a desire affects other people adversely?" Well, whether or not others are affected adversely is again only an opinion—even if they claim to be hurt, for example, such as when their relationship is ended by the other person. Does that really mean that they were affected adversely?

What about the learning, growing, and evolution that takes place whenever we feel emotional pain? If a relationship ends, people can feel hurt only if they choose and allow themselves to feel hurt. Remember too that nothing happens to any of us unless we're ready for it to happen. Accidents are not accidents, and so-called misfortunes are actually only stepping stones to loftier perspectives, made possible because of brand-new thoughts that took you through brand-new territory.

Challenges arrive when you're ready to grow and learn. At some deeper level, they are actually seen as ideal lessons for you to progress toward thoughts you've been thinking and dreams you've been dreaming. And if this is true for you, then it's also true for others.

Big Picture Thinking

You may still have some questions about "unsavory" thoughts and desires, but before we go there again, let's do some more "big picture" thinking. You might be saying, "Gosh, it seems I have too much power; I could either rip someone's heart out, psychologically or physically, or fawn all over them and love them to death." Seen like this, it would seem that you do have a lot of power over other people's lives, which possibly makes you wonder how they could be creating their own reality when you have such total freedom over how you behave toward them. Similarly, if the roles were reversed, it would seem that other people have a lot of power over you, given that they're free to behave with total freedom, in any manner they wish. So how does this affect our ability to construct our own realities?

Well, even though we each have that kind of free will, it doesn't mean that tomorrow is actually the entirely blank slate it seems to be. For instance, based on my beliefs and my view of the world, there are really only several ways for me to deal with people I come in contact with. For example, although I have total freedom, punching someone in the face is simply not a likely possibility, nor am I particularly capable of deliberately behaving in a mean, cold-hearted fashion; nor would I blatantly lie and mislead.

So, yes, I have the unlimited ability to act however I wish, but that doesn't mean that my actions aren't, to some degree, *highly predictable*—confined within a fairly narrow range of probabilities based on the beliefs I currently hold. Everyone *is* spiritually everywhere else at once, and because our awareness of all time and space reaches every single person on the planet, we know *exactly* what kind of people are in our lives and we know exactly what general *range of actions* they're capable of performing. Should this range begin changing in a way that no longer suits our thoughts, needs, and desires, then through the "accidents or coincidences" of our lives, the players will change. People remain in our lives, or they're moved in and out of our lives, based on the underlying thoughts, beliefs, and expectations of all involved, no matter how haphazardly or suddenly they seem to arrive.

The people now in your life are not there accidentally, nor are you accidentally in theirs. We all enter each other's lives pre-approved, with full knowledge of the *possible* roles to be played and their potential *likely* outcomes. Just because we aren't consciously aware of these decisions doesn't negate what is otherwise obviously deducible.

To get back to the question of whether or not our unsavory desires are also gifts, yes, they are, but that doesn't mean that their every manifestation will necessarily bring us peace and happiness— at least not in the short run.

Desires are just desires; they're not good or bad. But they sometimes exist as a result of our beliefs, which tell us that the things we want will bring us certain rewards. Yet we all know people who pursue things that *we* know won't bring them happiness; until they know it, however—until their beliefs change—they'll just keep chasing whatever it is they think will bring them happiness. And what better system could exist for learning that a thing or event is not what will bring you joy than ultimately manifesting that thing or event and learning it firsthand? While this may not be a fun lesson to learn, it will ultimately avail you new insights that were previously impossible to see with the earlier beliefs possessed, and thus our so-called unsavory desires yield fruit.

The Seemingly Unexplainable

You may still wonder, what of children who are violated or other situations where there do indeed appear to be victims of unpre-dictable, unearned tragedies? Even these extreme questions have answers; however, I don't want to deviate too far from the purpose of this book, which is about following your joy and living your dreams. Still, to give you a vague hint as to the direction I'd lead you before answering such questions, I'd ask you, "Are you sure you know all the spiritual implications to every 'horror story' you learn of?" Our logical brains, stuck in the physical world, struggle frantically to jus-tify, rationalize, and explain. But our spiritual selves know that there are larger reasons for things than what we can perceive with our physical senses.

I'm not implying that ugly, wicked, and despicably evil actions don't take place, nor am I suggesting they're ever justified or that aid and compassion shouldn't be immediately rendered to all those involved. But by considering the big picture, in light of the spiritual truths I've been sharing, we can begin to see that even the hardest questions have answers, and that there is order, healing, and there-fore love and perfection in every time and space occurrence.

Dreams Born in the Dream

On the other side of the spectrum are our dreams and desires that result from our beliefs, as opposed to coming to us as *gifts from heaven*, and the question might be asked, "What makes our belief-born dreams different than our inborn *gifts from heaven*?" Actually, there is very little difference. They're still from a divine source—ourselves in the here and now—and they still drive us on and inspire us to learn, grow, and be happy.

Differentiating between the two is a bit like understanding the difference between happy emotions and unpleasant ones, in that the happy ones might be considered more natural, while the unpleasant ones usually stem from limiting beliefs and perceptions.

For our dreams and desires, we can simply look to whatever it is they promise to see if they've been tainted by limiting beliefs. If their promise is happiness, fun, and fulfillment, then they likely haven't been tainted by limiting beliefs. However, if they promise recognition, status, justification, or something like that, perhaps *as a means* to attaining happiness, fun, and fulfillment, then somewhere along the way limiting beliefs got involved. These kinds of desires presuppose that something is missing—something that belongs to every one of us by divine right.

For example, if your desire or dream is to win over someone's heart as a means to achieving your own happiness, somehow you've come to believe that your happiness depends on the approval or the company of another, which simply isn't true. Whether or not you do lasso his or her heart, if this lesson isn't learned, your peace and happiness will never be stable, and deep down you'll know it. In this case, wouldn't it be even better to fail to win that person over so that you'd be pressed even harder to learn what you need to learn? Can you see that even while we may endure an emotional pain, it's always for our greater good? And this is true of all such pains. Rather than cursing them, use them to understand your beliefs and perceptions.

By understanding belief-born desires and why they're really motivating you, you can begin piecing together why you don't seem to have whatever it is they promise. If it's the feeling of freedom you want from a new possession or wealth, then could it be that ordinarily you feel somewhat trapped and limited? Or why might you yearn for appreciation and admiration unless, to some degree, you sense their absence from your life today? Ask yourself why. Because, as an eternal spiritual being, you really are quite free, and it's very likely that the only appreciation and admiration you ever needed earlier in your life came from within. So what's different today? How, when, where, or why did you stop seeing yourself as anything less than acceptable, lovable, and good enough?

Do you want a new job to garner respect? Do you want romance so that you can feel love? Do you want abundance in order to feel power or to avoid responsibility? First, understand what it is you really want emotionally, and second, ask yourself why you want it. If the answer is anything less than "to have fun and grow," then there's likely a lesson to learn, and it begins with understanding why you seem to think you're "without." Why, as the divine creator that you are, have you come to believe that something is missing in your life—that you're incomplete? Ask, because as you can now see, your current beliefs have manifested and desire has appeared to cure the sensed imbalance. This is fine, but if you don't understand that desire, its fruition may come more slowly. And when your dream finally does come true, it may not bring you what you are really after.

Whenever part or all your motivation includes the attainment or realization of something you feel you should already have or be, such as approval, health, or love, start looking to understand why you now find yourself without and what thoughts and beliefs of yours have so far precluded getting what you want.

All the answers you seek lie within. Daily, in moments of quiet, ask yourself for the direction you seek, and look for the answers in your feelings and intuitions. Feel with your heart and your mind; the "right way" will always feel good *and* make sense. Your mission in life—your purpose—is simply to be—*to be yourself.* And the only way you can be yourself is to begin listening to yourself—to your desires and dreams, and to your heavenly inspired feelings. After all, what else is there for you to listen to? What else is there besides your feelings?

You are not your thoughts. You are not your beliefs. You are not even your emotions, though all these have much to teach. However, the closest you can ever come to the wellspring that is you is through your desires and feelings. They're magical, they're unique—they're exclusively yours—and they should be honored. They hint at directions you might take and at just how fulfilled you can really be. They take you on a journey through springtimes and sunrises, as well as through life's murk and mire, and they point the way to enlightenment, highlighting areas in your life where you perhaps see yourself as less than you truly are.

Follow your dreams; they're yours for a reason, not the least of which is to make them come true.

Your *feelings* come to you through a window that opens to Divine Intelligence. Keep that window open, practice gazing from it, and open yourself to following your heart and thinking as you perhaps have never thought before. Begin appreciating its priceless view. And follow your dreams; they're yours for a reason, not the least of which is to make them come true.

6
Magical Universe

So you're likely sitting there, reading these words and thinking that you and your life are so real; thinking, probably, that over all, you're in control of this moment; thinking that it's your home, your office, your journey, your life. And you're right. You *are* in control, thanks *entirely* to the unending miracles that sustain and support you, right here and now; thanks entirely to a Universe that holds and protects the integrity of every cell in your body; thanks entirely to the trillions and trillions of atoms and their protons, neutrons, and electrons that make up you and your surroundings. This is *all* thanks entirely to the Universal principles that can unfailingly be counted on to consistently manifest your ongoing life, while simultaneously integrating your experiences with the *billions* of other people alive on the planet this very moment.

You *are* in control, and you're riding a wave of incalculable proportions. You are powerful beyond imagination, loved beyond comprehension, eternal and free to live the life of your dreams based on the thoughts you choose to think—*all thanks to the elements, principles, grace, and magic that now sustain you and your entire world.*

It's kind of overwhelming, isn't it? And to think that all these things that support you—that make your life even remotely possible—are invisible, lie in the unknown, and must be trusted to do their part. But do you trust them? Perhaps you do but only to the degree that you have to. Living would be impossible without some basic trust in life, so whether you admit it or not, you *do* trust them, but *how much* do you trust them? How much of your life and your manifestations are you willing to turn over to the unknown? Well, the more you turn over and the more you trust that everything is going to go your way, the more effortless your life will become.

Past Seeing, Beyond Believing

In a word, to me this kind of trust in the unknown is called faith— faith that the sun will rise tomorrow (and you along with it); faith that gravity will hold you to the Earth; faith that the spinning molecules that make up your body will not spin out of control and leave you; faith that your heart will keep beating and your lungs will keep you breathing; (and with some practice) faith that you are, and always will be, provided for; faith in the abundance and harmony of all your affairs; and ultimately, faith that your dreams will come true.

Faith connotes a recognition of spirit— an understanding that you are not here as some cosmic accident.

Faith in our magical Universe is what this chapter is about. It's faith in the magic that ensconces our lives—in all those things that are elusive, invisible, silent, abstract, and, most often, completely overlooked and taken for granted. Yet it is their presence that is evident in every facet of our existence if we'd just glance around and look for them.

Sure, you have to be able to trust or believe in yourself, in your family, in your equipment—whatever your profession—and in countless other things and people you come in contact with daily. But when it comes to trusting in the magic and miracles of life, in the unknown, and perhaps the unfathomable in concrete terms, *faith* is the word. Faith could be used interchangeably with the words *trust* or *knowing*, but faith connotes a recognition of spirit—an understanding that you are not here as some cosmic accident and a knowingness of your truly divine heritage. Faith acknowledges that you're not faced with living your life alone, and that you have invisible friends and energy to draw on for guidance and comfort.

Who or What Is the Universe?

I have to admit that it's somewhat challenging at first to have faith and believe in the magic of this unknown reality, particularly in a "conspiring" magic that's supposedly inclined to help and serve us. To our physical senses the unknown *is* just empty space, cold and impersonal. But because the unknown, or the Universe, is not physically detectable doesn't mean that it's sterile and lifeless. On the contrary, it's *alive. Aware.* And filled with love for you.

The Universe, or Divine Intelligence, doesn't lie in the vacuum of space. It comes from a "place" or a dimension that "precedes" both time and space, and from "there" it's created their intersection—this platform from which material manifestations exist. For our world, the Earth, to have such dazzling colors, sounds, and exquisite beauty, it shouldn't take much of a leap to consider that the wellspring of such a paradise would be equally—if not far more—radiant and spectacular. The unseen Universe must be a vibrant "place" that's bright and cheery, colorful, bountiful, and gloriously alive and aware all on its own, without even considering the countless entities and angels it must harbor. It's endowed with intelligence, and it's what you've been taught is "God," yet it exists without any religious trappings, judgments, and rules. Every grain of sand, the trees, the air, the water—everything, including all that is unseen—possesses this intelligence, this awareness; everything is this intelligence and awareness—an awareness that includes you and your thoughts.

We weren't cast here as a test to see if our strength, willpower, and stamina could get us through the turbulence of life. We're here to issue directives—whatever we wish—to a responsive Universe. Yet if we think we must go it alone, then the Universe and its principles will dutifully reflect that belief: *we will* feel alone. That's how much freedom we have.

Rather than just thinking that the Universe is alive and responsive, however, go further and remember that you are One with the Universe. Realize that the greater "you" extends beyond the confines of your skin to reach and touch everywhere you can imagine and beyond, into the unseen. You are alive in the Universe, and the Universe is alive in you. In this sense, it should become even more obvious that it does "conspire" on our behalf *because it is you*—the *bigger* you. The Universe yearns to see your smile and hear your laughter because you are the Universe personified, and *thus you are how it smiles and laughs*. Use it, call on it, commune and understand that you're heard.

The Universe is your ally, whether you see this or not. It roots for you, cheers for you, and loves you throughout every step of your life. It yearns for your happiness and fulfillment, and without a doubt, the cards of life are stacked in your favor *because of it*. I'm *not* saying that the Universe can reach over your shoulder and manipulate the deck independently of your thoughts and beliefs; this would violate your freedom, steal your power, and invalidate your responsibilities. But *as the Universe yourself*—as one of the original Adventurers who created this bastion of perfection amongst the stars—all the elements are here for you, your intents, and your purposes; *"you" put them here*. And chief among your aims was to *thrive*.

> *As the Universe yourself*—as one of the original **Adventurers who created this bastion of perfection amongst the stars—all the elements are here for you, your intents, and your purposes.**

Why else would you be here but to grow, to experience, to discover, to succeed, and to taste the bounty of your creativity? Is there any other reason you can think of that would have as much meaning, as much beauty, as much intrigue? Doesn't this resonate within you? Doesn't it make intuitive sense? You are here to thrive, and as was laid out in the little story introducing this book, "*Only by losing themselves and serving their illusions could the Adventurers then be driven emotionally—by their burning desires—to reclaim and know the depths of their divinity.*"

The Game Is Rigged

Granted, it may seem a bit naive to be naming or purporting the purpose of creation *from within the creation* when we ourselves are seemingly feeble, mortal, "lost" souls who so far have done little more than master our physical senses. Yet wouldn't it be even more naive to completely abdicate ourselves from speculating on the meaning of life? Isn't it equally absurd to *unquestioningly accept* what our equally naive forefathers have told us about the reasons for our existence, especially when those reasons made little sense in terms of the beauty, love, and compassion that is apparent everywhere in life? And wouldn't this be especially true when some of the "older schools" of thinking claimed we're here to be tested and judged and, should we fail those tests (which were quite impossible to pass), be condemned and rejected forever and ever? Such views were virtually all taught by leaders and chieftains who clearly had an unspoken agenda with which to control and at times manipulate the masses. Are they not the ones who used their views on the meaning of life to conquer, slay, and divide?

As with all "new" ideas, there are nuances you may not yet have considered that may take some time to digest. However, by turning within, listening to your heart and your own instincts, and by moving with your own agenda to understand reality and to liberate yourself from falsehoods, you can connect these stray dots with only a few strides and find great peace and empowerment.

Though it may have dawned on you already, I must note that what I'm about to share might sound contradictory to most people's view of the Universe or even to what I've laid out so far: *In all our affairs, the Universe (while infinitely loving and caring) cannot and will not trump your own abilities, interfere with your manifestations, or otherwise intervene as your life unfolds.*

As an analogy, consider a parent who sends a willing and enthusiastic fifteen-year-old to camp for two weeks so that the child might learn independence, social skills, and responsibility. How effective would the adventure be if only a few days into the program the parent showed up at camp, behind the scenes, and began meddling in the child's affairs to "ensure" success? Of course, if things at camp began going very poorly, there *would* be a need for the parent to intervene. Yet in time and space, however poorly things might *appear* to be going, as the eyes and ears of God—as divine ourselves—we not only have the phenomenal ability to change our fortunes on a dime through the proper use of thought, word, and deed, but no matter what happens, our return "home," our "salvation," *is guaranteed.* You could say we are loved so much that no matter how scared, bruised, and battered we become, the system has been set up in such a way, *with so much love*, that we *cannot* hurt our eternal, spiritual selves. The game is rigged ... in our favor!

Besides, if the Universe could intervene whenever we became scared, how could we ever, ultimately, *experience* our own power? How could we ever discover our true nature and heritage? You might answer, "Well, we could be shown," but that is not the nature of the adventure we have chosen. Or you might say, "Well, we could be told," but prophets and seers since the dawn of time *have been telling us*, yet they were typically "run out of town on a rail," often by the very organizations who claimed to be keepers of the truth. And while oftentimes parts of their messages were embraced, rites, rules, and rituals were tacked on later, as were the significantly flawed interpretations of earning, deserving, and sacrifice.

In this lifetime, the next, or the ones after, everyone eventually passes "Go and collects $200." In the meantime, however, we are all entirely responsible for ourselves, our manifestations, and our own procedures, hopping into the cockpit, powering the thing up, and aiming! And that's all you have to do to begin living the life you dream of living: just power up your thinking, aim (which implies action, albeit minimal compared to what will be done for you), and delegate the rest to the Universe—your Greater Self—and the principles that hold time and space together, having *faith* that they will perform flawlessly.

Reaching the Tipping Point

Our responsibilities are indeed paltry compared to what will effortlessly be done for us, yet nevertheless, taking some action—*consistent action*—is of paramount importance. Again, it's not so much because of what you might achieve but because taking action is how we put ourselves in a place of receivership of life's magic.

Whether you're thinking, speaking, or living, the Universe takes note, sees your true intentions, llows your actions, and knows all. *You're never alone.*

 instant you think new thoughts, the entire mechanism of the
Ue is thrown into motion. Immediately, players and circum-
s are arranged and rearranged to create the sequence of
cessary to bring about your dream. Then as you physically
 your dreams, there will follow life's so-called accidents,
s, and serendipities, deliberately calculated to predispose
ght people, at the right time, with the right ideas. You'll
d with precisely the right epiphanies, bright ideas, and
ssary to pull off your manifestation. Yet if you are not
g your life out in the world, at least moving in the
n of your dreams, there simply cannot be such
 "lucky breaks."
 much of what you already do (and what your
 nothing of life's workings do) may even be

happiness. It's the ultimate responsibility, a responsibility that was bestowed simultaneously with our receiving the absolute power to have, do, and be whatever our heart desires—the ultimate power. But lest you feel alone, tiny, and inadequate, do not forget that you are infinitely more than you've been taught; that you now have the ability to command all the elements to do your work (because you *are* those elements)—to metaphorically summon legions in the unseen to come to your aid (as all are extensions of yourself) and to literally move mountains (as they are just part of the illusions you've believed in). The entire Universe conspires on your behalf, using the principle of *thoughts become things*, to draw into your life whatever you have the ability to believe in.

Surviving Is *So* Last Year

It gets even better! On this "emerald in space," having created the props, placed the planets, and chosen your birth—*all for the purpose of thriving*—you can *know* that the stage is set for exactly that! You can rest assured that you are the perfect person to have all that you dream of having; that you were custom built for the possibilities that you alone dream of exploring; that whatever you need to perform, succeed, and find happiness is already in you! Of course, thriving has different meanings for everyone—to one it could mean self-love, to another it might mean accumulating material abundance, and to a third, it might mean both—but you can rest assured that whatever it means to you, you have what it takes.

Haven't you always found that you smile more than you frown; you laugh more than you cry; you've had friends more than you've been entirely alone; you've had money more than you've been flat broke; you've been gradually waking up to truth, rather than sliding into an abyss of deeper and deeper mysteries; and you've enjoyed health far more than you've suffered sickness? *We're all naturally and automatically inclined to thrive* in every area of our lives, and since the Universe and our physical lives mirror this inclination (conspiring on our behalf), as our lives unfold it's as if we're seemingly "pushed on" to greatness. It's just that we've slowed ourselves down a bit, being the spiritual infants that we are, because whenever it's come to creating change in our lives, not knowing any better, we've typically approached it by focusing excessively on what we don't like and what we don't have instead of focusing on our dreams.

Thriving, not surviving, is our default setting. Just look at our modern civilization's commerce, technology, and life expectancies. While there have been failings, you'd have to agree that in spite of our deep spiritual naiveties, we've still blown the lid clear off "surviving." *You didn't come here to survive; you came here because you wanted "it all,"* exactly as *you* define "all," and that's what you're going to get.

Thriving, not surviving, is our default setting.

Because you've likely never been told the truth, this may seem outlandish and fairy-tale-like. Armed with the truth, however, *you're free*. Life *is* easy. It's *always* been easy. And above all, life's mechanics are knowable. You needn't go forth in mystery, confusion, and self-doubt; these are just power robbers. Knowing now that your own inclinations are toward happiness and fulfillment—that this is what you are built for, that this is what the stage is set for, and that the entire Universe is in on the "game"—can you imagine the brand-new possibilities that suddenly lie before you?

Prayer

I'm not a big proponent for using the word "prayer." It's like using the word "God" in that it has so many connotations, meaning vastly different things to different people. I dislike the term because it usually implies that the one doing the praying is powerless and beholden to powers, or to a god—*outside* themselves—who picks and chooses whom he will help and when. But I love prayer's

implication that we are not alone and that we are being hear[d] are heard by this very same Universe, by every atom and mol[e] and by every entity that could possibly render you assista[nce] Whether you're thinking, speaking, or living, the Universe ta[kes] note, sees your true intentions, follows your actions, and knows [.] *You're never alone.*

Delegation

When I first began discovering the kind of material that I've been sharing here, I used to feel really alone—not because others didn't think like this (though few did) but because, when these concepts were blended with my "old school" thinking, the idea of creating my own reality was overwhelming. And although I immediately grasped that it was true, I heard myself thinking and feeling, "Gosh, how th[e] heck do I make my own reality? How do I become aware of *all* [my] beliefs and thoughts? If I make my own reality, then that mea[ns I] must do it alone, and what an enormous responsibility!" All [these] assertions were—and are—absolutely correct; it is a humong[ous job] and we *do* have total responsibility. *But we are permitted to [ask for help] and we can delegate as much as we like!*

In fact, delegation is absolutely mandatory in order [to get any-] thing done in time and space. Just as the pilot of a jumb[o jet has] control and responsibility for the plane and her passe[ngers,] she's required to delegate virtually everything th[at will] make the plane fly properly. She might turn the yok[e] or the rudder and flick a few switches to give the[] she didn't invent aviation or commercial flying[;] help build and test the plane and its millions [of] pieces; she didn't orchestrate the formatio[n] bought the plane and operates the airline[;] the ticketing agents and flight attend[ants;] the runways or the control tower. The[] beyond showing up several hours pri[or]

enough *when coupled with an awareness of how your thoughts become things*. But to exponentially increase the Universe's chances of reaching you suddenly and surely, do a few extra things. Act with faith and act *as if*, knocking on a few new doors and turning over a few new stones. Again, when such simple steps are taken consistently, *with the knowledge* of how they can and will be exploited by the Universe, it's as if a tipping point is *simultaneously* reached, and the subsequent results can and will be staggering and swift.

Thoughts That Stretch You

It's natural to become overwhelmed when you first begin to truly understand your power and responsibility. But when you also begin to understand that you have a loving system, powerful principles, and an aware Universe at your beck and call, it becomes a much less daunting task. Then the challenge becomes realizing just how much you can and should leave to the Universe.

At first this may seem pretty straightforward: asking and then having faith. But what you won't realize is that your initial requests are tainted with limited perspectives and old-school logic. Happily, once you see this, you can begin recognizing how much more you can ask for and expect from this magical Universe we live in.

As an analogy, think back to when you were a kid and you were asked what you would wish for if you could wish for any one thing. It used to be a torturous exercise because it seemed that whatever you picked would mean you couldn't have any of the other things you dreamed of. But then it dawned on you one day that the thing to wish for is to be granted more wishes! Then you could just keep on wishing and wishing!

This is how the Universe works: you can actually ask for a lot more than you might initially suspect. If you don't think you can ask for help, however, or if you think you can ask only for modest, selfless requests and that you really shouldn't overdo it, then that's all you're going to get. Think broader; let your imagination go wild when asking for things. Don't ask for enlightenment and then think that you must go to a solitary hilltop to practice receiving it; ask that enlightenment come to you effortlessly, while listening to your favorite music or driving home from work.

In addition, don't just ask for wealth and abundance and then think that you must bust your behind to do your part; ask that it comes to you quickly, honorably, and easily. Don't just ask for a new friend so that you can then have someone who understands you; ask for parties, celebrations, fun, and laughter. Don't just ask for a new job; ask for a career that thrills and challenges you every single day or one that makes a huge difference in the world. Don't ask to make a difference and then think you have to begin making personal sacrifices to do it; ask that it be a rip-roaring blast—the most fun you've ever had. Most people have no idea how many limitations they automatically attach to even the simplest of their desires.

Remember, you are not alone. You have at your disposal a living, loving Universe that's deeply tuned in to you—that can and must be delegated to—and by understanding its presence and having a renewed faith in its "magic," you can effortlessly begin commanding the elements to do your bidding.

Oops! Did you register what I just said? It's easy to just say, "Uh-huh, uh-huh," but I just said you have to have "faith in its 'magic.'" Do you now have faith in its magic? Do you now have faith in the unseen? Are you consciously aware that you don't have to figure out the *hows* or do anything alone? Well, starting today, if you can begin incorporating this kind of thinking into everything you do, welcome to the party!

Getting Grounded in Your Power

Unfortunately, it's easy to take the "magic" of life for granted and not feel its presence in our own lives. To help make its presence more obvious, realize that faith in this magic starts with an admission and recognition of *the miracle that you already are*—not just your unique personality, charm, and style (though these are miracles sure enough) but the very basic level of your existence. That you have awareness and perspective, and your thoughts and observations continually pour through you without any effort on your part. That's the starting point, and simply dwelling on your own miracle, which you are help-less to re-create or destroy (not even death or suicide ends the stream of your thoughts, which do not originate from the physical world), should be the starting point of your belief in magic.

Going a few steps further, begin to realize that, of all the things you think you've ever done in your life, you've actually done very few—except to issue directives based on your intents and expecta-tions that enabled the Universe to reach its hands into your affairs and get the real work done. Looking forward, realize that this very same magic can be counted on as you set your short- and long-term goals. By recognizing life's magic and how it's worked in your life already, you can begin counting on it to work today and in your future. This immediately means you can begin having more by doing less, leveraging the Universe and engaging the magic that *already* pervades your entire life.

Your Universal Bank Account

Imagine that I've just phoned you and told you that I've wired direct to your bank account twenty million dollars, tax-free. Imagine it! Believe that it's true for at least a brief moment. Can you see in your mind what the little slip from the ATM would look like when it prints your available balance? Twenty million dollars! Imagine all those zeroes! Imagine them on your bank statement and imagine balancing your checkbook with a beginning and ending balance that is eight digits long!

Now imagine the peace it would likely give you today. Just think, there'd be nothing you couldn't afford to have or do. There'd be nowhere on the planet you couldn't afford to travel to in style. There'd be no restaurant you couldn't eat at every day, no hotel you couldn't stay at for the rest of your life, no hobby you couldn't take up, no home you couldn't buy (almost!), no gifts for loved ones you couldn't afford, and never, ever again in your life would you have to worry about money! Think about this for a while and imagine the infinite possibilities. You might even put down this book for a minute to let your imagination really run wild with this twenty million dollars.

Kind of fun, isn't it? Now realize that the magic you currently have at your disposal *dwarfs* the power and freedom that that puny twenty million offers you. You probably quickly realized that you could spend twenty million in your lifetime, but with the magic of the Universe as your supply, you can make the twenty million grow into one hundred million again and again and still not scratch the surface of all you could have. Your supply is limitless, eternal, unending, and yours for the taking! It's already in your universal bank account, and better than money, it can be harnessed to draw more love, joy, and laughter into your life at a moment's notice. That should give you something good to visualize in the days ahead.

Of course, you need to believe in your universal bank account to use it, and because it's invisible, you must have faith that it's there. Act *as if* it is there and you'll then be able to draw on it. Just keep this in mind: though the potential of your universal bank account is limitless, it only has as much money in it as you decide to withdraw.

Now, our brain—logic—tells us that the more we take out the less we'll have, but that's because our brain is only accustomed to assessing *physical* reality. Its sense of logic doesn't work in the spiritual realm. In fact, the opposite is true with the universal bank account: the more we take out, the bigger the balance gets! If you go to your universal ATM for one hundred dollars, that's what it'll give you; but if you go for one million, it'll be there too—with faith.

This does not mean, however, that you should go out and spend more physical dollars than you have, racking up debt in the name of faith! It means that you must know that you do have a universal bank account, and that by using and drawing on it with faith—incrementally and gradually so that you ultimately become congruent with it in terms of all you think, say, and do—your physical accounts will soon begin mirroring it.

How? You start by *doing what you can*—by spending what you can without worry; by believing with faith that your coffers will be replenished; and by not hoarding for some rainy day. You also do it by window-shopping; by planning, preparing and paving the way for abundance to come into your life; by visualizing yourself living the life of your dreams; and by defining, perhaps with pen and paper, the life of your dreams. Have faith by moving forward and living the life of your dreams to any degree that you now can by following your dreams and desires and by listening to your hunches and intuitions and *physically* moving in directions that may yield more abundance. By insisting, demanding, expecting, and knowing that this magic is there to be called upon, inviting it into your thoughts with gratitude and giving thanks that what you want is already yours even though you don't physically see it yet, you prepare the way for unlimited withdrawals.

$$\infty$$

Evidence of lifes magic exists everywhere around us. To see for yourself, begin with your own life and your own inescapable awareness. Witness the miracle of your thoughts and realize that to think and breathe, to move about, to talk, sing, and dance, you must be a magical being—a spiritual being—far more powerful, deep, and resourceful than you ever before understood. By walking out into nature and observing its own effortless grace, beauty, and abundance, you'll witness even more magic. Nature, in fact, is overflowing with this wonder: flowers in bloom, species variety in a forest ecosystem, birds effortlessly flying across the sky. Seeing the splendor of a sunrise or sunset and watching the world respond accordingly—effortlessly—is nothing less than pure magic.

Faith in the Universe *is* a belief in magic, but once you understand the endless abilities of the Universe and realize that it offers itself to any and all who ask, the magic becomes far less mysterious and infinitely more friendly, dependable, and even predictable—hardly magic at all.

Learning to Turn Things Over to the Universe

We are so accustomed to doubting ourselves that we think it's natural to doubt things or processes that are seemingly outside ourselves. We think it's "natural," however unpleasant, to be concerned, to worry, and even to have backup plans, but these kinds of doubts actually *diminish* the otherwise flawless performances of the Universe on our behalf. The reason we worry so much is that we erroneously think that it is we, our physical selves, who have to carry out all our wishes. If that were true, then we *would* have a lot to worry about! But the irony is that our physical selves are little more than breathing lumps of clay that can't even begin to function without the help of the Universe! We can't walk and talk without the Universe, yet we think it's our job to make ourselves healthy, to provide for ourselves financially, to find peace and harmony by manipulating the hours of our days. And by thinking and behaving like this, we're telling ourselves—and the Universe—that we don't believe or have faith in its unending miracles.

On the other hand, with *magical universe thinking* built into your life, you can start enjoying and appreciating that everything is already just as it should be, and know that you are on your way to the manifestation of all your dreams. When you begin enjoying the present and all that it holds, you become less focused on the future and how you want it to turn out. After all, the Universe knows what you want, and by following your own natural rhythms and pace—your inner *gifts from heaven*—you can relax, having faith that all your future wants, desires, and dreams will manifest (before you even know what they are).

For those of us who aren't quite there yet—who like having goals and who see them as challenges—dream manifestation is at least a fun and enlightening hobby. By applying these understandings of life's magic to you and your life, you should quickly begin to realize that your job in the manifestation process is to primarily decide on and refine your dreams, not to painstakingly struggle as if you were working against the Universe to "make them happen."

Clarity Begets Clarity

Your job is to define as clearly as possible exactly what it is you want on both a physical level and, even more importantly, on an emotional level. But too many people I've met simply say, "I want to be rich" without giving any thought to why. They may reply, "It's obvious: I want to live without ever having to worry about money." There's nothing wrong with that, but once they achieve that, what are they going to do with their lives? The better you can answer these questions, the clearer your intent will be and the easier you'll find it is to think about—and then to bring about—whatever you're wishing for.

So what do you *really* want? Think about it now and really define it. I think you'll see that this question can sometimes spin off into an exercise on beliefs as well, but there's no harm done there. Understanding ourselves better helps us understand our truest desires. And the greater the clarity and certainty we have with our desires, the faster they manifest into our lives.

For me, whenever I go through these mental exercises (that is, first focusing on life's magic and then doing my part to define as clearly as possible what I want), I can sometimes feel myself hitting barriers. For instance, I get to this knowingness of my unlimited right to abundance and of my divine nature, but once I pull my head down from the clouds to apply it, planning some exotic new vacation or the purchase of a bigger and better home, I'll catch myself creating limiting thoughts, such as "Oh, I can't spend that much time traveling" or "I'd better wait until I have more money."

Whoa! These kinds of thoughts spring from limiting beliefs that have just reared their ugly heads, so I immediately begin exploring and asking myself why I think I should wait or why I feel I should put off my dreamed-of purchases.

The point is, by allowing yourself to be inspired by life's magic so that you can start dreaming really big, as soon as you start coming "down to Earth" with the application of your high ideals, you're in a peak state to catch and identify those beliefs that contradict the presence of this magic. This is actually a great place to be because you've finally exposed those invisible beliefs and you can then begin working on dismantling them. This kind of exercise serves two purposes: (1) to align your thinking with the truth about your power and the magical Universe you live in, and (2) to help you nab limiting beliefs.

**We may not be able to mentally fathom the logistics
of the Universe, but that doesn't mean that we can't
appreciate its magnificence, sense its benevolence,
or *rely* on its obvious perfection.**

Not Blind Faith

When it comes to having faith, just because this faith is in the unseen doesn't mean that this faith needs to be blind. Just because you can't see your thoughts doesn't mean you don't have them, and similarly, just because you can't see the processes that work the magic of life doesn't mean they aren't there. Blind faith means believing without reason or cause, and if this is the kind of faith someone has in the Universe, I can't imagine that it would be of much use. If you can't see or understand the cause or reason for anything, it becomes next to impossible to believe in it.

We may not be able to mentally fathom the logistics of the Universe, but that doesn't mean that we can't appreciate its magnificence, sense its benevolence, or *rely* on its obvious perfection. The faith that you adopt shouldn't be blind but a faith instilled with understanding. Understand that you can't be an accident and that the mysterious, loving forces that have brought you to this day are obviously still at play. Understand that everything is alive and that right now you are exactly where you should be. Then, even with these simple understandings, your faith will be bolstered, your confidence will be aroused, and optimism will set in, allowing the Universe its much-deserved freedom to fill your life with wonderful surprises and serendipitous "coincidences."

All That Is Gold Does Not Glitter

When you hit a slump or a lull, sometimes it can be hard to see the light at the end of the tunnel. But when you realize the nature of things and understand that your thoughts today will shape your tomorrows, and that those thoughts will be picked up and used to program a Universe conspiring on your behalf, what have you got to worry about? With these new understandings and the faith they automatically inspire, whenever you feel in a slump, allow yourself to begin thinking that wherever you are, with your new perspectives, things are inevitably about to get a whole lot better. The lull you're experiencing is just giving the Universe time to orchestrate a relatively complicated yet fantastic "surprise party."

This reminds me of the period in my life that immediately followed college graduation. I'd finished the accounting program with good grades and had done everything anyone could do to be in a prime position to get a great entry-level job with virtually any accounting firm, yet interview after interview, I failed to get an offer. I even came close to getting hired by some of the then Big Eight Accounting Firms, the most prestigious in the world, with two of them paying for me to visit their out-of-town offices (a sure sign that an offer was imminent), and yet I kept striking out. Months went by and it felt like eternity! I interviewed with almost every major accounting firm within three hundred miles of my home and . . . nothing.

I was so discouraged that I created three new resumes, all geared toward fields unrelated to accounting, because it seemed "it just wasn't meant to be." I had a banking resume, one for the insurance industry, and another to become a stockbroker, and *still* I couldn't get a job offer!

Well, I did get one offer from my father's CPA to work for $12,000 per year, which at the time was not a horrible rate, but even with my string of failed interviews I rejected it; somehow knowing I could do better. Besides, in my last year of college, I had dwelled on what it would be like to get at least $18,500 (the going rate paid by the Big Eight), and the offer of $12,000 was like a poke in the eye.

Finally, after three long, seemingly hopeless months, a family friend arranged an interview for me with P.W., which had just acquired a large new hospital as a client. It was unquestionably the most prestigious of the then Big Eight and probably the only firm I had not yet been interviewed by in my geographic search zone. The interview went fantastically well, and an offer for $18,500 immediately followed!

Talk about a blessing! I'm grateful to this day that those three months unfolded just as they did—that I hadn't been hired by anyone else—because it became obvious that time simply needed to pass before P.W. had an unexpected opening that would be perfect for me. This is the firm that eventually sent me to the Middle East on a foreign assignment, during which I enjoyed some of the most memorable times of my life. Upon returning to the United States from Riyadh, P.W. briefly sent me to Manhattan before finally sending me to Boston. Dream after dream after dream came true thanks to those three long months spent waiting; they were a blessing in disguise.

Now, what can you do with this story? Use it to instill faith during the lulls in your life. See these times as necessary reprieves that are allowing the Universe to shuffle around the players and events of your life in order to make some of your dreams come true. Don't dwell on these lulls, don't lose faith, don't lower your standards, don't get discouraged, and, most importantly, don't dwell on the apparent lack of progress you may seem to be making. As was true for me, even though you can't see progress doesn't mean it isn't being made. Know this: the Universe and all its mechanics are invisible, but things *are* happening. Even now as you turn these pages, miracles in the unseen are abounding on your behalf. If you doubt this, however, it means you doubt the *entire* Universe; your faith will weaken and perhaps you'll make some poor decisions that could short-circuit the gifts that were just about to be unwrapped in your life.

Chillin' Out While You Can

Now, don't start worrying that in the past you may have given up too soon on some of your dreams and are now hopelessly off course, because it's never too late to find euphoric happiness or to become wildly fulfilled. Maybe medical school is no longer a viable option, but with the kind of adventures that now await you, it's just as well, because the Universe is fantastically capable of dealing with exactly where you are today and delivering to you the life you've always dreamed you'd live.

Here's another thought along these lines: When you're in a lull, use the time on your hands to do some additional work with your thoughts and beliefs. Dedicate time every day to visualizing; start working on or updating your scrapbook or your vision board (if you have one), or maybe write out some of your beliefs. Don't start looking for problems, but be vigilant in ensuring that your thoughts and beliefs are in line with the life of your dreams. To do this, I use my dreams and the end results they promise as a starting point, and then I work backwards to my beliefs and thoughts of today, rather than rummaging around for limiting beliefs that may or may not be interfering with my life. Lulls can be looked at as gifts—the calm before the storms of glorious manifestation—and when you recast them in this light, they can even be transformed into some of the happier times of your life, almost as vacations between spurts of creative living.

Dwell In Spirit

Let me ask a question: If you could have anything your heart desires—anything, anything at all (except, of course, a specific person!)—what would you want? (And this time don't answer "to be happy" but pick a material possession or accomplishment.) What would be at the core of your dreamed-of lifestyle?

**It's never too late to find euphoric happiness
or to become wildly fulfilled.**

Now, whatever you dreamed of, do you have any doubt that the full "magic and sorcery" of the Universe might not be able to deliver exactly what you thought of? Do you think—maybe, just maybe—not even "God" could arrange what you've just asked for? Do you have any doubts along those lines? Of course not! You know that if it were up to God, the mystically charged forces of the Universe, anything would be possible—and that would certainly be true of granting your wish! The only real doubts you could possibly have, and very likely *do* have, are in yourself: you doubt your ability and/or your worthiness to achieve your ultimate dreams. Well, as to your worthiness, I'll talk about that in upcoming sections, but as to your ability, as I've alluded to before, *you should doubt it*. You (as in the *physical you*) can't do anything without the aid of the Universe, so there is no way the *physical you* can achieve whatever it is you want—never, never, never—unless, of course, you enlist the help of the Universe (which you've just admitted is capable of everything). So stop thinking that it's *you* who has to figure everything out.

If you really get what I'm saying here, you'll understand the profound importance of it. You and I, and everyone else, have led our entire lives thinking that things work the other way around—that we must, metaphorically, carry the weight of the world on our shoulders. But it's time to make a concerted effort to begin undoing this brainwashing. The following thought is worth posting around your home so you can remind yourself of it constantly: *Dwell in spirit.* Get used to taking your every challenge and problem there. And whenever you want something, immediately turn it over to the Universe and realize that the real work that needs to be done lies beyond your physical reach.

Expect the Unexpected

The next time you *visualize*, include the Universe and its magic. Don't just see yourself manipulating life; see the *unexpected* popping into your life and imagine the feelings you'd have after receiving some *awesome* curve balls from the Universe. Imagine fantastic coincidences and wonderful accidents happening in your dreamed-of circle of events that boost you further than you'd previously thought possible. Imagine receiving shockingly wonderful phone calls from complete strangers who are in a position to further your cause. Imagine telling friends of the miracle that happened to you the other day when you weren't paying close attention. Imagine opening a letter from some unknown company and finding it filled with incredibly wonderful news.

Include magic and surprises when you visualize! After all, it's present in your every waking moment, every day of the week. Right?

Yes, You; Yes, Now

As to your worth, people worthy enough to occupy time and space or those capable of thinking thoughts are automatically worthy of all that they can imagine, no matter who they are, no matter what they've done, and no matter how bad and undeserving they or anyone else may think they are! Basically, if you're still here, you're still worthy, because if you're still here, it could only be because you're still unconditionally loved—to a degree that's quite unimaginable—by the *entire* Universe. This is how to explain your existence; you are because *you are loved*. Actually, you're loved whether you're "here" or not, because in any realm of existence, you would still be of—or One with—God. There's no other possibility.

To make it even easier for you to comprehend how able and powerful you are, here's another way you can look at your life: Think of someone who now lives the life you want to live; think of celebrities or accomplished masters in whatever field you want to be accomplished in. (You might think of someone you idolize.) You don't have to pick just one person; think of many. Now ask yourself if the attributes of those people's talents, their gifts, were something that they personally had to manipulate on a physical level. Did they have to orchestrate the "lucky" breaks they received in their life? Do they do what they do as a result of their deductive brains? NO! They're just like you; physically, they can't even walk or talk without the aid of the Universe, whether they realize it or not! They just make better use of life's magic than most of us do by leveraging it better! Such people are inspiring examples of what the Universe can do *for you*. Through their beliefs, they've engaged the Universe to do all the things you previously thought you had to figure out for yourself!

Think of Tiger Woods on the golf course, Oprah Winfrey on television, or Kate Winslet on the silver screen. Think of the masterpieces created by Van Gogh, Ayn Rand, or Beethoven, and think of the legacies and the differences made by people such as Abraham Lincoln, Louis Pasteur, or Mahatma Gandhi. Where do you think all these souls got their material? How do you think their arts were performed? Why do you think they climbed to such stellar heights in their respective fields? Who do you think really did their work? And lastly, how do these people differ from you physically?

These people aren't (or weren't) any more divine or gifted than you. They all put their pants on one leg at a time, but for any number of reasons, they were able to believe and, *however humbly*, to act on their beliefs, which then brought the Universe into play.

Look at your own life too, and use every wonderful experience that has ever happened to you as proof that magic exists. Give the Universe credit for your past accomplishments and achievements so as to instill a knowingness that you are connected, because whatever great thing you've done before you can do again and again and again. Know that any dream you can muster is actually all in a day's work for the infinite, magical Universe, which holds you in the palm of its hand.

If you're still here, you're still worthy.

One of the things I sometimes do on weekends is drive through some of the gorgeous neighborhoods in Orlando where the homes sit on magnificent lots on beautiful lakes, and where the wealth and opulence literally ooze down their driveways and out onto the streets. Some of these palatial homes are just winter vacation retreats for residents who have similar homes elsewhere around the world, in even grander settings. I see these homes as reminders that living in such grandeur is so very attainable, even *ordinary*! Orlando, my hometown, doesn't have a few homes like this but hundreds (if not thousands), and so *do thousands of cities* across the United States and around the world! The people who live in these homes are no more special than you or I. The fruit of their dreams was provided by a Universe that yearns to provide the same to all. And as great as the wealth is that buys these homes, it's nothing compared to the wealth of the Universe.

There Is Only Spirit

In life it's like we're blindfolded (at least our physical senses are), because we're completely unable to see, hear, or touch life's magic. Yet to live your life—to live the life of your dreams—the secret is knowing that there is so much more happening on our behalf than the five senses can detect, and the way to know this is through faith. This is our greatest test: to know that even in the absence of physical proof we are spiritual beings; to know that although our thoughts are invisible, they will become the things and events of our lives; and to know that we are loved and provided for.

Many Eastern schools of spiritual thinking recognize how we misinterpret life's fantastic physical attributes and how we eat of the forbidden fruit daily. Sadly, their doctrines then label all that's physical as the culprit responsible for our problems, encouraging our detachment from material desires, considering them beneath us or below the spiritual level. But this only denies us our full spiritual connections. After all, any thought on the subject would reveal that all material objects are pure spirit anyway—that *thoughts become things*—thus the things of our life are really just the thoughts of our life. There is only spirit. The key to understanding life in time and space is to understand that it all springs from a magical inner world that we create through our thoughts, beliefs, intentions, and expectations, not through labeling or avoiding material things or trying to cancel out our desires. Yet because we can't physically nail down this spirit, faith is our ticket.

See the miracles in your life, expect them, count on them, and begin leveraging the magic behind the Universe; *that's what it's there for*. Then have a deep and profound faith that whatever you wish for shall be done "on Earth as it is in heaven," or to rephrase this, in matter as it is in thought.

You are divine, the Universe is loving, and your thoughts will *always* become things. WOW. Talk about control and talk about power—you've got both! Have faith, and know that just as the sun can be counted on to rise, so can the Universe be counted on to deliver.

Whether you realize it or not, you are, right now, in your home, at work, in a car, or on a plane, being carried by the magic of the Universe. It's always been there, it's always loved you, and it's always conspired on your behalf. You only have to know this and to have faith to begin deliberately using it.

**Have a deep and profound faith that whatever you
wish for shall be done "on Earth as it is in heaven," ...
in matter as it is in thought.**

Faith means you believe. You believe you are not alone, you believe you can and will stand in ownership of what you ask for, and you believe that the infinite wisdom and incalculable powers of the Universe are yours to draw on, to any degree that you can imagine. Ask for a little help and you'll receive it; ask for the world on a silver platter and it shall be yours. Actually, it already is.

7

The Elixir of Life

What is the elixir of life? I hinted at it in the last chapter when I talked about not having blind faith. To give you some idea, let me share an analogy. Let's compare taking a photograph to living the life of your dreams.

Picture-Perfect

Very simply, when taking a photograph, you aim, focus if necessary, and then click the shutter button, right? And if you've done everything properly, light passes through a transparent lens and leaves a replicated impression on film or your digital media card, which is later "manifested" onto something you can physically see (your computer monitor or paper). I'll bet you see the similarities to fulfilling your dreams already.

To live the life of your dreams, you must first aim and focus, deciding upon and thinking about what you want and then making some minimal effort in the direction of your dreams, which is like snapping the shutter button. From there, if your thoughts then pass through the lenses of your beliefs without being altered or tainted—if your beliefs are in line with your dreams—the impression is made. Finally, manifesting your intent into time and space is done with faith as you physically, perhaps patiently, see the process through to completion: faith that this entire chain of events will create a photo and faith that the principles at play in the Universe will perform as they're supposed to.

But my analogy isn't complete yet. There's one other element necessary for taking pictures—one that we all take for granted. It's quite simple yet essential. It's *understanding*: understanding the entire process; understanding that with the proper equipment and principles, and with you doing your part, you will get a photo; and understanding that if you do your part exceptionally well, it'll be a *great* photo—exactly what you'd wanted! Similarly, with full and complete understanding of the overall processes and principles at play and by doing your part, you *will* live the life of your dreams; it's simply unavoidable.

Without a basic understanding of what makes things work in time and space, how could you ever hope to *deliberately* affect change?

Understanding is the elixir of life. At the risk of repeating myself, the key to grasping your full power comes from understanding *that in life there are inviolate principles you can rely on, depend on, and literally bank on*; you don't need to know exactly *how* they work. With taking photos, you don't have to understand the curvature of the lenses, you don't have to know what material the camera's made of, you don't need to worry about exactly how light will leave an impression on the film or your media card, nor, generally, do you have to calculate how long the aperture should remain open. What you do have to understand is the overall concept of taking pictures: basically, how does the camera work and what exactly is required of you, the photographer? Similarly, without a basic understanding of what makes things work in time and space, how could you ever hope to *deliberately* affect change?

Without understanding life's mechanics, you have to worry about whether or not your dreams are meant to be, whether or not you're deserving, whether or not you're "lucky" enough. Do you

Without understanding, faith does little more than serve as a reminder of what it is you're hoping for, while faith that exists naturally instills confidence and expectation *because* of understanding.

Rewards and Responsibilities

you begin uncovering more and more of life's truths, so will you begin to understand the awesome potentials that are latent in all you think, say, and do. Automatically and effortlessly, you'll begin behaving in ways that are in line with beliefs that serve you. You'll think and daydream in line with your dreams. You'll worry less. You'll feel better. You'll laugh more. A harmony will begin overtaking you, and you'll begin to radiate a compassion and peace that will be readily detectable by others. *This* is what understanding promises. simply gets easier and easier, better and better. You have more in the Universe, more confidence in yourself, more acceptance the way things are, and finally you'll possess an understanding that gs *couldn't possibly* be better than the way they've always been. As wonderful as all that sounds, the process of enlightenment nevertheless comes with a price. You can't become more enlightened but an awareness of your total and utter responsibility for every that has ever happened in your life. Actually, that's not asking (I'd imagine you're already there), but sometimes we can kid lves when it comes to our responsibilities. For instance, we readily take credit for our failures than we do our successes. s true, we often tend to take on more responsibility for others eeing to their happiness than we do for ourselves. With true standing, however, you'll find that one of the greatest acts of responsible is taking really good care of yourself.

The Price of Knowing

sponsibility begins with self. Our first responsibility in life not to make the world a better place or to tend to those

keep finding yourself in the wrong place at the right time, or the right place at the wrong time? Are you "supposed" to be struggling as you sometimes do, perhaps as some form of penance or because it builds character, or is it only because you simply have a few limiting beliefs? There's no doubt that life can be very unpredictable without an understanding of the role you and your thoughts play.

Breaking It Down into Knowable Pieces

Again, this is not about trying to grasp *everything* suddenly and at once. Simply understand what you can. Understand what's before you. Understand today; that's enough.

For instance, you might not understand why you've been drawn to certain people who drive you absolutely crazy, but for now *you can understand* that, as creator of your reality, each one of those people has arrived in your life with your consent. They came as you summoned qualities, connections, or abilities within them that you had focused on; or they came as intermediaries—stepping stones in your journey to other experiences you've thought about.

Understanding *is* the elixir that reveals your place in eternity, and with it your beliefs can be aligned and your imagination ignited to achieve anything you can dream of.

You might not understand why a young child dies, but for now *you can understand* that reasons were involved and purposes were met, just as *you can understand* that death is only an illusion—an illusion that presses you to understand deeper truths so that such a loss will not obliterate your faith and hope for all else life offers.

You might not understand exactly how your dreams will come true, but *you can understand* that the hows and myriad logistics of such an accomplishment are beyond your normal awareness and can be left to the Universe and it's principles—as long as you do your part in thought, word, and deed. With deeper understandings, even though you can't yet explain every nuance of your life, you can still relieve yourself of the stress, fear, and anxiety that would otherwise accompany you as you pursue your goals.

Understanding *is* the elixir that reveals your place in eternity, and with it your beliefs can be aligned and your imagination ignited to achieve anything you can dream of. Without understanding, the simple principle of mind over matter becomes hocus-pocus, and sadly, your own achievements will be misunderstood. You will be left to secretly attribute your successes to timing, connections, luck, and coincidence or, just as foolishly, to hard work, selflessness, and sacrifices. You can spend hours each day hammering vivid imaginative thoughts before your mind's eye with little success in the long run because you don't understand that your beliefs must not contradict the object of your desire. Likewise, you can work to install new beliefs and act in line with your dreams, yet if you take no responsibility for where and who you are now, then what kind of authority do you really believe you have?

Whatever your level of understanding, it will not change the fact that you already create the life you lead from the thoughts you think; this truth can't be escaped. By understanding it, however, you acknowledge yourself to be the creator of your experience, from which point you can at least begin deliberately using life's principles to your advantage. The alternative is that you relinquish the power—but not the responsibility—of consciously shaping all that awaits you.

By understanding your past accomplishments, future ones become even easier to achieve. You won't have to guard your successes in fear and self-doubt once you have the understanding to succeed again. Worries evaporate when you see yourself as the conductor of the things and events in your life, all of which will flow and express at your direction, as they always have. And even better, the more you understand, the more your limiting beliefs effortlessly fall away like rain falling from a cloud, presenting you with evermore choices and avenues for prosperity.

Understanding to Bolster Faith

Now, I know that throughout most of your life, yo what you really need in this world to get ahead spiri faith, and I even reiterated that in the last chapter. It indeed take you anywhere you want to go, but as it stood by the rest of the world, faith *generally* mean *faith in lieu of understanding*. Yet as I alluded to ir blind faith can carry with it a burden of fear—fear in which you must have faith may somehow ne from you or that it could somehow betray you if measured up.

On the other hand, a faith *engaged by unders* but one that "gets" the general nature of reality behind all manifestations) allows you to confid effortlessly move through your life, living delibe like the god or goddess you truly are.

Faith is an integral, vital part of living in tim ally binds your moments together. It's the adh nows—between where you are and where alone decides which star you'll visit next ir wildest dreams when it *naturally* appears. faith—faith engaged *through understanding* your beliefs and therefore arises involuntarily.

As you begin uncovering more and m so will you begin to understand the a that are latent in all you think,

For example, if you understand that the inner world, then you'll naturally have fait ples that will convert your thoughts into your life. And if you understand your ow then naturally have faith in your existenc

less fortunate, but to live up to our own high standards, to act with faith that our dreams are "meant to be," and to maintain a tolerance and compassion for our own divine journey. By being so responsible to ourselves, the world *will* become a better place, and those around you will richly benefit, not just from the love you'll share but from the example you become.

You must want it. A second criterion for understanding, which fortunately is quite attainable, is that you must desire it! It must be a personal priority, and the tricky part is that you can't want it unless you first admit that the things you now think, know, and believe about life may be, to some degree, flawed. This can be a lot to ask for some because it means that you may have to suspend some of the ideals or philosophies you've become comfortable with over the course of your life in order to clear the way for illumination.

So, yes, understanding will likely mean that you have to push yourself outside your comfort zone and work at it, but the payoff is immense. Think of it: delving into a little self-exploration when you feel overcome by unpleasant emotions can lead to a banishment of those same emotions in the future. Truly understand why you feel depressed, and as you hold that reason to the light of truth, *poof!* It doesn't stand a chance. Understand why you feel powerless, in light of your divinity, so that you can quickly regain your power. Understand your broken heart (not just the pain but the cause), uncover its link to your definitions of happiness, and then let it go.

This kind of approach, using understanding in the face of unpleasant emotions, is kind of like pointing a flashlight at sounds in the dark: once you see what's going on, you realize how little you have to fear. But it does take effort, and usually, when you're feeling whacked by unpleasant emotions, exploring your beliefs and pinpointing your misunderstandings is the last thing you want to do, yet *nothing* can move you forward faster.

Understanding is a choice. Without it, you become transfixed by a world you've unknowingly created. Your mind becomes prey for the beliefs of others, and time and space events become a muddle of coincidence and luck that have you reacting to, instead of molding, the circumstances of your life. But with understanding, all things are possible. Life gets easy. You become lighter. And finally, it becomes incredibly obvious to you just how *fair* time and space has always been.

> **Understanding is a choice. Without it, you become transfixed by a world you've unknowingly created....**
> **But with understanding, all things are possible.**
> **Life gets easy. You become lighter.**

The Greater You

The next thing I want to address regarding understanding is the "Greater You," which to some might be called your soul. Whatever you like to call it, the point is that there is a lot more to us than we're even aware of. One way to look at the "Conscious I," the I that I think I am, is to imagine the Conscious I as just the tip of an iceberg. Have you seen pictures of icebergs? Although above the water we see only a little tip, there is perhaps one hundred thousand times more ice beneath the surface. Just as the tip of the iceberg might be said to be unaware of the millions of tons of ice that silently support it, so is the Conscious I relatively unaware of all else that we are, of all that supports our conscious existence.

For a long time, the idea of a Greater Self really challenged me in understanding the degree to which I make my own reality. I thought it should be obvious that our souls must also have their own leanings and desires, so I would wonder if my soul might wish to experience something as me (i.e., the concept of "sacrifice") that I might *not* wish to experience! The question that taunted me from time to time, particularly whenever I faced challenges was, is this what I want, or is this something my Greater Self has sought out for me and my growth? And if it is something that my Greater Self has sought out, then what happened to my free will and my ability to chart my own course without interference from elements that I'm not consciously aware of?

I've finally resolved that question with several realizations. The Conscious I does indeed create my reality *without* any interference from my Greater Self, *because this freedom and ability alone are what my Greater Self desired*: that my unique personality and perspectives would sojourn into time and space to savor and enjoy the magnificence of it all as led by my blossoming consciousness, desires, and preferences that emerged during the journey, however they emerged.

We each have a unique window to the world that is our own, that no one else can or ever will share. I believe that while my Greater Self "gave birth" to my awareness so that I might venture forth, it no longer gets involved with my desires and lessons. To do so would violate my ability to learn that my thoughts create my experience and my reality, thus violating its own expression *as me*. I *am* my Greater Self, and I desire what my Greater Self would desire if it were I in time and space (which of course it is!). My Greater Self's wish is simply that I exist with my own desires, which is the same as it existing through me, and from there, I've been given *full rein* over my manifestations and experiences. Of course, there is no real separation of self and Greater Self; this conversation is simply about the different perspectives my Greater Self has taken on, and *this life is all about my Greater Self*, freely expressing as Mike Dooley, without any limitations or agendas.

Our fortunes and misfortunes alike are exclusively a product of *our* beliefs and expectations, and we have complete control over these beliefs and expectations, installing and uninstalling them based on our understandings of ourselves, our lives, and our reality. We don't consciously seek out challenges; we consciously seek out end results or goals, and based on our beliefs and expectations, we move toward these goals. It's during such journeys that we encounter challenges—as stepping stones—whenever we face a truth with misunderstandings. In other words, our challenges are byproducts of our dreams; they are not imposed upon us by our Greater Selves.

The truth is we are all connected: We are One, and this One is the Greatest You. We hear "we're all One" all the time—so much that it almost has no meaning. But this idea is more than just a New Age concept; it's actually functional right now. Birds flying in formation, bees and ants working collectively—they don't work together *as if* they were of One mind; they actually *are* One mind. It's the same with each and every human. Physically we are separate, but spiritually, in ways we cannot now comprehend, not only are we connected but we're all One, reflecting different colors of the same light. And in this very moment, you are exactly who the Greatest You (aka God) most wanted to be, not a frail offshoot who must bow, curtsey, and yield to this "higher power" but an unbeknownst Lord yourself.

$$\infty$$

Let understanding spark excitement and joy for your sacred presence in time and space, and let it do the same for your phenomenal power to write the script of your life as each virginal now is born.

For the moment, grasp what you can. Just do your best. Use these new insights today. Let them bolster your faith, fill you with peace, and instill a certainty that your future will stem from your decisions and actions in the present, not the past. This will be enough; the rest of life's puzzle will make sense in due time.

**You are exactly who the Greatest You (aka God)
most wanted to be, not a frail offshoot who must bow,
curtsey, and yield to this "higher power"
but an unbeknownst Lord yourself.**

Ultimately, through understanding your reality, the props on your stage become props once again instead of demons, hurdles, and problems. Pain and sorrow vanish as you realize there are no good-byes, only reunions and discoveries. And you'll begin seeing the world around you as it's always been: an extension of yourself, intimately connected to everyone always, and camouflaged in a beauty so captivating that you briefly forget your role in its creation.

8

Abundance, Health, and Harmony

I don't believe that anything in life is meant to be other than what we think about, act on, and believe in, but if I were to make an exception, it would be this: you and I and everyone else in the world are meant to have abundance, health, and harmony in our lives. I realize this may sound a bit outrageous, but as I've made clear, I believe thriving is our natural state. When our thoughts are aligned with the Truths of Being, these qualities are impossible to escape. Can you imagine? Around every corner there'd be happy surprises, every day filled with good news, and every person in your life bearing gifts for your happiness and fulfillment.

In the previous chapter, "The Elixir of Life," I stressed the importance of *understanding,* and what I want to do in this chapter is get you to an understanding that abundance, health, and harmony are indeed your birthright—to get you past the notion that this idea is simply wishful thinking. When you truly understand this, as you go about living your life, any thoughts or beliefs that contradict the idea that abundance, health, and harmony are meant to be in your life will be exposed and fall away from your thinking. With faith *engaged,* opposing thoughts and beliefs will automatically be defeated, clearing the way for "right" thinking. By understanding that abundance, health, and harmony are reasonable benchmarks for your life, virtually everything you think will then be cast in their light, and your course will be set.

163

**What's going on here is a dance of becoming,
not a dance of remission, and every element and
compound, every beating heart and thought,
are all born of a greater intelligence.**

Your Heritage

You are a miracle. Every cell and atom in your body is divine and alive, intricate and sophisticated, efficient and perfect. Lack, illness, and discord aren't par for the course; they're not the goals for any of us. They're simply the byproducts of limited, fearful, and under-par thinking.

This place we live, Earth, is the emerald of all space: it's spectacular, living, and giving. It's alive with countless creatures that live in harmony in the air, land, and sea. It's teeming with intelligent life, an animal kingdom, a plant kingdom, and adventurers like you and me. It's lush with abundance and loaded with diversity—dazzling colors, sights, textures, and sounds; tantalizing sceneries from the plains to the mountains, from the seashores to the ocean floors, from the valleys to the glaciers and the deserts; sunrises and sunsets, snowfalls, rains, towering clouds, and crystal-clear blue skies. What's going on here is a dance of becoming, not a dance of remission, and every element and compound, every beating heart and thought, are all born of a greater intelligence.

Are you beginning to see, perhaps a bit more clearly, your heritage, your power, and your divinity? Are you beginning to see that with the power of your thoughts and the unending magic of this magnificent habitat, all things are possible?

The Universe has dreamed far, far more for you than you have dreamed for yourself. As I explained in chapter 6, "Magical Universe," you are far more likely, *by ten thousand times*, to succeed than to fail. Your *entire* life is proof of this "imbalance"; *your extreme predisposition to success*; your wild inclination to prosper; your divine propensity to thrive. Do you now realize that abundance, health, and happiness. It's the ultimate responsibility, a responsibility that was bestowed simultaneously with our receiving the absolute power to have, do, and be whatever our heart desires—the ultimate power. But lest you feel alone, tiny, and inadequate, do not forget that you are infinitely more than you've been taught; that you now have the ability to command all the elements to do your work (because you *are* those elements)—to metaphorically summon legions in the unseen to come to your aid (as all are extensions of yourself) and to literally move mountains (as they are just part of the illusions you've believed in). The entire Universe conspires on your behalf, using the principle of *thoughts become things*, to draw into your life whatever you have the ability to believe in.

Surviving Is *So* Last Year

It gets even better! On this "emerald in space," having created the props, placed the planets, and chosen your birth—*all for the purpose of thriving*—you can *know* that the stage is set for exactly that! You can rest assured that you are the perfect person to have all that you dream of having; that you were custom built for the possibilities that you alone dream of exploring; that whatever you need to perform, succeed, and find happiness is already in you! Of course, thriving has different meanings for everyone—to one it could mean self-love, to another it might mean accumulating material abundance, and to a third, it might mean both—but you can rest assured that whatever it means to you, you have what it takes.

Haven't you always found that you smile more than you frown; you laugh more than you cry; you've had friends more than you've been entirely alone; you've had money more than you've been flat broke; you've been gradually waking up to truth, rather than sliding into an abyss of deeper and deeper mysteries; and you've enjoyed health far more than you've suffered sickness? *We're all naturally and automatically inclined to thrive* in every area of our lives, and since the Universe and our physical lives mirror this inclination (conspiring on our behalf), as our lives unfold it's as if we're seemingly "pushed on" to greatness. It's just that we've slowed ourselves down a bit, being the spiritual infants that we are, because whenever it's come to creating change in our lives, not knowing any better, we've typically approached it by focusing excessively on what we don't like and what we don't have instead of focusing on our dreams.

Thriving, not surviving, is our default setting. Just look at our modern civilization's commerce, technology, and life expectancies. While there have been failings, you'd have to agree that in spite of our deep spiritual naiveties, we've still blown the lid clear off "surviving." *You didn't come here to survive; you came here because you wanted "it all,"* exactly as *you* define "all," and that's what you're going to get.

Thriving, not surviving, is our default setting.

Because you've likely never been told the truth, this may seem outlandish and fairy-tale-like. Armed with the truth, however, *you're free*. Life *is* easy. It's *always* been easy. And above all, life's mechanics are knowable. You needn't go forth in mystery, confusion, and self-doubt; these are just power robbers. Knowing now that your own inclinations are toward happiness and fulfillment—that this is what you are built for, that this is what the stage is set for, and that the entire Universe is in on the "game"—can you imagine the brand-new possibilities that suddenly lie before you?

Prayer

I'm not a big proponent for using the word "prayer." It's like using the word "God" in that it has so many connotations, meaning vastly different things to different people. I dislike the term because it usually implies that the one doing the praying is powerless and beholden to powers, or to a god—*outside* themselves—who picks and chooses whom he will help and when. But I love prayer's

couldn't stay at for the rest of your life, no hobby you couldn't take up, no home you couldn't buy (almost!), no gifts for loved ones you couldn't afford, and never, ever again in your life would you have to worry about money! Think about this for a while and imagine the infinite possibilities. You might even put down this book for a minute to let your imagination really run wild with this twenty million dollars.

Kind of fun, isn't it? Now realize that the magic you currently have at your disposal *dwarfs* the power and freedom that that puny twenty million offers you. You probably quickly realized that you could spend twenty million in your lifetime, but with the magic of the Universe as your supply, you can make the twenty million grow into one hundred million again and again and still not scratch the surface of all you could have. Your supply is limitless, eternal, unending, and yours for the taking! It's already in your universal bank account, and better than money, it can be harnessed to draw more love, joy, and laughter into your life at a moment's notice. That should give you something good to visualize in the days ahead.

Of course, you need to believe in your universal bank account to use it, and because it's invisible, you must have faith that it's there. Act *as if* it is there and you'll then be able to draw on it. Just keep this in mind: though the potential of your universal bank account is limitless, it only has as much money in it as you decide to withdraw.

Now, our brain—logic—tells us that the more we take out the less we'll have, but that's because our brain is only accustomed to assessing *physical* reality. Its sense of logic doesn't work in the spiritual realm. In fact, the opposite is true with the universal bank account: the more we take out, the bigger the balance gets! If you go to your universal ATM for one hundred dollars, that's what it'll give you; but if you go for one million, it'll be there too—with faith.

This does not mean, however, that you should go out and spend more physical dollars than you have, racking up debt in the name of faith! It means that you must know that you do have a unipersonality, charm, and style (though these are miracles sure enough) but the very basic level of your existence. That you have awareness and perspective, and your thoughts and observations continually pour through you without any effort on your part. That's the starting point, and simply dwelling on your own miracle, which you are helpless to re-create or destroy (not even death or suicide ends the stream of your thoughts, which do not originate from the physical world), should be the starting point of your belief in magic.

Going a few steps further, begin to realize that, of all the things you think you've ever done in your life, you've actually done very few—except to issue directives based on your intents and expectations that enabled the Universe to reach its hands into your affairs and get the real work done. Looking forward, realize that this very same magic can be counted on as you set your short- and long-term goals. By recognizing life's magic and how it's worked in your life already, you can begin counting on it to work today and in your future. This immediately means you can begin having more by doing less, leveraging the Universe and engaging the magic that *already* pervades your entire life.

Your Universal Bank Account

Imagine that I've just phoned you and told you that I've wired direct to your bank account twenty million dollars, tax-free. Imagine it! Believe that it's true for at least a brief moment. Can you see in your mind what the little slip from the ATM would look like when it prints your available balance? Twenty million dollars! Imagine all those zeroes! Imagine them on your bank statement and imagine balancing your checkbook with a beginning and ending balance that is eight digits long!

Now imagine the peace it would likely give you today. Just think, there'd be nothing you couldn't afford to have or do. There'd be nowhere on the planet you couldn't afford to travel to in style. There'd be no restaurant you couldn't eat at every day, no hotel you

implication that we are not alone and that we are being heard. You are heard by this very same Universe, by every atom and molecule, and by every entity that could possibly render you assistance. Whether you're thinking, speaking, or living, the Universe takes note, sees your true intentions, follows your actions, and knows all. *You're never alone.*

Delegation

When I first began discovering the kind of material that I've been sharing here, I used to feel really alone—not because others didn't think like this (though few did) but because, when these concepts were blended with my "old school" thinking, the idea of creating my own reality was overwhelming. And although I immediately grasped that it was true, I heard myself thinking and feeling, "Gosh, how the heck do I make my own reality? How do I become aware of all my beliefs and thoughts? If I make my own reality, then that means I must do it alone, and what an enormous responsibility!" All those assertions were—and are—absolutely correct; it is a humongous job and we *do* have total responsibility. *But we are permitted to delegate, and we can delegate as much as we like!*

In fact, delegation is absolutely mandatory in order to get anything done in time and space. Just as the pilot of a jumbo jet has total control and responsibility for the plane and her passengers' welfare, she's required to delegate virtually everything that's necessary to make the plane fly properly. She might turn the yoke (control column) or the rudder and flick a few switches to give the plane direction, but she didn't invent aviation or commercial flying processes. She didn't help build and test the plane and its millions of nuts and bolts and pieces; she didn't orchestrate the formation of the company that bought the plane and operates the airline; she didn't hire and train the ticketing agents and flight attendants; and she didn't build the runways or the control tower. The pilot does virtually nothing beyond showing up several hours prior to the flight for predeparture procedures, hopping into the cockpit, powering the thing up, and aiming! And that's all you have to do to begin living the life you dream of living: just power up your thinking, aim (which implies action, albeit minimal compared to what will be done for you), and delegate the rest to the Universe—your Greater Self—and the principles that hold time and space together, having *faith* that they will perform flawlessly.

Reaching the Tipping Point

Our responsibilities are indeed paltry compared to what will effortlessly be done for us, yet nevertheless, taking some action—*consistent action*—is of paramount importance. Again, it's not so much because of what you might achieve but because taking action is how we put ourselves in a place of receivership of life's magic.

**Whether you're thinking, speaking, or living,
the Universe takes note, sees your true intentions,
follows your actions, and knows all. *You're never alone.***

The instant you think new thoughts, the entire mechanism of the Universe is thrown into motion. Immediately, players and circumstances are arranged and rearranged to create the sequence of events necessary to bring about your dream. Then as you physically move with your dreams, there will follow life's so-called accidents, coincidences, and serendipities, deliberately calculated to predispose you to the right people, at the right time, with the right ideas. You'll also be infused with precisely the right epiphanies, bright ideas, and creativity necessary to pull off your manifestation. Yet if you are not physically living your life out in the world, at least moving in the general direction of your dreams, there simply cannot be such serendipities and "lucky breaks."

Simply doing much of what you already do (and what your peers who know *nothing* of life's workings do) may even be

harmony are already yours, in a kingdom you rule with the thoughts you choose to think? The starting point is not that you don't have any and you just want a little; it's that you have *everything* and you just want a little. What a concept! You are the prodigal child, and feasts, banquets, and celebrations await your return to riches unimaginable—to an inheritance you've completely forgotten was yours, right here and now on planet Earth. All you have to do is finally recognize the truth about your reality and who you really are.

The starting point is not that you don't have any and you just want a little; it's that you have *everything* and you just want a little.

Abundance Comes in Many Currencies

"What about those born in the poorest of countries? What happened to their birthrights?"

This question used to be raised by many of my audiences until I started addressing it head-on.

First, are you so sure they have it so bad? I've visited and spoken in some extremely poor countries, and perhaps the biggest shock I routinely experience is how happy and carefree the people are. South Africa is perhaps my favorite destination.

Joy radiates from even the poorest people in ways the typical Westerner *cannot even imagine*. As poor as they are financially, they have family, they have community, they have food, they usually have shelter, and they have each other. It would not surprise me if some of their elders whom I have been blessed to meet actually pity us in the Western world, with our towers of glass, wireless, high-speed internet, and so little free time. Are they really disadvantaged? Or do they have perhaps an entirely different set of priorities and values than we are accustomed to that makes them far richer than we can imagine?

Secondly, and this is a bit tricky because I don't want to be mis-understood, in cases of extreme poverty and disease, when you grasp that we are spiritual beings who live as many lifetimes as we choose, with *eternity* beyond that, it suddenly becomes a far less "disastrous" notion that we might have a lifetime (perhaps out of twenty thousand) that might be lived under truly "tragic" circumstances. We do not live only once, and for the extreme hardships you might occasionally choose to be born into, you might do so to shift your focus and your understandings to other facets of life that you may have remained blind to under any other circumstances.

I'm not for a second implying that the suffering we're aware of around the world is tolerable, acceptable, or natural. Everything that can be done *should* be done to aid our brothers and sisters, who are portions of ourselves. When anyone suffers, we *all* suffer. Of course, you might think, based on all else I've written here, "They are creators like I am; they chose to create their challenges. Who am I to deny them their chosen suffering?" But this line of thinking would be like ignoring the child who had disobeyed his parents only to become lost, sick, or hurt. Even though their predicament was of their own creation, there are abundant reasons to offer comfort and support.

This is not to say that those who create or choose to participate in calamities have done so for incompetent or childish reasons! In fact, one quite "advanced" reason might be to shock an otherwise slumbering world into paying attention to greater issues than "keeping up with the Joneses." Still, in the grandest possible scheme of things, stepping far enough back from any equation, we will nevertheless find order, perfection, and love as well as clear evidence that, as a rule, abundance, health, and harmony are our default settings.

Back to the point, this book is about you and your life, here and now. Hypothetical questions about African famines and social tragedies are both interesting and provocative, and while they indeed have answers within the context of *thoughts become things*, our highest priorities generally have to be *our own* lives, challenges, opportunities, and responsibilities. Of course, we can simultaneously reach out to others with assistance and love, but we'll be most helpful and at peace with the rest of the world, and thereby able to render true, sustained assistance, when we can first come to peace with ourselves.

It Takes Two

So at one end of the spectrum, we have a loaded Universe that, as you, literally conspires on your behalf to manifest your thoughts with an inclination and an ability to deliver whatever your heart desires. And at the other end, there's you, the thinker, who also wants to see your heart's desires manifested. That's it.

There are really only two stars in every one of our dramas: the Universe (and its unfailing principles) and you. Can you see that? And with what I've shared in earlier chapters, you should now realize that the rest of the people in your life are just players and teachers, existing in *your* realm solely because you've brought them there (including me), almost as if we were just bit actors and actresses helping to complete the play so that you can get on with your lessons and learning, fun and games.

So now, if you and the Universe both want the same things for you, and if these things can be summed up as abundance, health, and harmony, with the rest of us being far more passive in your life than anything else, then you can see that with your power and dominion over all things (unless you've done some limited thinking) your dreams *have* to come true. Whatever you want shall be yours! Whatever you can think to ask for you will receive! Your natural state of existence is to live in abundance, health, and harmony.

Of course, it's easy to say all these things and to feel their truth ring in our hearts, yet sometimes when we look around at our lives, it's disheartening to note that at times we do see lack, disease (or at least discomfort), and disharmony. So what's gone wrong? Where does the problem lie? Well, if there are really only two major stars—you and the Universe—in every drama, it would be safe to assume that the problem does not lie with the Universe; it lies within us. The good news, though (and sadly this is not true for most people yet), is that at least you and I know that something's not right, we know where the fault lies, *and we're doing what we can about it.* You've even spent the time and energy to find and read this book, which means that great and positive change is inevitable for you as you're becoming aware of your powers and your responsibilities.

> **There are really only two stars in every one of our dramas: the Universe (and its unfailing principles) and you.**

Here's a little exercise that will help you better see your natural state: Imagine that there's an identical copy of you—a clone—except that this clone has just one difference from you: it exists in a perfectly natural state (meaning it harbors no unnatural or limiting beliefs), and thus this radiant entity thinks no unnatural thoughts and produces no unnatural manifestations. Can you imagine how this radiant entity would think, how at ease it would feel, how quiet its mind would be? Can you imagine the harmony? Now, do you realize what would fuel this being's every thought? What would come first?

The answer is *desire.* This entity would quietly feel its desires coming forth, as these are the catalysts that start it all. Then, with your clone's desires floating around in its thoughts, unrestricted by limiting beliefs, do you know what would happen next? The desires would engage the clone's unlimited imagination, unleashing its full power because the being would have no limiting or contradictory beliefs or fears to contend with. The clone would then be thrown into *action,* helpless to stop itself from dancing life's dance, and in the process, predispose itself to life's magic and put itself within reach of an all-conspiring Universe. The heavens would open, eventually showering your clone with the manifestation of the thoughts inspired by its desires, and then new desires would arise, new thoughts would be engaged, and this happy cycle would continue indefinitely.

Can you see that your natural state would automatically avail you abundance, health, and harmony without any "effort" whatsoever? Can you see too that this is where you now belong—that this is what's *meant to be*? Without limiting beliefs and misunderstandings, it would never, ever enter your head to contemplate lack, disease, or discord.

The bottom line is that if presently you are lacking abundance, health, or harmony, the problem lies in your own thinking and thoughts. If there's a problem with your thoughts, it's because there's a problem with your beliefs, and if there's a problem with your beliefs, then there's something, or several things, you're not understanding.

To offer some clarity on these variables in our lives, I'll review each one separately. It's my hope that by focusing on what they are, instead of what they're not, you'll glean some new insights that may help you with your understanding of each, allow for the installation of new beliefs, and release you from any limited thinking that may have ensnared you in the past.

Since the material world is simply a reflection of an inner world, it's the inner world that needs adjusting, tweaking, and plucking when the outer world fails to please us.

Abundance

Typically, abundance deals with material things. Of course, it can just as easily apply to friends, laughter, creativity, and so on, but for this section, I'll be talking specifically about material things, even though you can apply the same concepts to abundance in any area of your life.

To start with the basics, what are material things? Material things are illusions; they're like the reflections we see of ourselves in the mirror, except that these illusions appear in time and space and what they reflect are our thoughts. So in case you've ever wondered how a thought looks, feels, tastes, smells, or sounds, wonder no more; just look around at the material things of your life and realize that what you are seeing, hearing, touching, tasting, and feeling are your thoughts that have been manifested.

Since the material world is simply a reflection of an inner world, it's the inner world that needs adjusting, tweaking, and plucking when the outer world fails to please us—and a good thing, too. Material abundance can be quite a heavy thing, and if you had to physically drag it all into your life, you'd need to be Hercules. Instead, you have only to think abundance into your life, remembering that thought, coupled with aligned beliefs, will automatically propel you into action.

I know this may be a challenging concept to grasp; it seems too easy. But remember, "things" are not as they appear. When you're getting ready to leave the house and you want to look your best, you probably spend at least a minute or two looking in the mirror. You check out your hair, your complexion, your color; if you're a woman, you might put on some makeup, if you're a man, you might shave, and then you'll be ready to go. Now, during such preparations, when you look into the mirror and see the things that need attention, do you reach out to adjust your reflection? Do you put your makeup or your shaving cream onto the glass in front of you?

So when you look at the material things in your life, at the abundance or lack thereof, why would you rush around manipulating the things of time and space to effect a change? It's just as crazy! What we need to do is go within. We need to work on our thoughts, our beliefs, and our understandings of life if we want to change the world of appearances. Until now we haven't, and this is because we've been raised and conditioned on the misconception that we must manipulate the physical world first to affect change.

We think that if we're experiencing lack we must figure out a way to haul some luxury into our lives. We think that when we want a new job we have to go out and meet the right person at the right time, in the right place, or find the right headhunter, or have the perfect résumé. We also think that if we want to meet some new friends we have to physically push ourselves in directions we don't want to go. These assumptions come from the idea that matter, the *things* of time and space, come first rather than our thoughts, feelings, and beliefs, convincing us that we must go out and physically manipulate everything and everyone. But the joke has been on us, and it's not funny anymore.

Our brain, the gray matter between our ears (as opposed to our thoughts), is an organ designed to help us assess the status of our manifestations, not create them, just as it's our brain's job to help us assess our reflection in the mirror, not create it. You don't have a brain to help you logistically manipulate abundance into your life— it can't! It's too small to be able to grasp all the likely paths, players, partners, and circumstances that continually evolve, moment by moment, every single day, based upon everyone else's thoughts as well! You have a brain to help you differentiate between what you want and what you don't want. And then by choosing to focus on (*and move with*) what you want, the logistics of such manifestations, considering every imaginable variable, are worked out for you in the "unseen." You might be thinking, "Well, if I don't like what my mirror shows me, then my brain tells me to comb my hair, to put on my makeup, to shave, or whatever, and then I do so." But that's exactly the illusion that has trapped you and the rest of us in the rut we now find ourselves in, thinking that it's *we*, our mortal selves, who do the things that the Universe actually does *through us*. Our brains, as much as ourselves, are useless in this regard.

Brains don't pass judgment; people do. Judgment comes from the spirit within us, the aspect of our entity that peers through our eyes. Brains aren't what animate us; spirit is what animates us, and brains don't have preferences. Spiritually, though, we do have desires and preferences, so if figuratively you don't like what you see in the mirror, it's the spiritual you making this call. And once you've come to this conclusion and have decided how to spruce up your look, what you've done is decide on the end result you'd like to achieve. Then this *vision*, say of combed hair, miraculously sets the hundreds of muscles in your arms and hands into play as you busy yourself looking pretty. You don't have to consciously think about how you're going to physically use your hands and arms; you just hold on to your vision of the desired end result and physically move in the *general direction* you need to move in. Instantly, following your unyielding intent and picking up on your motion, all the proper hand and arm muscles are thrown into action, grabbing a comb, brush, or whatever you need and running it through your hair.

In the world at large, the Universe takes care of the details that will bring you your objective, moving *your* muscles *and* the muscles and lives of other people whose dreams complement your own! Your brain just holds all your electrical circuits together and serves as the interface between the physical you and the spiritual you. It's not meant to figure everything out; in fact, it can't figure anything out. It's just meant to assist the spiritual you in assessing, through your *physical* senses, the physical world around you.

**Look around at the material things of your life and
realize that what you are seeing, hearing, touching,
tasting, and feeling are your thoughts that
have been manifested.**

Remember this when you begin yearning for something physical: it's not your job to sweat the details. *The Universe is your supply*, not dollar bills, not your status, not your family, not your friends, not your boss, not even your job, unless, of course, the Universe decides it will use any or all these "vehicles" for its arrival.

Because it's up to the Universe to provide for us, we can finally begin enjoying what we choose to do with our lives. And since you have the choice, "Follow your bliss!" as mythologist and author Joseph Campbell said. Not so much because your bliss will bring you riches, but because to the principles at play in the Universe, it simply doesn't matter what you do for a living. So why not do what you love and thereby enjoy the ride?

This concept of doing what you love can arouse countless limiting beliefs; you might even be sensing some right now: one has to work hard to get ahead in the world, one has to make sacrifices in life, one has to pay one's dues, and so on. But those are all fallacies—fallacies that can trap you into an unhappy life. Too often we link our dreamed-of end results to rules and conditions that need not exist. The only things that will actually avail us of the illusions we seek are our thoughts of the things we seek, not physical steps in a physical world.

To clarify, however, physical steps *are* a part of the equation, and they'll flow involuntarily, as we reviewed in chapter 4, "Life Is Waiting for You." The misunderstanding, heretofore, lies in our thinking that we must physically make our dreams come true; this is not the case. We must physically move so that the Universe's principles can *make* things happen—this is a BIG difference. This takes the weight of the world off your shoulders. The steps we "must" take are the easy ones: the baby steps that are simply an extension of our thoughts, our beliefs in motion, and these more often than not are the steps we *want* to take.

The truth is that abundance, too, is an inside job. Go there first to affect change. Become clear on what you want, and then go out into the world simply in the general direction of your passions. And as if on cue, the Universe will appear to grab the baton through the magic that dreams inspire.

Health

Your most intimate physical manifestation is your body, and what a miracle it is! Anyone doubting life's magic or the existence of Divine Intelligence has only to examine this awesome "machine" to enlighten his or her perspective.

First of all, your body is alive with an awareness all its own, infused with intelligence, that enables it to automatically and effortlessly grow up, adapt, and live on our planet. Within it are countless living cells, tissues, organs, muscles, and bones that respond to this awareness and its environment with their own awareness, working in concert with each other: breathing, eating, digesting, sweating, resting, sleeping, rebuilding, reproducing, thinking, seeing, hearing, feeling, smelling, tasting, heating, cooling, walking, reaching, grabbing, and more.

But perhaps the most astounding feat performed by your body is that it responds, with razor-sharp accuracy, to your thoughts and beliefs about it, giving you a living picture of what and who you think you are.

Your body is your manifestation, and its physical condition (like anything material in your life) reflects your beliefs and expectations about it. It's a living sculpture, and you're its artist. You are not what you eat; you are what you think, and this miraculous canvas creates and re-creates itself based on your ever-changing thoughts.

If you're concerned about your health, meaning that you might currently be unwell or that you might simply want to improve your well-being, then somehow, somewhere, you're not understanding something about your natural state, and this is causing an imbalance in the system.

When I was living in Boston, I heard someone on the radio "channeling" (channeling was discussed in chapter 5). Because the material sounded really good, I called and made an appointment for a personal consultation. During my consultation, I asked about many things, including my health. At the time, I seemed to have a perpetually upset stomach; I was underweight and basically just didn't feel good. I was told a number of things about my condition, but the insight that helped me the most was this: I was told I had approached my health questions with the presumption that something was wrong with me, or specifically that something was wrong with my body, yet I was then told that my body was perfect and behaving exactly as a healthy body should.

Well, this really stumped me, and I had to think about it for a moment. Then a light went on in my head that made me laugh out loud. The message given was that a really perfect body (a healthy body) will respond to its environment, its food intake, and its sculptor (me) with signs of discomfort, illness, or fluctuating body weight as a signal that it is not being treated or viewed properly. Perfectly flawed, if you will.

This was a subtle message, but how true and important it was and is. What it means is that we *all* have healthy, perfect bodies *all the time* and that sometimes they get out of whack *because of us*, not because of them. By blaming our bodies, we not only shirk the real issues but we create brand-new limiting beliefs that weren't even there to begin with! We all start out with perfect bodies and keep them our entire lives, and we don't suffer poor or irregular health because they become imperfect. They respond according to how we view them, ourselves, and our lives. This is really what *Infinite Possibilities* is all about: *thoughts become things*, and this includes "things" like our physical health.

Weight Concerns

One of most common complaints I hear from people about their bodies is their weight. Although there is always a spiritual issue that would precede weight becoming a challenge, its existence is often first seen *physically* in the guise of overeating or under-eating. And sometimes by tackling the eating challenge, inroads can be made to dealing with the deeper issue—if in fact it doesn't automatically resolve itself once the ideal weight is reached. Just because there is a deeper spiritual cause to weight gain or loss doesn't mean that it is so profound and complex that a few quick fixes to your perspectives and physical routines can't often resolve it.

Let me offer some thoughts that may *complement* whatever else you're currently doing to deal with any weight challenge you might be facing—some things to supplement, not replace, all the conventional wisdom on weight issues that's already available.

1. *Relax!* In the grand scheme of things, *your problem is quite simple*. After all, you're not faced with trying to grow a new limb or adding five inches to your height; you just need to adjust your weight! So many people face their weight problem as if it were the most difficult and complex challenge in the world ... and then it becomes the most difficult and complex challenge in the world—really difficult, virtually impossible to handle—*primarily because they've come to view it that way*. So the first point is to chill out and realize that, with the proper perspective, the challenge you face is, in truth, a very small one.

2. *Don't make or believe in excuses.* Overeating or under-eating is not "natural"; just that realization alone should ring bells in your head. Thinking otherwise creates acceptance and complacency, countering natural tendencies that would otherwise ease you toward balance. This perspective reminds you that your body is *inclined* to be an ideal weight, that you've been pushing it against the grain with your recent eating habits; and you'll realize that once you begin listening to it, its innate balancing mechanisms will be allowed to work *for* you, *enhancing* your own efforts as you strive toward your goal. Covering up unnatural eating habits with clichés, such as "It's just the way I am" or "I come from large people," minimizes your challenge, skirts your responsibilities to self, and, far more damaging, installs beliefs that sabotage your attempts to lose weight.

In the past, I would often work hours and hours into a starving hunger, several times a day and almost every day of the week, just not wanting to be bothered or interrupted by my need for food. I used to even think this was a badge of honor, something to be proud of, but what nonsense, especially when I was already underweight! When I started to finally get my head around how *unnatural* and unhealthy it was to let myself go hungry, that my work *and* social life were suffering because of it, my old attitudes became more embarrassing than empowering. The same, of course, is true for those who overeat.

Now, you obviously have reasons (sometimes reasons you hide from yourself for this kind of physical imbalance), so you should also explore and work with your beliefs, perhaps with guidance, to find or replace these root causes. By working backwards from the outer symptom toward the inner dilemma, accepting that overeating or under-eating is not natural, you can start making inroads toward changing your behavior and understanding your beliefs so that you can ultimately stop playing the weight game and move on to new frontiers.

3. *Realize that your body is not you!* Your body is *your creation.* Separate yourself from the definitions you've painted for it, because it has an awareness and needs all its own. It needs you, it relies on you, and it exists solely to serve you. Your physical body depends on you for its very existence and deserves the utmost care. This line of thinking can also help you separate your emotions from food. For instance, if you were feeling particularly sad one day or depressed or angry, you wouldn't go over to your beloved cat or dog and triple its food, would you? Would you make him or her starve for a day? So why do that to your body? Remember to combine logic with love when you consider your behavior, emotions, and decisions. Then listen in and trust. Think about your behavior, get logical for a moment (however overrated it may be), get rational, get spiritual, and begin to apply some divine, loving intelligence to your situation.

4. *Notice everything you say and do about your weight to avoid reinforcing any negative programming.* Avoid saying things like "I'm helpless," "It's no use," "I have a slow (or high) metabolism," "It's hereditary," "It's my thyroid," "It's difficult," or something a friend of mine used to say: "All I have to do is look at food and I gain weight!" Those thoughts will strive to become things, your body will react, your metabolism will slow, and you'll be far worse off than you were.

Fortunately, it doesn't matter if these things were once true; from now on they're not, and you must cease giving them their power. Even if you are now one hundred pounds overweight, never again utter the words "I am overweight," because this statement will only continue to perpetuate the manifestation. Your body is perfect and supremely capable of achieving its perfect weight; it's just that until now you've unknowingly misprogrammed it, and you've got about one hundred additional thoughts clinging to you for life. Drop the thoughts and the weight will drop too.

5. *Model your behavior after your dream self.* Splurge, indulge, and treat yourself to the occasional delicacies you crave *as if* you were already at your ideal weight. These acts of faith, or acting *as if*, powerfully tell you and the Universe that there's a new game being played. They demonstrate a confidence that you are in control, and they create that feeling of having already succeeded. As your dream self, enjoy a slice of chocolate cake after dinner, not the whole cake! Not even two slices, because if you really were your dream self, even two slices would be too much and unnatural! It goes both ways: by modeling your behavior in such ways, you create thoughts that will serve you in the direction of change you wish to experience.

Begin deliberately saying things as if you were at your dream weight. Go ahead and say things that don't even make sense on a physical level, like "Thank God I'm so thin!" This isn't a lie; it's the truth. Spiritually, there does indeed exist another you who is at the perfect weight, and you summon it forward into your physical reality when you make statements that recognize it. By saying you're overweight or underweight or by making jokes about your body or your condition, you project these comments into your future and thus your reality. You must immediately begin thinking, speaking, and acting in line with your dreamed-of weight. Go ahead and obsess over the new wonderful you; eat, sleep, and breathe it, and that's what will be projected into your future. Forget where you are and where you've been, and live in the reality of your new dreamed of image.

6. ***Focus less on your weight and more on living a well-rounded life. (No pun intended.)*** This is also advice I give people who seem to be consumed with either finding a new romantic partner or manifesting abundance. They want what they want so greatly that it's blinded them to the rest of their life, who they already are, and all they already have—to the point that the rest of their life begins to suffer. Pretty much no matter what your weight is, you still have a life NOW! And your life deserves attention. Don't put off the fun stuff, the challenging stuff, or anything else because you aren't yet pleased by your weight. On the contrary, keeping your life balanced will be one of your greatest assets when it comes to affecting weight change; through achieving balance, your weight loss may well even happen automatically.

7. ***Eat less.*** Conversely, if you want to gain weight, eat more. Yes, it's simplistic but wildly overlooked! I apologize to those who readily understand that both overeating and under-eating are the first symptoms of a deeper issue, and I address this to those who still find the physical element of their weight gain or loss an isolated mystery. As I've already stated, the deeper issue is usually the ideal starting point for affecting meaningful change, yet the second-best place to begin is controlling food intake. It's rather amazing that today there is actually diet pet food—as if the *amount* of food your beloved pet eats is of paramount importance, or as if the fact that Baxter is overweight has some mysterious root cause that requires a very special blend of modified processed foods to be remedied. There is no overweight pet on the planet that cannot eventually, and usually relatively quickly, be reduced to its ideal weight by simply feeding it less. And the same is true for people wishing to lose weight.

8. *Exercise!* I won't even elaborate, except to point out that in this regard you most certainly do not have to go crazy, join a gym, or run marathons. The slightest effort in this regard, done under a doctor's supervision, will pay huge dividends in keeping your body healthy and in balance.

Harmony

Oh, how much finer life becomes when we can find harmony. But the thing with harmony (and it's just as true for abundance and health) is realizing that it does not have to be found. It already exists; it's within you, it surrounds you, it's your natural state.

I had a strange experience a few years ago. I had been listening to Pachelbel's Canon in D, one of my favorite pieces of music, and, as sometimes happens when I listen to it, I was overcome by a joyous, blissful feeling that is almost impossible to describe—like happiness turned up a million degrees. After I turned it off and went into my yard to do some chores, I somehow slipped into an altered state. Suddenly I again "heard" Canon in D playing in the recesses of my awareness, and simultaneously I perceived the bushes and plants around me gently swaying to the melody and exuding their own joy that was equally inexplicable. In that instant, I felt I knew more about the reality of plants than will ever be found in a book. I knew then that this was their joy, their peace, and their harmony *all the time*. I remember thinking how impenetrable it was. It even occurred to me, as silly as it may seem, that even if a tree were to be struck by lightning or uprooted by a bulldozer, this trauma wouldn't have any effect on its blissful state of awareness: just being and radiating a joy that's invisible to our physical senses. I also sensed that even if a tree were to slowly wither and die in a drought, it would still know only this bliss.

That episode only lasted several seconds and I haven't experienced it since, but it reminds me to this day how things really are, not just for plants and trees but for all life. There exists this love, joy, and harmony in every living thing: every atom, every cell, every insect, every creature. It's only when we mask it with the perceptions of our physical senses, our judgments, and our beliefs that it becomes invisible. It's also alive right now in you, just a breath away from recognition. Harmony doesn't need to be found; it needs to be uncovered from within and permitted to capture your attention. And to help you unlock the doors that may sometimes keep it from view, here are three thoughts:

1. *Acceptance.* If there's something ruffling your feathers, fighting it won't make it go away. If anything, fighting it will keep it at the forefront of your thoughts and thus in the forefront of your ongoing manifestations. Accept that you have challenges and that the things in your life are as they are. As I said earlier, that doesn't mean you have to love them or that you can't change them, but you do have to accept them in order to move forward. Acceptance means that you stop struggling against the Universe, because no matter how justified you may feel, the Universe will win. It also means recognizing that whatever is on the plate before you is there with a lesson to teach, and it means you're willing to revisit it in a higher light to find that lesson and peacefully embrace it.

2. *Be self-referring whenever you encounter life's turbulence.* Realize that you, not whatever it is that's bugging you, is masking life's joy and harmony, and only you can remove the blindfolds that keep them from your awareness. The circumstances of our lives don't bring us pain, fear, or worries; it's only our perception of the circumstances that bring these things. By accepting what's before you and working on your perception of it, you can and will be elevated to a higher, more harmonious understanding of the situation.

3. *Remember that everything in your life is exactly as it should be.* You're never thrown into a situation or given an experience accidentally. In fact, you're never thrown into anything; you only create experiences and situations or avail experiences and situations because you are ready to face the consequences and see things in a new light. You are the reason things happen to you, and by accepting and looking at your life with self-referral, you can begin understanding that everything is as it "should" be. There are no accidents and the Universe doesn't make mistakes. Life is our playground and study lab where we get to try out our thoughts, and if it doesn't already, one day this will all make sense to you. You'll realize that nothing was ever lost; that you have been kept whole; and that, as an eternal spiritual being, you still have forever before you.

**For whatever you want, rid yourself of
any conception of *how* you'll get it.**

Don't Mess with the Cursed "Hows"

Whether it's abundance, health, or harmony we're after, our obsession with the hows in life is what gets us into trouble. To demonstrate this, let's move this talk back toward material abundance (even though the same concepts apply to health and harmony), and I'll give you a little test. Let's say that you're dreaming really, really big about whatever it is that you really, really want to manifest into your life. Go ahead and pick something outrageous right now that you'd like to experience or have.

If you're like the rest of us, you'll initially feel that in order to manifest what you've just thought you wanted, you're going to have to *figure out how* to get it. If you're a realtor, you're already thinking about what kind of listings you're going to have to get; if you're an author, you're already thinking about the bestsellers you're going to have to write; if you're a salesperson, you're already thinking in terms of commissions and bonuses; and if you feel you're currently stuck in a dead-end job or if you're unemployed, you're probably feeling stressed out because you have no idea what the heck you're going to have to do to be able to afford your grandiose dreams.

So, without messing with the cursed hows, what *do* you have to do to get this thing you want? This is the test. What *will* you have to do to achieve this dream? No matter what your profession, or whether you lack one, I hope you just thought, "I'll have to engage the invisible forces of the Universe to do this for me," knowing full well that whatever you dream of is a cinch for the Universe, just as it's virtually impossible for the physical you. Often our first failing when dwelling on abundance, health, or harmony, is immediately thinking and stressing that we're going to have to figure out how to bring them into our life.

For whatever you want, rid yourself of any conception of *how* you'll get it. Remember when, straight out of school, I thought I was going to get fired during my first three months working at P.W.? Well, once I realized I was making a bad situation worse with my negative thinking, I began visualizing every evening when I got home from work. And remember that I told you I didn't know what to visualize, because as a bad auditor, I didn't know what good auditors do (or I wouldn't have been a bad auditor)? Well, that impasse was a blessing because it led me to focus on my desired end result: walking up and down the hallways of P.W., beaming with joy. Not knowing *how* else to get out of my position as a bad auditor prevented me from telling the Universe *how* to save me, which would have limited it from seeking the absolute highest and best solution. As it turned out, the solution was something *I could never have plotted in a million years*—being loaned to the tax department!

I focused exclusively on the end result—being happy at work— and that's exactly what I got when I let the Universe figure out the hows, or the details, of its achievement. Had I insisted that I become a "good auditor," it's much less likely the Universe could have even used the tax department as my salvation as my thoughts on becoming a better auditor would have kept me in the audit department!

I then went on to tell you that after I averted an early termination at P.W., I began working on a little scrapbook to help me visualize all kinds of things I wanted in my life, including the places I wanted to go. Basically, that little scrapbook held photographs of my desired end results, *not the means of their attainment.* It held pictures of my dreamed-of lifestyle, which is the hidden trick to the power of this kind of tool: it immediately gets your thinking to the *end result.* I looked at these pictures and visualized for about ten months, when finally, after a short seven-day period, decisions were made that swept me off my feet and landed me in a Middle Eastern city I had never even heard of, much less dreamed of or visualized. As it turned out, that tour of duty in Riyadh, Saudi Arabia, was perhaps the one thing that could have made my dreams come true the fastest. It was *how* my dreamed-of lifestyle would be realized, yet it was far beyond anything I could have imagined happening. Not only that, but it was a *how* that was in keeping with my own adventurous nature, and a fantastic time was had.

You're never thrown into anything;
you only create experiences and situations or
avail experiences and situations because you
are ready to face the consequences and
see things in a new light.

By letting go of the *hows,* not only do you free up the Universe to figure out things *for* you (in ways that may leave you speechless), you also free yourself from all the fears, worries, and stress that go along with trying to manipulate time and space.

There's another challenge that goes with trying to plot your course. As you stress about every little detail of your progress, you are slowly drawn out of the now and begin living in and worrying over the future. But if you turn the hows over to the Universe, you can begin enjoying the present. By delegating and leveraging the Universe, you not only ensure that tomorrow will turn out for your highest and best, but you free yourself up to begin enjoying all the wonders that life already holds for you. This applies to every area of your life, not just your career but also your health and the harmony of your affairs.

Don't mess with the cursed hows.

You *Can* Do This

Now, let's ratchet things up some, because you're not reading all this to make your life a little bit better; you're reading this so that you can get busy making your dreams come true, and at a minimum that means living in abundance, health, and harmony. Depending on where you are now, it may seem like you have a long way to go, but realize that the actual distance you have to travel isn't physical. The challenge you face lies in shifting your thinking and understanding. You want to go from thinking the kind of thoughts that have delivered you to this day to thinking the kind of thoughts you'd think once your dreams have already come true. And while they may be two entirely different classes of thought, *they're still just thoughts.*

> **By letting go of the *hows*, not only do you
> free up the Universe to figure out things *for* you ...
> but you also free yourself from all the fears,
> worries, and stress that go along with trying
> to manipulate time and space.**

So let's talk about this new kind of thinking. Thinking is similar to any physical task we perform. We get used to doing it in certain ways; we have our comfort zones, our routines, and our habits. Yet right now, by reading this book, you've acknowledged that you're ready for some changes, and the message I've been sharing is that any such changes must first take effect in thought. Although I've shared a variety of ways to approach this, I really want to help you move quickly and easily into thinking in some new directions. The following are five easy ways to begin thinking new thoughts, with an emphasis on *what* to think (as opposed to *how* to think).

A Palette of Thoughts

Create for yourself (and why not start today?) a huge palette of thoughts to dwell on. What I mean is that you can develop now, ahead of time, a list of thoughts to think in the near future when you visualize, when you run errands, when you daydream, whenever. Take some time now to creatively provide yourself with a palette of thoughts to choose from later on. Even though you'll only visualize once or twice a day, no longer than five or ten minutes at a time, it will make everything simpler if you have a list of the many nuances of your dreamed of life.

For example, if you want to lose weight, instead of just visualizing yourself being thin from time to time, create lists now of the hundreds of positive ramifications that being thin will bring into your life. You might think of what it will be like shopping for new clothes or trying to decide what to do with all your old clothes that no longer fit. You might think of the reactions of old friends and the reactions of new friends when they learn of the changes you've made. Think of picking new goals that would only seem attainable or worthy of dreaming once you are *already* at your ideal weight; think of how going for a walk or exercising will be so much easier; or imagine helping and inspiring others to achieve as you have. Think of everything that will be positively different, because virtually everything will be!

Create this huge palette of thoughts now so that you have all this "thought ammunition" to bounce around your head in the days, weeks, and months ahead. In addition to making lists, you can enumerate these positive scenerios on alternating pages of your scrapbook. It's easy, and you can create this kind of palette for every dream you have.

For abundance, think of the "help" you're going to have to hire to run your affairs: the accountant, the lawyer, the nannies, the lawn care companies, the swimming pool people, and more. Think of how you'll find them. Think of how you'll interact with these people and perhaps their families. Think of what else you'll be doing with your time. Think of the kind of goals you'll be setting for yourself once you're financially set for life. Delve deeply into imagining your life and affairs under these new circumstances. Make these palettes so large that you always have things to think about, to wonder about, and to consider. They should be so large, and your thinking along these new lines should become so predominant, that going forward you won't even be able to watch television or drive past a billboard without considering the ads in the context of your new life.

Think BIG

As I mentioned lightly in the beginning of this book, think big, yet pace yourself. Beyond simply inspiring yourself, when you think big your dreams send your thoughts *beyond known limitations*. By aiming high, it's like reaching above the clouds of doubt, because you have no idea what kind of limits may even exist way up there.

For me, the abstract thought of "living the life of my dreams" gives me far more inspiration and *less resistance* than focusing on just getting my next book published and distributed or on a new speaking opportunity because it shoots me past all my known arguments. And while the thought of living the life of my dreams is abstract, it's still easy to imagine lots of related details—hearing my friends' voices as they congratulate me, seeing the shine on the chrome of my new car, arranging the new furniture in my corner office, meeting with an architect to discuss renovating my London flat, feeling the sweat pouring off me after an excellent country run! What's important is that we not make these details more important than the big picture: *living the life of our dreams.*

Give Yourself Incremental Goals

Actually, there's nothing wrong with exclusively dwelling in the clouds of your wildest dreamed-of end results, but these visualizations may seem so far removed from your present life that you may find it hard to believe that you could ever really close the gap, and consequently, you could become overwhelmed. Break down your lofty goals into several bite-size pieces so that from time to time you can also work on more immediately manageable achievements, empowering yourself and building your confidence as you make progress toward your dreams. A word of caution, however: this is not to be misconstrued. I'm not suggesting you create incremental hows (e.g., "I'll write a bestseller so that I'll then be able to splurge on a family safari in Kenya!"). What I mean is that you should have some incremental *end results*; there's a big difference between the two (e.g., "My first book's first draft will be complete by the year's end! By summer I will have an agent. It will be a book that thrills readers the world over!"). Or, entirely independent of your dream to become a writer, you'd imagine, "This year we'll vacation in Mexico! Next year we'll safari in Kenya!"

Of course, you can dream big *and* fast. The point I am making is not to make one dream *how* another dream will come true. There's no reason you cannot dream of your first book becoming a bestseller; it happens all the time. But this example was purposefully "loaded," because writing a bestselling book is a classic and common example of *how* many people see their other dreams coming true. The only reason one should aspire to write a book to begin with is either because they earnestly have something to share or because they love writing.

Happiness's Greatest Secret

To the best of your ability, enjoy your life as it already is. It's not the realization of your dreams that will bring you happiness; most people adjust their dreams as they go, raising the bar higher and higher, and so it should be. Ever hear of a millionaire who didn't strive for his or her second million? We're naturally insatiable creatures; reaching one goal, we immediately fix our sights on the next.

These pursuits are adventures. They keep us growing and they keep us alive, which means that by perpetually changing our goals and dreams, the only constant in our lives is the journey we're on—a journey without end and one that is partly based upon attaining "things" we do not yet have. So the trick is learning to find happiness even while you do not yet have all you want, because you never will! Do you see? If we postpone our happiness until our present dreams come true, it becomes a habit without end—our achieved dreams constantly being replaced by new dreams. To enjoy life means to enjoy the journey even though the journey itself implies that we are incomplete. This is happiness's greatest secret; master it now and you can coast into "the rest of your life."

Ground Yourself in Truth

Spend some time every now and then just dwelling on the fact that your natural state is abundance, health, and harmony (five to ten minutes is enough). Think on their nature and their pervasiveness in life itself. See life sending to you all that you want, because it does. Consider nature itself, with its peaceful sceneries and its prolific productions of greenery, flowers, and fruit. Reflect on how little the animals in the wild have to worry about their survival, food, and shelter. And recall every incident in your life in which you were miraculously provided for. Dwell on life's magic and strive for that certainty of knowing that you are perfect, you are loved, and all is well. This thinking will take you past limits you don't even know you have, and more and more it will enable you to begin seeing proof of *life's harmony and abundance* all around you.

Water rises to its own level unless physically prevented from doing so, and your level includes an endless supply of rich abundance, perfect health, and blissful harmony. These elements are your birthright, and they belong in your life right now. You are special, you are divine, and you are oh-so deserving. Life will carry you on—it already has—and to direct more abundance, health, and harmony your way only requires an understanding of the true nature of who you really are, where you are, and why you're here.

Can you see yourself living in the home of your dreams, owning fabulous cars, frolicking on a South Seas island or in the Caribbean in the winter, taking in Broadway shows in Manhattan, traveling internationally every year (first class, of course!), skiing the Swiss Alps, hiking in the Himalayas, joining safaris through the Masai Mara? How about sailing, scuba diving, playing tennis, golf, or polo—can you see those too? You could be staying at the Hermitage in Monte Carlo; attending Wimbledon, the Masters, or the Super Bowl; buying wonderful gifts for family and friends; financially helping those in need; incorporating your own charitable organizations; funding scholarship programs; feeding the hungry; housing the homeless. Can you see yourself living like this? I can.

Now imagine feeling good about your body, being fit and trim, working out, jogging, playing sports, sweating, and loving it. Can you envision yourself posing for pictures and loving the results (medicine-free, hospital-free, doctor-free, pain-free)? Never, ever having to think about your health when deciding upon future adventures, vacations, jobs, and travel while supporting others in their quest for a healthy life? Can you see yourself like this? I can.

Your life can be stress-free, when every day you feel satisfied with everything you did and didn't do, always knowing that you've done enough and always feeling that you are exactly where you should be, breezing through your days with a powerful sense of grace, feeling your connection to the Universe, and appreciating that you really do have all the time in the world. Can you see yourself like this? I can, and so can the Universe.

To enjoy life means to enjoy the journey even though the journey itself implies that we are incomplete.

You are a miracle, you are prone to succeed, and the cards are stacked in your favor. By embracing these simple truths, you'll unavoidably meet with the abundance, health, and harmony that is even now everywhere in your life.

9

Relationships

*I*s there anything more challenging or more rewarding than relationships—at home, at work, at play, and in love? And isn't it interesting that while we tend to define our relationships in terms of the people in them, the one thing all our own relationships have in common—the ultimate common denominator—is ourselves?

In this chapter, we'll begin by talking about the relationship we have with ourselves, the common denominator, because when we have peace with ourselves, we can have peace in our relationships with others; understanding ourselves makes it easier to understand others. And more so, when we can be happy with ourselves, we can more readily be happy with others. I'll also share some specific insights into the relationships we have with partners, especially romantic partners, so that you might begin to develop an awareness of what it is your heart truly desires and how you can best bring it about. Whether or not you're now in a romantic relationship isn't important, because as you'll see, for the most part these ideas apply to all relationships.

Our Relationship with Ourselves

The key, of course, is self-love. And the only way to love yourself is to first be yourself: authentic, genuine, and natural, which will lead

to understanding yourself, which as in all things, brings appreciation, acceptance, and compassion.

Where you are is never who you are.

Listen to Yourself

Follow your feelings, your heart, and your mind. Forget about
appearances and what other people think, because no one else can
know the secrets in your soul nor the promise that you came here
to fulfill. This reminds me of something that occurred during the first
year of TUT. Business was slowly growing (we had no salaries yet)
and we had moved the world headquarters from my one-bedroom
apartment into a two-bedroom apartment, with boxes of T-shirts
from the floor to the ceiling in every room.

Every day at 5 PM, UPS would come by to pick up the day's
orders. The driver would usually have to wade through the boxes
in my living room to get to my makeshift office. One day he noticed
my framed Florida CPA certificate hanging on the wall and asked me
in a shocked voice, "You're a CPA?!"

"Yep," I said, kind of proudly.

"Well, what the heck are you doing living like this?!"

That was a hard moment for me. The answer, of course, was that
I was following a dream. I had embarked upon a journey to a fantastic place, and the couple of years I had to spend in the apartment
were just stepping stones. But the driver couldn't see the journey; he
saw where I was as my destination, and for a moment, I saw things
through his eyes and totally lost my confidence.

Of course, where you are is never who you are. Yet often where
you are is all other people ever get to see of you. Only you know
the truth about who you are.

To be yourself and to love yourself, you must *listen to yourself*
and realize that *you* are the ultimate authority on you—the chief
executive officer of your life who is infinitely more capable of seeing
your life's big picture than anyone else could ever be.

Be Patient with Yourself

This is not just a Universe that compassionately watches you like a doting parent but a Universe with superpowers that are yours to leverage. Every tiny thing we think, say, or do is amplified by a million powers back at us; the Universe rewards your efforts exponentially. Think of it: by simply visualizing and taking baby steps, you command the entire Universe to orchestrate miracles of synchronicity, to rearrange the actors and actresses of your life, and to make possible breathtaking coincidences and happy accidents that will yield whatever you were initially thinking about.

This is when faith comes into play—between your first baby steps, and the manifestation. During this part of our journeys, we must live, to the degree possible, as if we knew that our dream's manifestation was inevitable, even while the physical world around us still mirrors our prior thoughts and expectations. We must accept that time is necessary for our *thoughts* to *become things*, without drawing the conclusion that "nothing is happening," "it's not working," or "I must not be doing this right" when we don't see near-instantaneous results.

Turning our life around is like turning around a jumbo jet in midflight: the pilot may turn a hard left, but at almost six hundred miles per hour it's going to take some time before that plane is pointing in the opposite direction, and it wouldn't help matters if after the first minute, the pilot quit, saying, "I don't get it. She won't turn around; seems to work for everyone else but me."

Give your manifestations time.

To be yourself and to love yourself, you must *listen to yourself* and realize that *you* are the ultimate authority on you—the chief executive officer of your life.

The Universe is your able and competent servant. Have faith in it and be patient with the progress the two of you make. As I said earlier, just because you can't see all that's now happening for you behind the curtains of time and space doesn't mean it's not happening, yet becoming impatient with yourself can undo all that work.

Keep Busy

Sometimes the best way to instill patience is to keep busy. Have you ever gone sailing and the wind just died? Suddenly the sails started drooping and there isn't the slightest breeze to fill them again? The most frustrating thing about losing the wind is that you don't know when it's going to return. You might sit still for minutes, but it could also be many hours. If this has ever happened to you, one thing I know is that *you knew* that the wind would return at some point—maybe not as soon as you'd like, but you knew it would return—and it always did.

Now, it wouldn't have done any good during the lull if you had cursed the elements, would it? And it wouldn't have done any good if you started doubting your sailing abilities or if you had begun losing your faith in the wind and worrying whether it would *ever* return. The same is true of the lulls we experience while pursuing the life of our dreams. We all want so much and we all want it now, but when it doesn't appear as quickly as we'd like, it doesn't do us any good to begin doubting our ability to manifest whatever it is we want or to lose faith in the Universe.

The thing to do is to take advantage of the calm by doing things that you wouldn't be able to do if the wind were howling. Go fishing, go for a swim, take a nap, eat a meal, make some phone calls, wash down the boat—do anything except worry and doubt. By busying yourself, not only will you be productive but you'll also take your mind off the lack you're facing.

In life, use what time you *do* have to do what you can. Always *do what you can*. These are among the most powerful four words in this book because when you do what you can, new avenues become available, new vistas and vantage points are created, and your immediate focus becomes the present.

Accept Yourself As You Are Today

Accept all that you've been; you've only ever done your best, given your understanding at the time. And all that you've done has made possible your enlightened perspectives of today.

Accepting also means forgiving yourself for your so-called mistakes. Of course, this is only possible if you've already accepted total responsibility for your life, and it doesn't mean being angry or disappointed in yourself. It just means realizing that you have been, *and therefore always will be*, at the helm of your ship. It means that while you may not yet fully grasp every situation you've ever experienced, you still claim each as your own creation.

Forgive yourself through understanding—understanding that you're not here to be "perfect" but to experience the human adventure, part of which, at this time in our civilization, means fumbling around in the dark, trying to make sense of things. Take responsibility and accept yourself, *thereby empowering yourself* to change whatever it is that doesn't now please you. No matter what rejection you've faced, no matter how trying your life has been, and no matter how greatly you think you've erred, offended, or violated, *today you are poised for greatness*. You've made it this far, and for the lessons learned and the truth discovered, the best is yet to come.

Stop Seeing Your Desires as Needs

Desires point you in the direction of where you *want* to go, while needing too often carries the implication of lack or incompleteness. Desire typically has you looking forward, while need casts your attention to unsatisfactory present circumstances.

Whenever you'd like change in your life, let your focus be on its acquisition and upon your anticipated ownership of it, rather than your disappointments or what you're missing. Focusing on the lack perpetuates the lack and gives you reason to be disappointed, and so immediately you begin your journey toward change unhappily.

Focusing upon what you want, however, especially if done playfully and as if you already have it, empowers you and lightens you up with anticipation. Plus, it positively charges the principles in the Universe that will bring your desire to you.

Whenever you want change, come from a place of desire and strength, not of need and incompleteness, so that the ensuing journey can feel like one of adventure and choice.

Chill Out!

I remember when I learned these truths almost thirty years ago. At first there was the elation over discovering my power and the wondrous Universe we live in, but then there quickly followed a realization of my responsibility to think and then to live with my powers of manifestation, and I was overwhelmed. I became aware of my every negative, frightening, limiting thought, and I felt absolutely doomed unless I fought them back, one by one, tooth and nail!

Today I know better. I still have times when fear arises and when uncertainties spark runaway trains of self-doubt, but as I laid out in chapter 6, "Magical Universe," I now understand that we are inclined to succeed. We are all naturally far more buoyant and optimistic than we give ourselves credit for, and simply entertaining a negative thought does not mean it will manifest. Not only does it have to win out over our countless other thoughts about success, happiness, and love, but it goes entirely against the grain of our natural disposition to thrive.

We've chosen to be born into primitive times. Spiritually speaking, it's as if we've just crawled out of the caves. Fear and pessimism are rampant in the world around us, yet as I pointed out earlier, look at the phenomenal strides our civilization has made *despite* living in such darkness. Even now, there is far more light, globally, nationally, and individually. And with this awareness, we realize we needn't panic over our every worry, fear, or doubt; we can indeed chill out, enjoy the journey, and have far more tolerance and compassion for ourselves in the process.

Trust the Universe

Trust the Universe, its principles, and the greater aspects of yourself to be working on your behalf with your overall best interests in mind. You don't have to specifically ask for something in order for great things and wonderful surprises to start happening in your life.

When I first began to grasp how life really worked, in addition to my initial concerns about my fears and worries, I found I suddenly had something else to worry about! Knowing that *thoughts become things*, I began to worry that if I wasn't clever or creative enough to *think* of something ahead of time, I'd never get to experience it! Or I worried that if I dreamed of one thing, as it manifested it might limit me in areas I hadn't thought of. But then I remembered all the pleasant surprises I'd already experienced in my life, as you have, and how perfectly they fit into everything else that was going for me.

Simply *being* happy or *dwelling* on happiness will inspire the Universe to *make* you happy *in all the ways that you define happiness*. If material abundance is part of how you define happiness, then the Universe knows you will not be fully happy without it, and it will draw it into the equation. In this case, with the desire for happiness *plus physical efforts made on your behalf to be happy*, you needn't even visualize abundance to suddenly find yourself swimming in it. The Universe knows you inside and out, and in a sense it knows things about you that you don't even know about yourself. Whenever you ask for something (thinking new thoughts), not only can it be delivered but it will be delivered taking into account *all the other aspects of your life*, without your having to give thought to every nuance or detail ahead of time.

You also needn't worry that attracting abundance into your life, for example, will come at the expense of your health or relationships. The Universe automatically knows how to orchestrate every manifestation, taking into account not only your entire life but all the lives that are touched by your life. Of course, if abundance is your dream and you begin messing with the cursed hows, sweating the details, blocking off options, and tying the hands of an otherwise unlimited Universe, your pursuit of wealth may indeed jeopardize other areas of your life. But when you move forward with an understanding of how life really works, life balance becomes effortless.

You needn't become obsessed with your thoughts; just be aware of them. They're not going to betray you, nor will the Universe. Free up your mind, let it wander, let it wonder, and let it explore reality on its own. Trust. We're all creative, spontaneous, and playful, and so are our thoughts and our manifestations. With our innate spiritual autopilot set on success (our natural inclination) and the profoundly accommodating Universe working 24/7 on our behalf, good times and wonderful surprises are par for the course.

Our Relationships with Others

Before I get to our relationships with others, I need to cover some basics so that we're on the same page. First of all, and for the record, I trust you now recognize that life is just too mind-bogglingly perfect, miraculous, and splendid to be an accident. Right? And with this line of thinking, it becomes impossible to think that your own birth and all its circumstances were an accident. Life is far too exacting, purposeful, and meaningful for there to ever be any kind of "accident." Nothing is ever left to chance—and *your* birth was no exception. *You* set the course, *you* chose your parents, and *you* chose when and where you'd be born. We all did.

Now, you might object to this idea, thinking that your "awareness," or your personality, is brand new—that it began on the day you were born. After all, it seems logical to deduce that since we can't remember anything prior to our birth, we must not have existed. Yet you do believe, I'm quite sure, that "life" is eternal. And if life is eternal, aren't we actually speaking of consciousness? And haven't we already determined that consciousness not only exists independent of time, space, and matter, but that it actually creates

u see, any event that affects more than one person must be
ved" via the beliefs and expectations of all involved. For
le, why didn't Jesus use His profound powers of healing to
ll lepers at once (banishing the disease entirely) instead of just
He came in contact with? The reason is that *He* didn't do the
g; He merely invoked the healing powers within those who
to Him with the desire to be healed and the belief that it was
ble. He didn't heal the whole world overnight because he
dn't—the whole world wasn't ready to be healed. Their beliefs
expectations prevented it. The point here is that when operating
shared reality, as we all are, our affect *on other people* is entirely
rmined by those other people, and when the masses are
lved, any experiences must fall within the beliefs of the times.

None of this means you can't *shatter* world records, heal yourself
m disease, accumulate vast fortunes, or begin doing things that
e never been done before, because the global consciousness does
eed expect such accomplishments and even miracles. But when
manifestation of your thoughts would affect other lives, you're
erating in a shared space that also contains their thoughts, beliefs,
d expectations.

As I mentioned before, those in your life who may be affected
y your thoughts already know what you're up to, just as you
now, deep down, what their dreams are and the directions their
ives *may* go. Your hopes and fears suit them; theirs suit yours as
well. This is equally true of your place in the world's population.
All of us have been drawn together by like thinking and complementary objectives, both in our closest circles of friends and in
broad, global terms.

In a situation where you *would* like to affect the course that a
specific person will take, your thoughts can influence them only if
they grant you that power through their innermost beliefs and
expectations about life. This is the privacy you would insist on,
after all, if the roles were reversed and someone was trying to
affect *your* life. Nevertheless, if you do wish to exert such influ-

them? If you're with me so far, then perhaps you can now see that
you are eternal; that there will never be a "time" from this day forward that you do not exist in spirit. Hanging on? Good. So you can
now take the leap and realize that if you will spiritually exist
forevermore, into time's future, in part because time is simply an
illusion, then mustn't you, similarly, have always existed in time's
past? Hold on, this really is going somewhere. You weren't just
born in 1935 or 1985 to live for eternity; you *came from* eternity.
You existed before there were the illusions of time and space; you
had to if you are their cocreator today. If this weren't true, your
essence or spirit would be as artificial as the illusions that support
you. If you did not transcend time and space, you would wither
without them.

And now that you can "see" that you had to be "around" before
you were born, don't you think you had something to do with the
circumstances of your birth?

**Nothing is ever left to chance—and *your* birth was
no exception. *You* set the course, *you* chose your
parents, and *you* chose when and where
you'd be born. We all did.**

You chose every wonderful (and not so wonderful) parameter
of the life you're now living for the emotions, insights, and understanding you're now experiencing. You set the stage. It's not that
tomorrow is set in stone, for *truly anything* could happen next
based upon your own *evolving* thoughts, beliefs, and intents, mingled with those of the population.

The point of all this is that the people in your life, those you
have relationships with—from your parents, siblings, and childhood
sweethearts to your children, coworkers, and present-day love interests—are not there accidentally; they are and were your choice,
directly or indirectly, *as a function of all your thoughts, beliefs, and
desires*, and so too were you a part of all their choices. So when it

comes to assessing and learning from the relationships of our lives, it's important to see them from the perspective that these people (*especially* these people) are in your life with your blessings and with something to teach you.

None of this means that birth relationships must be revered and held above all others. And it doesn't mean that you must indefinitely maintain these relationships, for it could well be that one of your challenges was to break some patterns that existed in past experiences. All relationships result from choices—birth relationships as well as relationships forged during the adventure of life—and you're free to change your choices from one day to the next based upon your own needs and desires.

If your childhood was filled with unhappy memories and you're asking yourself why—*why would I choose such unpleasantness*—the answer is simple: you wanted the challenge, knowing full well the rewards it promised—perspective, sympathy, compassion, appreciation, awareness, and understanding. I'm not suggesting here that one must endure hardship to grow and progress, but if that's what you've encountered, you will be rewarded. And very likely, by the time you've found this book, you *already have been rewarded* to some degree.

When you consider that a lifetime is, well, "just" a lifetime and that you live as many lifetimes as you like, perhaps you can understand why some people choose to immerse themselves in extreme circumstances—even in brutal and "wicked" hardships—because, after all is said and done, they will return (just as we all will), to the beauty and remembrance of their divinity. Add to that thought the idea that anyone choosing a lifetime with a rough start can follow it, if he so chooses, with a lifetime in the lap of luxury, and it then becomes even easier to understand.

To each his (or her) own; we all make these decisions for ourselves, and though we may live again and again in time and space, *each of our lives is precious and important, imparting treasures of knowingness that could not be obtained in any other life, by any other person, ever.*

I want to make it clear, however, that n̲ past decisions, and just because a life may so far doesn't mean there's some hidden age̲ tinue that way. In fact, every challenge an̲ opportunity to overcome and to live in abund̲ mony; we needn't learn to live with these chall̲ and drag them with us throughout our life. beginning, presenting new opportunities to ris̲ we make these kinds of decisions based on adopted and the thoughts they inspire.

There is one last topic I'd like to go over befo̲ to maximize the joy in our relationships with o̲ one—one that we've all locked horns with at one̲ our lives—because it deals with other people and how their choices may or may not mesh with our o̲

Living in a World Full of Creators

Keep in mind that when it comes to deliberately ca̲ niche in life and visualizing the life of your dreams, ju̲ touches many others, so do your thoughts.

Generally, to be manifested, your thoughts must fa̲ most *basic* parameters of the cultural and social beliefs̲ to avoid violating the experience of a fellow adventure̲ ple, if you wanted to turn your cat into a dog, grow and̲ arms, or levitate yourself over New York City (assu̲ occurrences would be witnessed and experienced by̲ couldn't happen until the mass beliefs held by the share̲ tion permitted it. The good news is that global awarene̲ shifting into higher and higher levels, and people are waki̲ their spirituality and resonating with the truth of their po̲ magnificence. All kinds of new possibilities and potentials a̲ ing into play that *will* allow for some new thinking and thu̲ stunning manifestation.

ence, your potential success will also depend on your motivations and desires.

If your intentions are well-meaning, your thoughts will help the one concerned, for they will be received with the love that sent them forth, stirring hope and awareness of the options available to them. If, on the other hand, your motivation is self-serving (and there is nothing wrong with self-serving motivations), it's far better that you forget the specific person and instead visualize your desired objective.

For instance, as I mentioned before, if you aim to discover "true love" with a specific person, don't visualize that person; visualize true love and all the consequences you think it will have on your life. Intensely imagine the feelings it will evoke once achieved and its impact on your daily affairs. Don't dwell on your idea of who the person is who will unleash true love within you; focusing on him or her only distorts your wish to find love. When you focus on the person, you're actually focusing on the hows of its attainment rather than leaving the details—the means—to the Universe. Just see the end result; see yourself happy with a wonderful companion.

In Love

Until now, I've focused on the relationships we have with our self, how people get into our lives, and what kinds of effects we actually have over one another. For the remainder of this chapter, I want to get into some specifics, particularly those dealing with romantic relationships—how, through understanding and honoring ourselves, we can extend this love to our partners and further the adventure.

Here are five thoughts that are all too often misunderstood or overlooked. They're aimed at helping you manage and appreciate your relationships.

1. *Honor yourself between relationships.* This first point about being in relationships is actually about when you're

not in one! I think one of the saddest things in life is when I see others trying to *fit in*, no matter how high the cost to their integrity. Too often, in my experiences, it seems that our society and culture operates under the false premise that people should, ideally, be in a romantic relationship. This cultural expectation doesn't care about whether they're ready for one or whether they want one, but states that generally, people "should" have a romantic partner. Of course, this means that if you don't want one, there's something "wrong" with you, and that you can't possibly be as happy as you would be if you were in a relationship. I'm not saying that friendships aren't natural, nor am I denying that sharing time with a loved one can enhance virtually any experience. But this mass assumption can be hurtful to those who are alone, and it can make it particularly challenging for those of us who are, regretfully, influenced by popular mass beliefs, to find happiness in our own company. Each of our lives has seasons, and what is right for one person may not be right for another.

Whether you are single by nature or whether you are between relationships, your life now affords you opportunities for growth, adventure, and self-discovery that *do not* exist presently for those in a relationship. Enjoy this time. Use it. Appreciate every moment while being unconcerned about what anyone else thinks.

2. *Measure your relationships by the love that's been shared.* Too often relationships tend to be measured by how long they last instead of how much love or fun was experienced. There's the belief that "great" relationships withstand the test of time. Since when has a clock or a calendar been the measuring unit for love, emotional growth, or happiness? Quality is what counts, not quantity. This is not to say that you can't have a quality relationship that also lasts a lifetime, nor am I saying that adversity in a relationship should lead to its abandonment. But these two benchmarks—

quality and quantity—usually have very little, if anything, to do with each other. What's important in any relationship is that it is a fulfilling, rewarding experience in terms of either learning or happiness.

3. *Understand your motivations.* Entering a relationship when you're not ready or for the wrong reasons can make it an unhappy experience from the start. We have an obligation to ourselves to understand what motivates us, and that obligation extends to our partners as well. Are we moving through our lives motivated by fear or a sense of adventure? Do we want a relationship so that we can hide from the rest of our life or to blend with it? And—the most common question—is the relationship meant to add to our happiness or create it?

Relationships can't make you happy; they only intensify whatever you already feel about yourself and life. Other people are like a mirror: they reflect your attitudes about life and yourself back to you. A happy person entering into a relationship will likely become even happier, and an unhappy person entering into a relationship will likely become even unhappier.

What exactly is being mirrored? It's not your behaviors, your looks, or your outer expressions but the beliefs and the perceptions you have of yourself. This is often the case for people with low self-esteem who are further abused in their intimate relationships. They think of themselves as flawed, unworthy of love and appreciation, or even deserving of punishment, and these thoughts are not only picked up by the other person but, depending on their disposition, may be expressed, possibly in the form of abuse. Of course, it is more complex than this, but the point is that what you bring to the relationship is what you will gain from it, whether it's happiness, sadness, or self-doubt.

In the same vein, it's futile and usually dishonest to enter into or stay in a relationship believing that it will make the *other* person happy. How often have you heard people say, "I just want to make you happy"? Too often! No one is, nor should they pretend to be, in a relationship to make someone else happy. That kind of statement typically hints at their own unhappiness, usually within their relationship. Your first objective, for the benefit of yourself and your relationships, is to make sure that *you're* independently happy. When you're happy and joy is your motivator, the rest of the details in your life will take care of themselves, and usually, though not always, those around you will be happiest.

4. *You decide what's meant to be.* Why is it that in most areas of life, people believe in free will, infinite possibilities, and our inherent, natural-born freedom, yet when it comes to relationships, they believe that some are meant to be? It's probably the romantic in all of us, and in that sense, when everything is rolling along smoothly in your relationship, it's pleasant to fantasize that perhaps the Universe saw the two of you as being such incredible complements that it preordained the union. Yet should the relationship become challenging, the notion of your union being "meant to be" can mischaracterize everything! If the relationship ended, was failure involved? Was there an error on one side or the other? Should it be "saved" no matter the cost (since it was "meant to be")?

Nothing in time and space is meant to be, except for what already exists in the present and all that awaits in the future that will be determined by your ever-evolving beliefs and expectations. Tomorrow is a blank slate. It has to be; otherwise there'd be limits and constraints on our ability to create our own realities.

5. *Relationships are an adventure.* Just as in life, in an adventure there is hope, challenge, promise, and mystery. Relationships are not "work," per se, as we so often hear. I understand the point trying to be conveyed when they are called "work," and yes, all relationships, like all adventures, are an ongoing labor of love. But given that most in our society still consider "work" to be a four-letter word, attaching this label or characterization to your relationships is unwise. A firm belief in anything, including the presumption that relationships are "work," will bring about that reality. The truth is that relationships don't have characteristics until the people in them define them. They're not easy or hard, challenging or rewarding, work or play until someone says so. A bigger truth here is not that relationships are this, that, or the other thing; it's that individuals in relationships see them as this, that, or the other thing, and so they become.

As a side note, rather than working on the relationship, each person "should be" mindfully "working" on his or her own life perceptions, which is true regardless of whether or not we are in a romantic relationship. It's just that such relationships create a fantastic opportunity for exactly this, as your partner so often reveals to you your own perceived strengths and weaknesses, and understandings and misunderstandings. It's not that the relationship is work; it's that it creates ideal conditions for us to learn about ourselves. Yet if the "work" becomes arduous and is blamed on the relationship, rather than seeing it as the next step in understanding yourself, you'll mistakenly ascribe such growing pains to coming from the partnership, not understanding that it simply facilitated your own natural, inevitable awakening to truth and self-discovery. Such thinking would then color your future partnerships in the same light, as laboratories of pain, thereby *making them* laboratories of pain. *Thoughts become things.*

Thoughts for Adding Romance to Your Relationship

Here are ten simple thoughts to consider for making the most of your romantic relationships, in addition to all the other guidelines and ideas that may already be serving you. These are quite straightforward, and even if you've heard them before, when now combined with the spiritual insights that have been shared thus far, they may begin to make even more sense.

1. *Beyond what's "necessary," shed all behavioral expectations you may have for your partner.* Of course, when entering into any relationship, you do so for your own wishes and desires, and you can rightly hope to *expect* they'll be met. For instance, you expect to be loved in return, to be respected, and perhaps to have complementary roles that contribute to the partnership, creating something that no one person could create. But apart from what you can't live without, rid yourself of all behavioral expectations that your partner will have to live up to, and instead keep your main focus on yourself—your own standards and behaviors—so you can add to the relationship rather than take away from it. Doing so will enable you to become your best; you'll release your partner from our culture's sometimes implied "job" of entertaining and making you happy, and you'll create room for the unexpected. Unnecessary expectations create narrow definitions or preconceived ideas of what "should be," and in addition to limiting your experience, they take your attention away from the beauty of what is. Fortunately, we can change our expectations as quickly as we can change our thoughts.

2. *Dwell on what's right.* Nothing can doom a relationship faster than dwelling on what's wrong. In life you get what you think about, so if you're constantly focusing on what's wrong in your relationship or in the other person, look out! You just magnify it and project more of the same into the future. This is a scary thought, because we all know what it's like when something starts bothering you. You tend to fixate on it and mull it over a hundred times in your mind.

By dwelling on what's wrong, you actually characterize your future. It can take a lot of willpower (or, even better, *understanding*) to get yourself out of that kind of loop, but which do you want more—to be right and justified or to have a better relationship?

By the same token, don't dwell on your differences. So often I've heard friends say, "We're so different; I don't know why we ever got together!" What's ironic is that from my perspective they're like two peas in a pod and are actually far more alike than not. Chances are that if you've been drawn together with someone to the point of entering into a serious relationship, you have far more in common than you've even realized, whether or not your similarities have manifested into the same extracurricular activities or not. What you likely *do* have in common is life assumptions and core beliefs, and it's likely just as true now as it was when you first met.

Another irony here is that it's the little differences between partners that actually attracted them to one another in the first place. That's often what's fun—the adventure of seeing things from someone else's perspective *while still sharing the same core beliefs*. After all, we don't want clones; we want someone who may help balance out our life, not shadow it. Yet it's sometimes these little differences that are dwelled upon and therefore magnified way out of proportion and context, to the point of becoming the very justification for ending the relationship they once helped launch.

Conversely, in a world where our *thoughts become things*, dwelling on what works, what pleases you, your similarities, and what is "right" will not only expand its presence in your life but will literally maximize the chances of drawing more "positive" behavior from your partner.

3. *Don't assume.* This might sound like a childish admonition, but it's at the core of many unhappy relationships. If you're assuming something about another, *it means you're guessing*. And if you're guessing, it means that communication and, more importantly, understanding has broken down in the relationship.

In the absence of actually knowing what's going on, we make up the missing pieces, and usually when we make stuff up, we tend to listen to our fears more than what we know to be true. Then we begin reacting to our own assumptions and behaving in ways that mirror what we erroneously believed to be true. Your partner picks up on your new beliefs and your assumptions, and starts reacting to your assumption-based behavior until finally you actually create the reality that was triggered by your fears—*a reality that did not previously exist*!

Of course, the biggest challenge here is knowing when you're assuming something; no one consciously decides to assume anything. Instead, we react to what we think are truths. So here's the trick: the next time the truth about a situation or your partner starts troubling you, take a time out, go within, reexamine the so-called facts of the situation, and reconsider where you might have them wrong.

4. Accept that there will be challenges. Enjoy and appreciate the challenges in your relationship, because by their mere existence, they create the perfect opportunity for you to master the areas of your life and yourself where you have the least understanding. As I made clear earlier in this chapter, our relationships and our partners are not accidentally in our lives. You don't just get stuck with someone abusive, you didn't just randomly marry someone who became a workaholic, you didn't just happen to fall in love with an introvert. Your partner's qualities are often the very qualities that will bring about the perfect challenges that help you grow where *you* most need—and want—to grow.

5. Let the other person love you in his or her own way. This is presumably what attracted you in the first place—your partner's unique personality and how he or she expresses him- or herself. Actually, this rule could also fit within the "expectations" rule. Don't expect to be treated exactly as you treat the other; it's not fair and it only draws your attention to your own *perceived* shortcomings of the other person, creating issues where there were indeed none.

> **Unnecessary expectations create narrow definitions
> or preconceived ideas of what "should be," and
> in addition to limiting your experience,
> they take your attention away from
> the beauty of what is.**

If you concoct rules that need to be met for you to feel loved, then you're going to spend more time marking your scorecard than expressing love *in your own way*, and you'll minimize the efforts that *are* being made on your behalf. Be thankful for what you have, be all and give all that you can, focus on being better yourself, and let the chips fall where they may. At least you'll know that you did your best.

6. *Talk smart.* Talking—communication—some say, is the most important ingredient for a successful relationship, but I would add that it's critical to choose your words wisely. Your talking can do as much damage, if not *more*, than silence.

First of all, never just complain or criticize; there's nothing constructive about either. Complaints and criticisms are one-way, dead-end conversations that create resentments and feelings of inadequacy, no matter how tactfully they may be presented. Instead, make constructive suggestions for what you would like to see differently, rather than speak about what you dislike. And whether or not there's a conflict, develop the muscle that consistently offers compliments on all that you do like. By first demonstrating your compassion and appreciation, you become a partner and an ally, paving the way for conversations rather than conflicts.

When unpleasant behaviors must be discussed, learn to separate them from the person; understand it's the behavior that's upsetting you. Then you can share your feelings, without implying that you were intentionally violated and without making your partner feel attacked.

Second, lose the notion that someone is right and someone is wrong, because given your unique perspectives on any given difference, you both have a valid point of view. Let your talks be aimed at collaborating and understanding each other's experience more than justifying your own.

Finally, be sure you understand your own motivation in wanting to talk. I know what it's like when something is bugging you and you know it shouldn't be bugging you, but darn it, it is. You feel you've reached your limit, yet without further trying to understand the issue and your reaction to it, you decide, "We have to talk about this." That kind of talking is just grabbing the monkey off your back and throwing it onto your partner's, and while it might make you feel better temporarily, the pendulum will surely swing back your way.

If you've got issues, first do your best to understand why you're upset. Are assumptions involved? Expectations? Are there any other elements that perhaps you alone have control over? If not, then at an appropriate time and in an appropriate way, discuss these concerns as your own and not as a relationship "problem."

By first demonstrating your compassion and appreciation, you become a partner and an ally, paving the way for conversations rather than conflicts.

7. *Accept responsibility for your feelings.* This isn't about what happened; it's about how you reacted to it. Remember, your emotional reaction to anything is based on your perception of it. If something disappoints, the disappointment originated within you, and *only you* have the power to change how you're feeling.

Often when we're upset in relationships, our knee-jerk reaction is to try to snuff out the external cause of that disappointment. I'm not suggesting that you have to put up with everything; far from it. We all have preferences with regard to how we'd like our life and relationships to go, and *preferences are both good and natural*. However, when they're applied to your life's situation and they cause you pain, you have choices about how to respond, and the first course of action is to reexamine your understanding and perspectives, which is virtually impossible if you blame others for how you feel.

8. *Fight fire with kindness.* Anger is destructive, as I said in chapter 3, "Blessed Emotions," and when two people are angry, twice the damage is done, not just personally but to the relationship as well. I'm not saying that you ought to respond with flowers every time you're insulted, nor am I suggesting that you just ignore trouble. But when you realize that another person's anger results from his or her own limited perceptions, it's easier and better to approach the situation with compassion.

When someone is angry with you, it's because somehow he feels threatened; he's usually afraid of somehow losing his grip on the situation. When you retaliate with anger, it only reinforces his belief that he stands to lose something important. By responding with kindness, perhaps by issuing an immediate and sincere apology or by gently inviting him to talk, you're no longer seen as the problem but as the solution. Kindness truly is power, and it's a powerful person who can live by a code of kindness at all times.

9. *Have your own life and your own interests, and strive to be as fulfilled outside the relationship as you hope to be within it.* Now, this may sound like the most obvious thing in the world, but it's sadly absent for so many people in relationships. Let there be space and a degree of independence with regard to your exchanges with life beyond the relationship, whether you find this from your work, your hobbies, or other activities. If you're building all your hopes of happiness on the temple of another, you're actually shirking your responsibility to be happy by shifting it to the one you love. Living only to be with another person isn't an act of love, it's an act of fear—fear of life itself.

And here's something really, really important about "having a life": it must include interacting with people. These people don't have to be friends; they can be coworkers, fellow club members, church members, fellow volunteers—anyone—but we must have these social interactions in life if we don't want life to pass us by. By all means enjoy solitude—time in the garden, time with your pets, good books, or even watching television—but whatever it takes, stay involved with the world and people.

Relationships should be to life what an excellent dessert is to a fabulous meal; they should never be the meal itself. Your relationships should add to your life, not be your life.

10. *Make your own happiness job number one.* Nothing else you might ever do in your relationships could be more important to you and, just as important, to those you love. Of course, this brings up the issue of selfishness and it's a question I often get, because some people equate making yourself happy to hedonism, decadence, and greed. Hardly. That's just our old-school programming. We are spiritual beings. *Our natural instincts are compassion, love, and charity.* If these premises weren't true, there's no way we'd survive, much less thrive, throughout eternity. In fact, our civilization would never have come as gloriously far as it has without them.

There still seems to be a pervasive belief in the world that if one person succeeds, it must be at the expense of another. This sure wasn't true when Thomas Edison discovered the light bulb or when Steve Jobs introduced the iPod and iPhone. And so too will you exponentially add to the joy of your relationships when you make *your* happiness job number one.

There is no guarantee for the success of particular relationships because they will always, in some aspect, depend on someone outside of ourselves. But by doing your part—by staying true to yourself and making your own happiness a priority—you'll be better prepared to overcome misunderstandings held by others and yourself, and in time, you'll be drawn to those of similar persuasions and passions.

When you don't know what to do, don't do anything!
Wait. Wait until you *do* know, because if you stay true
to yourself, eventually *you will* reach the
point of knowing.

Irreconcilable Differences

What of relationships that seem to have irreconcilable differences? Just the thought of that hurts, doesn't it? And the reason it hurts so much, other than compassion and love being your natural-born inclination, is because we tend to look at everything in such black-and-white terms. No relationship is ever truly over, and as hard as it may seem to believe sometimes, no love is ever lost. We are eternal, we are timeless, and so are our connections with one another. We're fooled by our physical senses into believing that something is gone, blinding us to what has been gained, but whether or not we sense the gain, it's still imparted.

No love is ever lost because whether or not the relationship continues, the good compounds and its effects will outlast any pain or suffering in the long run. What truly hurts when a relationship ends is our pride, but as I said before, this kind of pain is priceless when it comes to uncovering our so-called invisible limiting beliefs. Use the pain, trace it back to its source, and get a handle on why you feel less when obviously you're the exact same person you were prior to feeling it.

We are eternal, we are timeless, and so are our connections with one another.

What if you're in a relationship that seems to have irreconcilable differences, and you want to know if you'd be better served by moving on? This is a tough call, and the best advice is the age-old adage my mother likes to use: *When you don't know what to do, don't do anything!* Wait. Wait until you *do* know, because if you stay true to yourself, eventually *you will* reach the point of knowing.

Your relationship must be serving you, either directly or indirectly, for it to be worth having. And when I say serve, I mean you must be either having fun or learning, or preferably—though not necessarily—both.

Our work is how we create and contribute and it's how we make the biggest difference with our lives.

At Work

Can you guess what your most important relationship is at work? It's the relationship you have with your work itself. Everything and everyone else comes in a distant second place. Your work, whether it's at home raising kids or in the office of an employer, is what you give back to the world. In spiritual circles, we hear so much that you should give, give, give in order to receive, receive, receive. I think we need another word in our vocabulary—one for giving yourself to life—because normally the word "give" implies charity, and that's not the kind of giving I'm talking about. I'm talking about plugging your-

self into life so that the world will continue to turn, giving your t
talents, and passions, and if you're getting paid for it, great. Our w
is how we create and contribute and it's how we make the biggest
ference with our lives.

Look at the big picture for a moment. Our civilization, through
much of the world, has finally reached a point where most of
don't have to live off the land. We've got so much momentum goi
that our society has created an endless number of jobs, all of whi
are vital for us to be enjoying the quality of lives we already have. V
all work *together* seamlessly, magically, without even realizing ho
one hand washes the other or how valuable and indispensable o
own contributions are. It's like we all carry batons in a great rela
race, though we're completely unaware of the end destination and c
the importance of each and every runner. Working is *giving* in th
truest sense of the word, no matter how underpaid or overpaid yo
may feel, and your relationship to your work should begin with
understanding its indisputable value to others as much as to yourself.

At Home

For your relationships at home, particularly with your children, keep
in mind this important perspective: children must be respected as
spiritual beings with a lineage as long and as ancient as your own.
They are fellow adventurers, simply sharing your time and space,
and each is unique with his or her own lessons, objectives, and journeys ahead. Don't try to force children or your relationships with
them to fit any preconceived ideas. Not every child will be intellectual or academically inclined, emotionally compassionate, outgoing
and friendly, or even playful and "happy," but whatever the child's
unique personality, it's part of the chemistry he or she chose to maximize his or her learning and happiness in this lifetime.

**Children must be respected as spiritual beings with a
lineage as long and as ancient as your own.**

Accept your children for who they are and your relationship with them for what it is. This doesn't mean that you won't offer guidance or even lay down some hard rules; you have a responsibility to do both. And it doesn't mean there shouldn't be an ongoing attempt to make their life and your relationship with them better and better. It just means appreciating their differences, approving of them, and encouraging them to march to the beat of their own drummer.

∞

Few things in life can be a catalyst for so much pain or so much joy as our relationships with one another because these relationships so harshly expose our beliefs in the duality of our physical world, where everything seems either very good or very bad, while we seemingly stand helpless before it. But we're never helpless to change the circumstances of our lives, as long as we do not look to the physical world to effect these changes. Look within. Seek first to understand, and thereby love yourself.

As spiritual beings, we must go within to effect changes, which means working with our thoughts and beliefs about other people and with our beliefs on how they affect us. When becoming aware of these beliefs, *watch yourself and listen* to all you think, say, and do, because the shocking truth is that you're actually eliciting certain behaviors from everyone you come in contact with based on your beliefs, perceptions, and dispositions in each evolving moment.

To make the best of your relationships, realize that the people in your life are chosen: they have been chosen by you to enhance your learning and happiness just as you've been chosen by them, perhaps to light their darkened path. I'd expect that while reading this chapter, you wished a time or two that whomever you might be in a relationship with right now would take to heart some of the points I've made. But you know people don't open up to new ideas—even helpful ideas—until they're ready, which means that very likely you're the one who's going to have to lead the way for the moment.

And you're the one who will sometimes have to settle for not having the last word. It'll come back to you, however, not only in the way of having better relationships, but when all is said and done, you'll see how your patience and goodness rippled out into humanity, raising us all a notch or two higher into the light.

10

Tools and Techniques

*A*lthough I generally avoid formal methods and rituals, there are a number of little exercises I've found myself doing on a somewhat regular basis that may be helpful to you when it comes to working with your thoughts and beliefs. They are simply suggestions for ways you might engage your imagination and ultimately harness the principle of *thoughts become things*.

Of course, I've already suggested numerous things you can try, such as visualizing, belief bulldozing, mantras, affirmations, and so on, so instead of repeating myself, I'll revisit them with additional insights, as well as share a few new tools.

None of these are very rigid; they may even seem lightweight to you, but they can be (and should be) adapted to your particular style and temperament. It goes without saying that there's no right or wrong way to gain mastery over the illusions of time and space, and what works for one person, or for me, might not be at all useful to another.

You don't have to do the following exercises on a daily or predictable basis, either, but they're helpful to know and to have available when you feel the need or desire to do them. There are no rules—and this should take away any pressure you may feel that you *have to* "do something," because you really don't have to do *anything*. You're already crafting your life day by day, and you're already growing and getting better and wiser in every moment; this is inescapable.

Creative Visualization

Visualizing just once or twice a day for five or ten minutes is ideal. And I've already told you that perhaps the most important things you can imagine are the emotions you expect to feel once your dream has already manifested. Let me just add a few points that might help you expand and enhance your visualizing experiences.

Scrapbooks and Vision Boards

Long before *The Secret* suggested vision boards, I was making scrapbooks from plain white sheets of paper, with glued-on pictures cut from fancy magazines of images I expected to see in my dream life. So I will make references to scrapbooks, even though the same can be applied to vision boards, which are just large-scale scrapbooks made of poster board.

The power of a scrapbook lies in the fact that it's filled with images of the *end results* you wish to possess or experience, completely side-stepping the *hows*. You don't create your scrapbook with pictures of *how* your dreams are going to come true—of you hanging out in a singles bar or pounding the pavement looking for a new job; you put in it photos of the fruits of your dreamed-of life.

Scrapbooks most certainly do not have to be just about acquiring material things.

Now, to make your scrapbook even more useful, you can add quotes, either your own or passages from favorite books, any kind of inspirational writings, or anything that inspires you. I usually alternate pages with a photo and a quote. You might also use some actual photographs from some of the high points in your life—happy photos of you and your friends or any other photos that bring back good memories, such as *emotions of being in control, at peace, happy or carefree*—feelings you'd like to experience more of. For that matter, you can take photos of cheerful, smiling faces from magazines—the kind of faces you'd like to have in your life to help you imagine the joy you're after, because scrapbooks most certainly do not have to be just about acquiring material things. And while you're at it, definitely include a recent photo or two of yourself amongst all the other images. Remember, this collage is about your life; naturally then, the person of honor should be present! And this will help you associate *yourself* with the images you choose.

Another addition to my scrapbook are brief notes I've written to myself as if they were notes from someone else, like congratulations, thanks, or job offers that would be written to me if a particular dream of mine had *already* been achieved.

I even have fake checks I've written to myself, from real people and real companies, for huge sums of money as payment for whatever services I'd like to perform for them (e.g., royalty payments and speaking fees).

The last bit of advice I have for your scrapbook is to be constantly updating it. After you stare at any photo for a while, it'll likely lose some of its luster and some of your enthusiasm. So don't just add new thoughts and photos to your scrapbook; take out the old ones that no longer have the same emotional impact. Your scrapbook should inspire and excite you as a happy thing to turn to.

Oh, and one more bit of advice on scrapbooks: give it a rest every once in a while. You don't have to use a scrapbook to help you visualize. Sometimes just getting a new issue of a great magazine will do just as good a job, and at other times, just closing your eyes and creating your own pictures is best. Remember, there are no rules.

Getting Primed

Just before you start visualizing, do your best to enter into that feeling of truly understanding that you are a divine creator and that all things are possible. This is a state of understanding that you *really do* deserve whatever you have the "audacity" to believe in, possessing the certainty that your thoughts *always have become* and *always will become* the things and events of your life. Remind yourself that the realization of your dreams is not something you have to orchestrate; all you have to do is determine, define, and focus on the end result, and the Universe will figure out the details. The Universe and its principles will be receiving the impressions of what you want, picking up your thoughts when you visualize and taking over from there; *it's the law.*

Another thing you can do before visualizing is remind yourself of all your prior successes in life, especially similar successes with regard to what it is you're now after. You can also do this whenever you face challenges, reminding yourself of times in the past when you prevailed over similar adversities, whether you're about to visualize or not. List them if it helps, and write down or think of all the other times in your life when you received help that you needed: when the Universe stepped in on your behalf, when you maintained the necessary faith to bring about the changes you wanted, and when you triumphed in the face of fear. Looking at these lists and thinking of your successes before you visualize will help you have the right frame of mind and bolster the belief that you can, indeed, have whatever it is you want.

Getting into the perfect frame of mind isn't always easy, so don't beat yourself up if you're feeling a little stressed or harried before you start. Whenever possible, do what you can to get that right feeling—listen to music, read some deep and profound words, or briefly listen to an audio program. The difference in your visualizing, including the results it will eventually yield, can be great because you'll face much less resistance from limiting beliefs by starting like this. Such beliefs will all have been, at least temporarily, diminished by the state of grace you've just invoked. Eventually, you'll get used to thinking from these perspectives, whether or not you're about to visualize.

Beyond the Dream

Something else I sometimes do when visualizing is think *beyond* the point in my life when my dreams will have come true. I think of my life as if all my dreams have already come true, and then I think and wonder about what new goals I'll be dreaming up then. I'll wonder about what kind of thoughts I'll have when I'm more enlightened. I'll wonder about what kind of people I'll associate with. I contemplate my future priorities, *all of which presupposes that my dreams have long since come true.* I see myself way out there in the future, accomplished and helping others, and I imagine what my life will be like as that other person. From that future per-spective, I send back thoughts to my present self like, "Oh boy, Mike; stay the course. If you could only see what I can see now, you'd pass out cold! Keep plugging and enjoy the journey, because no matter how great the setbacks may be, this—where I now am—is where you're now headed, and it will be worth every bump in the road along the way!"

Because this kind of thinking takes for granted that your dreams of today have already come true, these kinds of thoughts—these presumptions—will strive to become part of your life so that you can actually experience that sense of accomplishment. And the only way you can experience that sense of accomplishment is *to have* such accomplishments beneath your belt. Focusing on these end results, and in particular their related emotions, is what inspires the magical Universe to figure out just *how* to get you there—and it will, with faith. It never fails.

Getting Playful, Having Fun

This last thought on visualizing will actually open the door to other exercises: visualizing, or thinking thoughts about your dreams as if they've already come true, need not be an isolated exercise. I know I suggested visualizing no more than once or twice a day for five or ten minutes, but that's referring to a dedicated visualization time in a quiet room in your home or office. In addition to this, however, at random points throughout the day, by all means have pleasant, happy, casual daydreams—without the formality. Remember, the reason that visualizing works is because your thoughts do become things, and *thoughts become things* whether or not you're visualizing.

All your thoughts, including your daydreams, jockey for their place in your life, so put up reminders around your home or your office or in your car, your briefcase, or your purse—everywhere you go—that will constantly feed your thinking mind with the kind of thoughts you want to be thinking and experiencing. Use photographs from magazines, photos from your personal photo album, and inspiring quotes. Anything that you might put in your scrapbook you can also post on the mirror in your bathroom, your refrigerator, or your computer monitor.

Organize your life so that you're faced with constant reminders (thoughts) of how your new life will be, as well as reminders of life's magic. Think, "Oh yeah, there's my new Porsche," not "Look at that. Wouldn't it be nice?" Don't even think "Won't it be nice" to imply that it will be in your future; say, "It *is* nice," as if it's now in your present, and as if it's now parked in your garage!

Note Cards and Bullet Points

Here's something else I often do to help focus and stimulate my thinking along the lines of *what I want* to be thinking. I used to do it with just a notepad, but now I prefer using three-by-five-inch index cards. I write down extremely detailed bullet points with descriptions of the things I want, and when using these cards, I usually have one card per subject. For instance, one card might be for my work or career, another card for the kind of new car I want, another for the next home I'd like to buy, another for the kind of enlightenment and wisdom I'd like to possess, another for my short-term goals, and one for some long-range goals. You can categorize these cards any way you like.

Right now one of my favorite cards is one on which I've written down three different goals I'd like to achieve that are not very far-reaching, but if all three were to manifest in the very near future, not only would I be thrilled but it would also powerfully confirm that I'm on the right path. These are reasonable goals and yet they stretch me as well.

What three relatively simple things could happen in your life, within the next twelve months, that would be a confirmation of the path you're on, thrill you, and leave you powerfully charged as you look to the future? Write them down together; these are the intermediary goals I spoke of earlier.

On another card, I've written down compliments and praise I've received from various people by category—some recently, others long ago—that affirm to me, through other people's eyes, that exciting things are awaiting me and that my potential is unlimited. When rereading them, it's as though I'm reliving them; I *feel* like I'm receiving them all over again. They tug on my heartstrings, inspire me, and help me add emotion to my thoughts.

On another card, I've written what my next home will be: it will be on a chain of lakes and modern, with a fireplace, a pool, great landscaping potential, nature trails, a modern dock, a boat ramp, a boat-house, a well with crystal-clear potable water, excellent views, a tile roof, and high ceilings. It will be a solid, well-built structure above the flood plain and need little to no maintenance, and on and on, including every imaginable desired feature. Writing this card is like drawing word pictures. As you create these lists, you can almost see what you're describing.

These cards or lists not only inspire you when you make them, but they can be referred to later on and may be used as a basis for either visualizing or daydreaming. In fact, right now, in the back corner of my desk against the wall, I have a pile of several dozen cards that I'm constantly adding to or modifying, or I'm removing cards that are old and no longer inspire me. As with your scrapbook, keep the mix fresh. And like your scrapbook, there are no rules here; sometimes I don't touch my cards for weeks or months at a time, and other times, I use them every day.

Acts of Faith

Acts of faith are extremely powerful. To refresh your memory, acts of faith are physical demonstrations that are in line with your dreams: demonstrations that imply that your dreams have either already come true or are about to come true. For instance, making a scrapbook is not an act of faith but occasionally splurging with confidence is, even though the old you says, "Hey, you can't afford that!"

Let me help you draw the line with what's reasonable behavior here. By all means, stretch yourself outside your normal comfort zones when performing these deeds, but at the same time you need not jeopardize your overall financial stability, health, or peace of mind. Don't turn your acts of faith into acts of recklessness! For instance, as I mentioned earlier, incurring debt in the name of faith is absolutely unnecessary. See chapter 4, "Life Is Waiting for You," for lots of ideas that do not require spending money to demonstrate having abundance. It's a fine line and one you have to intuitively define for yourself.

As I suggested earlier, you can write down acts of faith ahead of time and begin performing one or two every day, and as you more consistently become aware of how this all works (life, that is), you'll automatically, "on the fly," begin seeing opportunities that will allow you to act just a little bit out of step with your old ways of thinking and/or in line with the new beliefs you wish to instill. Either way, it's worth attempting at least one such act of faith every day, because 99 percent of the time, acts of faith cost little or nothing to perform but their effect on your psyche is immeasurable.

Beliefs

With beliefs being at the core of how to create change in your life, let there be no end to the type of exercises you practice and invent that will help ensure yours are in alignment with the life of your dreams.

Inner Dialogues

First and foremost, your number one tool in uncovering limiting beliefs comes from developing an ongoing awareness, throughout all your days, of the things you think, say, and do. It's like having a sentry on guard or a watchdog who filters your every thought and looks for limitations, or perhaps it's like the antivirus software your computer uses that checks every program and attachment you open for infections.

Now, you might think this is just too easy for uncovering long-buried, deep-seated, limiting beliefs, or perhaps that it's ineffective since many of our beliefs are indeed invisible. But working with your beliefs isn't hard, tricky, or difficult unless you believe it to be so. It's easy, fun, and simple, right?

Make the commitment to yourself that you will always be on guard when it comes to observing the things you think, say, and do, and *you will* surprise yourself with what you find. It's a habit worth developing. And when you do catch yourself with some limited thinking or behavior, to expand upon what I shared earlier, don't just say to yourself, "Oh yeah, there I go again: I've got to stop thinking like that!" Realize that your thought or behavior was the result of a limiting belief, *and that belief is still there.* Once you catch yourself expressing limits, do something! Ferret out that belief, liqui-date it, bulldoze it, replace it—do something, because you are so close! This is the time to start writing down your list of beliefs if you are inclined to make lists. But whether you write or not, you should start thinking and asking yourself why you thought as you did. What was the trigger? What are the feelings? What lies beneath the limiting thoughts, what beliefs were adopted, and how else can you look at the situation?

For all the times you wonder whether or not you have limiting beliefs, and for the times you'd like to take a proactive approach, a little trick is to begin asking yourself some questions. Ask the exact same questions that you would ask a master—an awakened Christ or Buddha—about yourself, your life, and your challenges. Get as specific as you like. For instance, you could ask, what are the greatest lessons I might learn from this situation? Why did I choose this lifetime? How else can I approach finding creative, fulfilling work? Why am I feeling powerless, brokenhearted, or confused? What am I not seeing that I *could* be seeing concerning abundance, health, and my relationships?

Usually I pretend that I'm asking the question to my Greater Self, or higher self, but if you want, you could actually write the questions to the Universe, to God, or to any spiritual deity you honor. Then (you guessed it) answer those questions yourself. Just act as if you were answering the questions as the Universe, God, or your higher self. Or pretend that this question was posed to you by a dear friend and that she expects and needs you to answer it. If you're not sure how to answer it, then *pretend* you know the answer and give it. Make up and say whatever feels right. Just try it, because I know you'll be surprised with the results. Again, there are no rules here, but this is an exercise that works best for me when I record the questions and answers, either on paper or typed into my computer.

What also works best for me is following each question with an immediate answer, rather than first writing out a whole bunch of questions, because what often happens is that a dialogue actually develops. Initially, my answers will sometimes include questions back to myself in response, which forces me to reexamine my thoughts or perhaps the underlying presumptions or beliefs that prompted the first question. Sometimes this will go on for a while, but at some

them? If you're with me so far, then perhaps you can now see that *you* are eternal; that there will never be a "time" from this day forward that you do not exist in spirit. Hanging on? Good. So you can now take the leap and realize that if you will spiritually exist forevermore, into time's future, in part because time is simply an illusion, then mustn't you, similarly, have always existed in time's past? Hold on, this really is going somewhere. You weren't just born in 1935 or 1985 to live for eternity; you *came from* eternity. You existed before there were the illusions of time and space; you had to if you are their cocreator today. If this weren't true, your essence or spirit would be as artificial as the illusions that support you. If you did not transcend time and space, you would wither without them.

And now that you can "see" that you had to be "around" before you were born, don't you think you had something to do with the circumstances of your birth?

Nothing is ever left to chance—and *your* birth was no exception. *You* set the course, *you* chose your parents, and *you* chose when and where you'd be born. We all did.

You chose every wonderful (and not so wonderful) parameter of the life you're now living for the emotions, insights, and understanding you're now experiencing. You set the stage. It's not that tomorrow is set in stone, for *truly anything* could happen next based upon your own *evolving* thoughts, beliefs, and intents, mingled with those of the population.

The point of all this is that the people in your life, those you have relationships with—from your parents, siblings, and childhood sweethearts to your children, coworkers, and present-day love interests—are not there accidentally; they are and were your choice, directly or indirectly, *as a function of all your thoughts, beliefs, and desires*, and so too were you a part of all their choices. So when it comes to assessing and learning from the relationships of our lives, it's important to see them from the perspective that these people (*especially* these people) are in your life with your blessings and with something to teach you.

None of this means that birth relationships must be revered and held above all others. And it doesn't mean that you must indefinitely maintain these relationships, for it could well be that one of your challenges was to break some patterns that existed in past experiences. All relationships result from choices—birth relationships as well as relationships forged during the adventure of life—and you're free to change your choices from one day to the next based upon your own needs and desires.

If your childhood was filled with unhappy memories and you're asking yourself why—*why would I choose such unpleasantness*—the answer is simple: you wanted the challenge, knowing full well the rewards it promised—perspective, sympathy, compassion, appreciation, awareness, and understanding. I'm not suggesting here that one must endure hardship to grow and progress, but if that's what you've encountered, you will be rewarded. And very likely, by the time you've found this book, you *already have been rewarded* to some degree.

When you consider that a lifetime is, well, "just" a lifetime and that you live as many lifetimes as you like, perhaps you can understand why some people choose to immerse themselves in extreme circumstances—even in brutal and "wicked" hardships—because, after all is said and done, they will return (just as we all will), to the beauty and remembrance of their divinity. Add to that thought the idea that anyone choosing a lifetime with a rough start can follow it, if he so chooses, with a lifetime in the lap of luxury, and it then becomes even easier to understand.

To each his (or her) own; we all make these decisions for ourselves, and though we may live again and again in time and space, *each of our lives is precious and important, imparting treasures of knowingness that could not be obtained in any other life, by any other person, ever.*

I want to make it clear, however, that no one is at the mercy of past decisions, and just because a life may have been challenging so far doesn't mean there's some hidden agenda stating it must continue that way. In fact, every challenge and hardship is also an opportunity to overcome and to live in abundance, health, and harmony; we needn't learn to live with these challenges, prolong them, and drag them with us throughout our life. Every day is a new beginning, presenting new opportunities to rise up, and every day we make these kinds of decisions based on the beliefs we've adopted and the thoughts they inspire.

There is one last topic I'd like to go over before getting into how to maximize the joy in our relationships with others. It's a tricky one—one that we've all locked horns with at one time or another in our lives—because it deals with other people and their choices and how their choices may or may not mesh with our own.

Living in a World Full of Creators

Keep in mind that when it comes to deliberately carving out your niche in life and visualizing the life of your dreams, just as your life touches many others, so do your thoughts.

Generally, to be manifested, your thoughts must fall within the most *basic* parameters of the cultural and social beliefs of the times to avoid violating the experience of a fellow adventurer. For example, if you wanted to turn your cat into a dog, grow another pair of arms, or levitate yourself over New York City (assuming these occurrences would be witnessed and experienced by others), it couldn't happen until the mass beliefs held by the shared population permitted it. The good news is that global awareness is now shifting into higher and higher levels, and people are waking up to their spirituality and resonating with the truth of their power and magnificence. All kinds of new possibilities and potentials are coming into play that *will* allow for some new thinking and thus some stunning manifestation.

You see, any event that affects more than one person must be "approved" via the beliefs and expectations of all involved. For example, why didn't Jesus use His profound powers of healing to cure *all* lepers at once (banishing the disease entirely) instead of just those He came in contact with? The reason is that *He* didn't do the healing; He merely invoked the healing powers within those who came to Him with the desire to be healed and the belief that it was possible. He didn't heal the whole world overnight because he couldn't—the whole world wasn't ready to be healed. Their beliefs and expectations prevented it. The point here is that when operating in a shared reality, as we all are, our affect *on other people* is entirely determined by those other people, and when the masses are involved, any experiences must fall within the beliefs of the times.

None of this means you can't *shatter* world records, heal yourself from disease, accumulate vast fortunes, or begin doing things that have never been done before, because the global consciousness does indeed expect such accomplishments and even miracles. But when the manifestation of your thoughts would affect other lives, you're operating in a shared space that also contains their thoughts, beliefs, and expectations.

As I mentioned before, those in your life who may be affected by your thoughts already know what you're up to, just as you know, deep down, what their dreams are and the directions their lives *may* go. Your hopes and fears suit them; theirs suit yours as well. This is equally true of your place in the world's population. *All of us* have been drawn together by like thinking and complementary objectives, both in our closest circles of friends and in broad, global terms.

In a situation where you *would* like to affect the course that a specific person will take, your thoughts can influence them only if they grant you that power through their innermost beliefs and expectations about life. This is the privacy you would insist on, after all, if the roles were reversed and someone was trying to affect *your* life. Nevertheless, if you do wish to exert such influ-

point, answers start gushing forth and I am always more enlightened for my efforts, possessing a greater *understanding* of myself, my perspectives, and my beliefs than before the exercise began. For the elixir of understanding, the world quickly seems right again.

If you insist that these steps are hard or difficult or that your beliefs are invisible, then that is what you'll find. Instead, keep telling yourself that you're amazed with the results, that it's easy, that you have exposed limiting beliefs, and that you're making excellent progress.

Intellectualizing

This exercise works best when you're facing a particular dilemma. Perhaps you just can't seem to break through to a life of wealth and abundance, you're facing a particular fear, or you're facing a challenge, like losing weight. This is another exercise that might be better written down, but whatever works for you—like mulling over the issues each morning when you drive to work or at night as you go for a walk—is fine.

This exercise calls for you to enumerate all the reasons, physically and spiritually, that you "should" or can be experiencing the opposite of the challenge you're facing. For example, if abundance continues to elude you, engulf yourself with all the reasons why this should not be an issue in your life. List your traits and qualities that are of value to the world; if possible, recall experiences when it was not an issue; remind yourself of the absolute fact that wealth, like poverty, is exclusively the result of your life's focus; list evidence of how easy wealth has been for countless others to acquire; and so on.

Draw on other successes in your life where you clearly *did* bring about desired results in terms of health, friendships, or happiness, and realize that attracting dollar bills, sales, or contracts is no more challenging than attracting health, friendships, and happy times.

Ask yourself questions such as, "What has kept me, *so far*, from relating to and approving of my creativity? My intelligence?

My_____?" Then whenever you bump into a limiting belief, latch on to it and don't let go until you clear all its failed logic from your system!

This kind of intellectualizing of your beliefs can be useful since it's more in line with the ordinary workings and leanings of your rational thinking process. It's a practical exercise that can sometimes reveal the absurdity of the thoughts and beliefs that may have held you back so far.

Be creative and let loose, knowing all the while that your thoughts of today are what paint the pictures of your tomorrow. *It's the law.*

Make Believe

Here's a technique you can try that's fun and easy, though it requires at least two people (preferably people you're close to who won't think you've lost your marbles). I used to do it with my mother and brother when we worked together. We'd meet every week for breakfast to get focused and psyched up about the company and our dreams, and toward the end of our breakfast meeting, I'd usually launch into the fantastic things I'd been up to, like meeting with distributors in Japan, Switzerland, or South America. I'd go into details about the exciting deals we were working on and the large contracts, and I'd talk about the trips I'd made in my private jet. I'd suggest that, for our next couple of family business meetings, we should meet over tea at the Ritz in London, since we all had projects going on in the United Kingdom, and on and on. Of course, none of this had happened yet; it was all a fantasy, but I talked *as if it were all real* and they listened attentively as if it were all real. They'd ask serious questions, as any business partner would, and I'd have answers. Then I'd turn the tables on them and ask my mother what was new in Hollywood, where she had countless offers to turn some of her books into movies, and she'd launch into meetings she'd had with Steven Spielberg over rewrites, gala events she'd attended, and more.

Andy would also get involved. He'd complain that my private jet was too small for his entourage and brag that he was getting a larger jet, which he'd let me borrow as needed. We'd plan more rendezvous around the globe: "When I get done in Thailand ...," I'd say, and "Andy, when you wrap up your deal in Paris ...," and "Mom, when you're done with the shoot, let's meet up in Hong Kong for some fun." Now, I know you're probably thinking I'm even crazier than you'd first imagined, but we really had *fun* at those meetings, combining our fantasies with readings from books that inspired us and sharing new insights or breakthroughs we'd actually had that week. By the time the meetings were over, we'd each be walking from our table with our heads in the clouds.

Similarly, I remember a time when my brother was exhibiting our T-shirt line at the MAGIC apparel tradeshow in Las Vegas, and to help get him psyched up thinking the good thoughts, I sent him a fax through the hotel front desk he was staying at (this was before email existed) that read in huge handwritten letters, "Urgent!! Andy—Must borrow Learjet! How do I reach your pilot? Mike."

Although none of us have yet been inside a private jet, all of us have trotted the globe on company business, and right at this very moment my mother has two Hollywood producers interested in turning her book *Grown Men* into a movie. Again, you can see that working with your thoughts and coming up with ways to think thoughts that will serve you can be both fun and easy. Be creative and let loose, knowing all the while that your thoughts of today are what paint the pictures of your tomorrow. *It's the law.*

Tuning In

This technique is totally different—one I use to help me with decisions as well as to exercise my inner senses. Whenever I'm faced with a choice (any kind of choice), I try to frame it into a yes or no question; then I'll clearly ask that question, close my eyes, take a few deep breaths, and visualize the word "yes" and then the word "no." I'll play with those visuals in my mind, bouncing them around to see them as clearly as I can, and whichever of the two words seems bigger, more dominant, or closer to me is the answer I believe that the Universe, or my Greater Self, is showing me. I've heard of other people doing variations of this, some suggesting that when you breathe out you exhale the question, and when you breathe in you'll get either a yes or no. You really should at least try this, and in whatever variation you like the most, because I have to tell you, I've been really shocked by how accurate and helpful the answers are. In fact, I can think of a time or two when I didn't follow the advice of the answer I received and how I sorely regretted it later!

I use this technique often, sometimes several times a day, even for little things, such as choosing brands when shopping or whether or not to make certain phone calls. The more you do it the easier it gets, and the great thing about doing it with little decisions is that you can begin trusting your answers and honing the use of your inner senses for when you have some bigger decisions to make. Where do the answers come from? Here's the important thing to realize: they come from within, *from you*. This is not an exercise that forces you to give up any of your power or authority but one that increases each.

Our inner senses are like our physical senses in that if they're not used, you start tuning them out and ignoring them. Maybe it would be better to compare them to our muscles: if not used they atrophy, and we become dependent on only those muscles that we do use. By beginning to use this yes or no technique, you begin flexing an inner muscle that may have never been used before, and with practice you'll get to a point where you'll become accustomed to referring to your *feelings* whenever you have a decision to make—*without even having to orchestrate this test*. You'll instinctively and automatically begin feeling out your options in the same manner that you automatically *think* them now, when you intellectually face decisions.

Goal for the Day

Here's another exercise for building some inner muscles, and this one works on the muscle of faith. Pick a goal for the day—something extremely attainable that you unquestionably believe could happen that day, though something that could just as easily not happen. You might choose to finish a particular task or maybe you wish to start a new one. You might choose to hear a particular compliment, like on your hair, or to find something, like a dollar. Anything!

For instance, even as I was creating the audio program that preceded this book, I was actively selling it as a subscription, with one recording (chapter) being mailed out to each subscriber each month throughout the year. Often, virtually every day, I'd pick a number of online orders I'd like to receive, and I was astounded at how often it worked, to the exact number.

Here's what I did: I'd get really centered in a quiet place each morning, and I'd have a personal conversation with the Universe, or God (really, it was like a prayer). I'd tell the Universe the quantity I'd like to sell, *usually stated as a minimum*; talk about why I wanted it; give my personal reasons—what it would mean to me—and even review how reasonable a request it was. What differentiates this exercise from simply praying or thinking is the intensity and clarity of my focus. I *really* talked directly to the Universe and understood clearly that it heard every word. Then I'd mentally see, vividly, a picture of myself filling the orders, and as an act of faith, I'd get the exact number of programs I wanted to sell, wrapped up and ready to go.

One of the reasons this exercise can be so powerful is that by making this a reasonable request (as *I* define reasonable) and a believable request (according to *my* beliefs), I'm even more convinced that it could happen, which ramps up my beliefs about my inevitable success. With the proper beliefs, the definition of what's reasonable can accommodate any request, and with practice and confidence, your requests (and mine) can increase without limit to include anything we like.

There are some important points to be mindful of with this exercise: You must give yourself credit when you get exactly what you want. You must do this because it means you understand your role in shaping the events of your life, and conversely, you must take responsibility when things don't pan out. Now, this does not mean getting mad at yourself or throwing your hands in the air, saying, "Well, I just don't know what I did wrong!" It means you try again tomorrow, with an *even clearer* focus, a *more precise* request, *better* visualizations, and perhaps a new act of faith.

If you have to make your requests more reasonable or more believable, then fine; do whatever it takes. The only thing here is that even after lowering your expectations, you must still give yourself credit for instigating the magic of the Universe. This might be harder if your request seemed very easy to fill, because you could rationalize it away and say, "Oh, that would have happened anyway." The best safeguard against rationalizing away this magic is to stick with this kind of exercise every day—to do it often—and you will see patterns or nuances that emerge with your successes, and you'll build this muscle of faith, a faith that you can ask and then receive the ultimate accomplishment.

Meditation

If you're like I used to be, the sound of this word immediately brings some guilt, because you feel like it's something you should already be doing but aren't. Well, to help you feel better about that, let me remind you first that there are no "shoulds" when it comes to living in time and space or acquiring enlightenment. Secondly, to one degree or another, you already do meditate in a variety of ways, although you may not sit cross-legged while *ohhhhmmmm*-ing.

There's a misconception, I believe, that meditating is something one must do to advance and grow, but to repeat myself, there is *nothing* one must do to advance and grow; there are *no* rules. And meditation has so many mysterious connotations to it that it can almost seem like it's something beyond the normal person. In reality, there are as many different types of meditation as there are moods.

Actually, *life* is one big meditation. It's *all thought*, focused one way or another. "It's all good," and whether you meditate the way yogis do or not has little to do with your spiritual evolution and the enlightened insights you can possess.

Listening to music, reading, jogging, walking, daydreaming, going to the movies, absorbing ourselves in a fantastic meal, spending time in nature, maybe even calmly smoking a cigar to get the day started are all forms of meditation. All these things calm and ease the mind, and they allow for different kinds of focuses that cannot necessarily be experienced otherwise. I think what's important is not how people spend time in thought, even if that means stilling their thoughts, but *that* they do, as often or as infrequently as they find beneficial.

Do I spend some time every day clearing my mind of all thoughts? No. Would this form of meditation be beneficial? Sure, but so is eating carrots, and I hardly ever do that, which doesn't mean I don't otherwise eat well! One day I may just commit to such an exercise on a regular basis (clearing my mind, *not* eating carrots!). Until then, the point I'm making is that I am no less spiritual or any less determined to understand myself than those who *ohhhhmmmm*, and I've learned to appreciate that I have my own ways, as unorthodox as they may be.

Getting Out of the Gates

I'd like to offer some techniques (or just some thoughts, really) for dealing with what would usually be considered the more "ordinary" challenges we face on a daily basis.

Overcoming Resistance

Nothing can kill a great idea faster than just sitting on it! It's true for most of us that when starting a new project, whether it's small or career changing, we often feel our own resistance. For the most part, that resistance is fueled by doubts or fears that create hesitancy. After all, no one wants to waste time on one pursuit only to change his or her mind days, weeks, or months later; lots of energy can be wasted. Still, even at times when we know what path we want to take, we may hesitate and in the hesitation lose our focus, ultimately risking the manifestation of a dream.

Just Start It!

The advice I have here is to just *start* whatever it is you wish to start. You don't have to think in terms of finishing yet, and one of the best ways I've gotten myself to just start something without getting too overwhelmed is to kid myself into it. I blatantly lie! I tell myself that all I have to do is break the ice and no more; I just have to exert a teeny, tiny bit of effort, and once done, I can back off until the next day. Then invariably, once I've started, I actually want to push a little further, then a little further, and the next thing I know, the project is well under way. What gets me here is that I know I'm lying to myself when I coax myself into "just starting," but it works anyway!

The first time I ever did this was when I was training for a marathon. My alarm clock would go off at 3:30 AM so that I could run before work, but honestly, at 3:30 AM. my only thought was to smash that clock and go back to sleep, rationalizing that I could run after work instead. But that wouldn't have worked and I knew it, so at 3:30 AM I would tell myself that I didn't have to run if I didn't want to but that I must at least get up to use the bathroom. Somehow it's infinitely easier to get out of bed to use the bathroom at that hour than it is to get out of bed to run twelve miles, but once I was out of bed, it was relatively easy to throw on my shorts and shoes and take off in the dark to run. It worked every time, even with the same dumb lie.

Of course, I tell myself all kinds of lies when it comes to starting projects ... or perhaps a better way of looking at this is that I change my focus and perspective, which is not really lying at all. I take my eyes off what seems like an overwhelming task, choosing instead to simply focus on the next step, and this can work on every imaginable project before you. When it comes to getting started, just focus on what's immediately at hand, not what you're going to have to do tomorrow or next month. One day at a time, one hour at a time, or *one minute at a time* is all that's necessary to begin the longest of journeys.

Seeing with New Eyes

Another technique for overcoming resistance is seeing the task at hand with a new pair of eyes. I had an experience when I was about twelve years old that I remember to this day.

Bicycles were always in my life as a kid; I was adventurous and I practically lived on mine, riding far and wide until I got a flat tire. I was clumsy with repairs to the point that my repairs usually needed repairs. It was an overwhelming task to me, and one I'd put off indefinitely. To me a flat tire automatically meant "no bike" for *months*, until a tough young neighbor—a kid a year younger than I was—showed me another perspective.

His name was Billy, and he had some really cool dirt bike wheels that I wanted to buy for my bike for a couple of dollars each. At first he wanted too much money for them, but then one day he lowered the price. The only problem was that the tire on one of the wheels was now flat. "Aha!" I thought. "No wonder he wants to sell them; they're junk!" I knew that if I bought them, they'd sit flat in my garage forever, so I said, "No way. This one's flat! Are you crazy?!" Billy was confused. He looked at me and said, "So what?! Fix it! Takes five minutes!" No way. I was *not* going to be tricked! "It's easy," he said. And then, frustrated with me, he added, "Watch!" Then and there, in about five minutes, Billy stripped the tire, removed the tube, inflated it, stuck it in a bucket, found the hole, deflated the tube, and applied the patch. "Let the glue dry, and you can ride on it tomorrow," he said, not knowing how he'd impacted my life.

I went home with my new wheels and tires, feeling really foolish. "Why had I always made such a big deal about fixing a tire?" I wondered. I thought of all the months I'd ever gone without a bike because of the false perception I'd created. Similarly, we can spend so much time justifying why something is hard or how it can't be done when we really could have done the entire job in the time we wasted defending our feeble positions.

One day at a time, one hour at a time,
or *one minute at a time* is all that's necessary
to begin the longest of journeys.

Now ask yourself, what in life do you think is hard? Is it parenting, enjoying your job, a task at work, understanding your spouse, losing weight, getting out of bed in the morning, quitting smoking, or making a million dollars? It's time to see it all with a new set of eyes, because like flying, landing on the moon, or cloning sheep, nothing is hard or even impossible, nor can anything become easy or within reach, until we say so.

Make a Commitment

A third technique for overcoming resistance is to make a commitment to yourself. Don't give yourself a way out; burn your bridges, as they say. The creation of the audio program that preceded this book was an example of how I burned my bridges. One December I suggested to my email subscribers that I would create a twelve-hour audio program entitled *Infinite Possibilities: The Art of Living Your Dreams*, with one recording to be released each month in the coming year.

Immediately, in one day, I sold almost $5,000 worth of subscriptions to people who had paid online and in advance before I even knew exactly what would be included in the first recording, which at that point was due in two weeks! I couldn't back out without contacting everyone and issuing refunds, which I had no intention of doing. So I started and continued, releasing one recording at a time, and again, I often kidded myself into the next month's script. Come on, Mike, I'd think, just write a few paragraphs, that's all; just start it. And invariably, by physically taking just the first step, momentum was created, resources were summoned, and the second step was a cinch.

Inspire Yourself

Numerous books have been written about getting inspired, so I won't try to compete with them here. I have just two simple suggestions to add.

First, don't ever lose sight of the rewards you're after. Understand that everything you're doing today—*everything*—is preparing you for the treasures that lie just up ahead. Whether it's apparent or not, *everything* you do is preparing you for the life of your dreams, and all that you've been through and are now going through, even the painful or frivolous stuff, is exactly what you need to prepare you for what's coming next. Had you manifested your dreams too quickly, for instance, they might have all slipped through your fingers just as fast. But now you're being readied and the groundwork is being laid. This is how to view the path you've walked so far and the steps you take today—as training and preparation for the "best of your life."

It's like this: If you were climbing a ladder and you forgot where it was leading, you'd be far less inspired to go any farther than if you remembered that every rung on that ladder would bring you closer to the realization of your goal, just as every day does, no matter how challenging it may be or how off course you may seem. Constantly remind yourself of why you're now doing what you're doing, imaging the anticipated glory, sense of accomplishment, and the wonderful byproducts it will draw into your life.

Secondly, don't lose sight of the bigger picture—that life, the journey, is the greatest adventure. Now, I don't want this next comment to startle you or sound morbid, but you're—we're—all going to die anyway, right? So get going! Make haste! The sun's now shining and it's your turn on stage, though it *won't* always be. If you see this line of thinking as I do, hopefully you'll be inspired, because what it really means is that you've got nothing to worry about; nothing to lose by reaching, stretching, and trying whatever it is you want to try. It's true that you're eternal, and there will be other chances, other lifetimes, but *none* will be quite the same as this one, nor offer the same rewards. Plus, the unimaginable glory that awaits you at the end of this life will be magnified by your every effort *today*. Life rewards effort exponentially, so the less time you spend idling your motor, the greater the rewards will be.

Stop Stressin'

These days, the topic of stress also warrants a book in itself, so I'll just offer a few thoughts. To me, stress is primarily the product of our *believing* that we, the physical aspects of ourselves, must *physically* surmount every obstacle in our path, rather than recognizing that the real work of our lives is done at spiritual levels. Stress results from our obsessive desire to *physically manipulate* our time, our space, and our lives. Instead, understand that you have only to *direct* your life and your manifestations. How else could you ever begin living the life of your dreams without such an ability and power?

We just get off base and forget that directing the courses of our lives cannot be done physically; it's sparked from within. We may also remember that we should not attempt to control specific people, places, and things but instead focus on the broader aspects of what we want in terms of abundance, health, and harmony, letting the Universe manage the details. It's these details that stress us, but they're the domain of the Universe, not our physical selves.

Life is a spiritual game, and it must be played spiritually in order to win; the key is recognizing this, even though our lives are expressed physically. As you now read these pages, you're physically oriented in a physical world, and so you would logically compare wherever you now are to wherever you'd like to go, which you also see as a physical destination. You deduce, then, that in order to get from physical point A to physical point B, you had better start manipulating all things physical to make the journey. But this is where our illusions trick us: A and B are just reflections of an inner spiritual world (like mirages), and so it's the inner spiritual landscape that must be manipulated to get from mirage A to B.

**It's astounding how well things work
when you stop resisting or insisting.**

When Life "Isn't" Working

What do you do when you seem to be making no headway in your life—when it seems that every door you open slams shut? The best example I've had of this was back in our retail t-shirt selling days, when the industry began changing and nothing we did could stem the tide or give us an edge. I won't go into all the different crazy angles I tried, but they included direct selling, sales promotions, new locations, and innovative selling arrangements with some of our wholesale customers. Many of these efforts required almost a year to implement and test before we realized that they just weren't going to work.

In the end, the solution we chose was to finally and drastically change course—to close the stores and get out of the business altogether. Of course, there were still other alternatives, but this was what we chose for a variety of reasons, including the fact that we could financially afford to without any unpleasant repercussions. With hindsight, we now see that closing down the operation was long overdue. At the time, however, it was torturous. It was like something had died, or worse, that we were euthanizing a dream. It felt like quitting, and in a sense we did quit.

But sometimes when life doesn't seem to be working, it's because you've gotten so swept up in *how* you want things to go physically that you end up losing sight of what you're really after spiritually. You begin refusing to allow the Universe, your dreams and thoughts, to figure out the *hows*, preventing it from showing you every possible alternative, including the ones that question or even threaten the very path you're on. You begin demanding that things, physical things, go a certain way, and to make matters worse, you keep reminding yourself that all things are possible, *thoughts become things*, and that dreams are meant to come true, perhaps rationalizing that the challenges and difficulties you're experiencing are just par for the course. But for us (and I think this is often easy to see in the lives of friends and contemporaries), we ended up becoming more and more narrow-minded about how we wanted things to unfold, and the things we were insisting on materially weren't manifesting for a variety of deeper reasons that we couldn't see at the time.

Life is a spiritual game, and it must be played spiritually in order to win; the key is recognizing this, even though our lives are expressed physically.

Looking back at how well the transition has gone for each of us, we've realized that had we put off the decision any longer, we would have only put off the exciting paths we're now individually on. The fun had left us long before we closed our shops; each of us had moved on in our dreams to other ideas of how we'd like to live our lives, yet we wouldn't let go of the very business that was keeping us from moving forward, rationalizing that if we could pump up the profits all would be well and kidding ourselves into thinking that that was necessary in order to pursue our other dreams.

It's astounding how well things work when you stop resisting or insisting. If you're *not* honest with yourself, you're going to manifest warning signals everywhere, and the very sands beneath your feet will begin shifting.

Now, this is a tricky subject, because there could be any number of reasons that could seemingly prevent life from working for you, but I think they'd all fall into two categories: either you are on the right path but your beliefs are in conflict or you haven't listened to your heart—your deepest burning desires—and the path you're on needs a new direction. Either way, honesty and self-exploration will help you find your way.

These are my tools and techniques. They're simple, for sure. But if you believe they're too simple or not challenging enough, then let me suggest that you might be thinking that enlightenment and spiritual awakening should be a hard and arduous undertaking. And if that's what you're thinking, then please think again. Both enlightenment and waking from our spiritual slumber should come naturally and easily; you don't have to hide yourself in seclusion to spark new thinking. You just need some new thinking!

There's really only one way to grow spiritually, and that's through thought. And there's really only one way to manifest the life of your dreams, and that's also through thought. Any exercise that can positively affect your thoughts—by enhancing your dreams or expanding your awareness—is gold. Whether through structured routines or over a morning's cup of coffee, taking some time to stretch your philosophical muscles will inevitably hasten the day when your dreams come to pass.

11

Questions and Answers

*T*his chapter gives me a chance to share with you some of my correspondances with people who've had questions about the kind of material I've shared so far. The people who asked these questions, perhaps for the first time in their lives, have become aware of their awesome power and responsibilities. I often get many of the same questions again and again, so I'm sure that at least some of these might be similar to questions you may still have.

Is setting deadlines for the Universe okay? For example, can I not only ask the Universe to make me a millionaire but also to be one by the end of this year?

Yes and no. It's okay to ask, but I think more damage than help can be done with time frames. When you start dealing with time frames, you start meddling with the physical side of things, which is the domain of the Universe. You run the risk of tying its hands from finding the best possible route between you and whatever you're asking for. If, when you're visualizing, you see your dream *already* manifested, you've already told the Universe that you're ready for it *now*! But if you come up with a date, what if the Universe could handily beat it? Or what if the manifestation of your dream is all but inevitable, but because you've given it a time frame that clashes with some of your other desires and beliefs, you miss the deadline?

Then you're not only risking the crushing disappointment of the missed deadline, but because you aren't aware of your pending success, you may also begin doubting whether or not you'll ever get what would have otherwise been a certainty. When setting deadlines, you risk damaging your confidence in the Universe and perhaps your belief in the overall achievability of whatever it is you wanted, derailing what would have been an effortless manifestation!

Of course, there are instances when picking dates may seem unavoidable. The first is when you're given a physical deadline, such as having to pay your rent by a certain date. In this situation, I'd still suggest taking your eye off the date and instead focusing on your desired end result: having a wonderful roof over your head where your financial obligations are being met in a harmonious way (rather than insisting that it be a particular roof and that a particular landlord receives an exact sum of money by an exact time). Get away from the details of how and when; those are for the Universe.

The second situation where you might use dates is perhaps when setting goals. For instance, what do you hope to achieve over three years, five years, or ten? But these kinds of goals, by their nature, are structured with much looser time frames, and you already know when you're setting them that they'll likely be adjusted as your priorities change. In this case, dates are more like guidelines than deadlines, which is good.

Having just said all that, I do believe that a truly enlightened person would have no problem manifesting just about anything within a time frame, but until you're walking on water, there's just no need to go there because it creates all kinds of stress and anxiety. Picking dates is almost as bad as dealing with the "cursed hows." It's risky business, and you would do well to avoid doing it whenever you can.

Another question I receive a lot of is from people who feel that at some point in their life they were much more advanced—more naturally tuned into the magic of life—than they are now. They feel they've lost something and they want it back, and my reply is always the same:

You still have it. Often it's our advancing maturity or spiritual development that sends us on a journey into new territory, which can sometimes be scary. But the fears that develop later in life aren't there because we've lost something; they just begin appearing as our awareness expands. You unquestionably have the same penetrating insights today that you've always had; these can't be lost. It's just that now your insights have to contend with a wider grasp on reality—on your true nature and responsibilities, moving from theory to application—and this is just the natural evolution that every soul must make on its way to a mastery over all illusions.

To help you see this, you wouldn't want, I hope, to now have a lesser awareness, would you? I mean, anyone can be dumb, brave, and determined. You've passed that stage; you've graduated. Now it's time to be wise, brave, and determined!

> **Opportunity does not knock only once;**
> **it knocks every single moment of every single day**
> **for every single one of us.**

I also get a variety of questions that contain doubt and regrets about past decisions. And my advice is usually this:

Don't look back. No matter what decisions you've made, the Universe, your thoughts, are now dealing with them on your behalf. It's conspiring and handling all the details at full throttle to make all your dreams come true, right from where you are today. It is supremely capable of dealing with whatever decisions you've made, and it doesn't slap its forehead with exasperation and say, "Now look at what you've done! You've made my job a nightmare!" No, to the Universe, *all* jobs are easy; magic is its forte! It hasn't given up and neither should you; it hasn't judged you and neither should you; it doesn't look back and neither should you. Help it out, free it up, be happy, and look forward. It's still aiming for all the infinite joys that lie ahead because it knows that all things remain forever possible. It's never too late for anything. Opportunity does not knock only once; it knocks every single moment of every single day for every single one of us, and what a lot of damage has been done by thinking otherwise!

Simply learn from the past and see whatever happened as if it were part of a calculated training program designed to enlighten you with new perspectives and prepare you for even greater opportunities that imminently lie ahead.

How do I deal with all the uncertainties in my life?

By trusting the "unknown." After all, it's the wellspring of all things, including every wonderful thing that's ever happened or that will ever happen to you. The unknown is your friend, made of divine intelligence, home of infinite possibilities.

Whenever you don't know what lies around the corner, you can choose to be frightened or happy about it, and whichever you choose will affect, influence, and even decide those mysterious moments to come. Also remember that just because you can't see something wonderful with your eyes or detect it with your physical senses doesn't mean it's not there. Always, just beyond our physical senses, the Universe churns with all its magic and miracles. It's not just sitting there on idle; it's in the middle of orchestrating your life. Right now, because of your natural-born inclination to thrive, things are happening invisibly—things you can be happily looking forward to—so start looking. Every wonderful thought that you've ever thought is now busy at work, looking to fit itself into your life.

To judge the progress of our lives strictly by using our physical senses means we're not looking within to define who we are and where we're going. It means, instead, that we're looking at mirages for meaning. This is life's ultimate test—to see without looking, to hear without listening, to know without going, and to be without becoming. How? By confidently unleashing the power of your imagination into the unknown, into the cast net of invisible principles, and *understanding* that wonderful results are inevitable.

Always, just beyond our physical senses, the Universe churns with all its magic and miracles. It's not just sitting there on idle; it's in the middle of orchestrating your life.

I need some help. Just how do I contact the Universe?

It starts with just being quiet and following your feelings. Really, it's about getting in touch with yourself, because you are your own point of contact with the Universe. Spend some time totally relaxing every day, breathing deeply, and letting your mind wander anywhere it likes without rules. Give some exclusive time to yourself, just feeling and thinking whatever you like, *and forget trying to be spiritual*. Just be yourself.

I'm really at the end of my rope. My life is great, yet I am constantly fatigued and unhappy. I feel like I'm losing my optimism and desire to have change. I can't seem to shift.

Do something—*anything*. Take action. Be the shift. *Stop waiting for it*. It's not enough to claim that life is wonderful, to see its beauty, and to spin dreams that may one day come true all by themselves. They won't. Join a club, take a class, ask for a promotion, move across town, adopt a pet, volunteer, mingle, network. Dare yourself, challenge yourself, *engage the magic of life*.

How does the dreamer awaken from the dream?

Of course, the questioner is asking about the dream of life, but to answer this, let me first share a recurring nighttime dream I've had.

In this dream, I suddenly become aware that I might be dreaming. And with this realization, I begin looking around at the sights and the colors; I notice what's near and what's far, and I listen to the sounds; maybe a bird will fly by or a breeze might blow the limbs of a nearby tree, and so I rationally think to myself, "No, I can't be dreaming. This is all way too real; there's too much detail; my surroundings all look exactly like they do when I'm awake." The next thing I know I lose my focus as well as the suspicion that it's a dream, and I'm waking up minutes or hours later. So was it a dream? Yes. Did it differ from real life? No! And this provided me with two new concepts. First, dreams are real—every bit as real as the life you and I lead; and second, *life is a dream* that's every bit as illusory as the dreams we dream at night.

**This is life's ultimate test—to see without looking,
to hear without listening, to know without going,
and to be without becoming.**

To answer the question about how to wake up from the dream of life, I asked, "Is a dream less real than so-called reality? What differentiates the two?" Waking up *within* a nighttime dream is more a matter of realizing that you are dreaming than snapping out of it into waking reality, and it's the same in life. We chose *to be here*; to have a time and space focus. We aren't here to snap out of it, but rather to wake up *within* the dream—*to realize we are indeed dreaming* and that we are our own dream weavers, thereby accelerating our manifestations and lessons and having the most fun possible.

This, you could say, is the heart of living the life of your dreams: realizing that we are our own dream weavers and living accordingly by watching and becoming aware of our every thought, word, and deed because these all dictate how the dream will unfold. And for the hardcore enthusiast, consciously attaining this level of awareness will come as all experiences come—first by imagining it; then by claiming it; and ultimately by acting it, demonstrating it, and living it.

Be the shift. *Stop waiting for it.*

How can I better cope with the pain of disappointment?

Sometimes it's hard to convince yourself that disappointments are "natural" and actually helpful in the long run. But by *understanding* the situation and seeing things "rightly," the pain will vanish. When you understand the pain, it means you *understand* how you've incorrectly interpreted a situation. And with true understanding, you realize that you are no less than you were before the incident occurred—you still have the same freedom to create your own happiness and the pain you felt was a lesson to teach you just that.

It may not seem easy, but you can do this. Push yourself. Do what it takes. Dwell on the questions raised by your disappointments and insist upon their answers.

Nothing seems to be working, so I've been wondering, Can we change our minds about what we wish for, or is this giving up?

There's nothing wrong with changing our minds, it's one of our greatest freedoms, and sometimes exercising it can propel us faster into new and exciting territory.

Whenever you're feeling really confused about what you want, the first step is to be really honest with yourself and to start listening to the voice within. It's very tempting to blindly pursue a dream with your heart and to shut out all common sense or intellect. But when this approach leaves you spinning your wheels or bouncing off obstacles, it could be that your intellect can help you adjust your life rudder. At a minimum, the intellect can help you to chart a path of least resistance between otherwise invisible limiting beliefs. If you feel awkward or uncertain about a direction you're going in, it would never be because the direction is unachievable; *all things* are indeed achievable. But it could be because you have opposing beliefs in that direction or instincts trying to alert you to hazards ahead, and if you ignore these signals in the name of the *thoughts become things* principle, you could be cruising for a bruising.

**When you love the path,
your dreamed-of destination becomes
almost incidental, and happiness
becomes a daily affair.**

When people who have achieved great success in any field are asked what it was like in the beginning, having risked it all, they often reply that they were completely unaware of the risks because they were so focused on what they wanted *and so totally in love with its pursuit*. The lesson here is not only to fall in love with your dreams (this should be a given) but to also find a path you love, which can hardly be done if you are feeling intellectual resistance. When you love the path, your dreamed-of destination becomes almost incidental, and happiness becomes a daily affair.

Knock on every door and turn over every stone when choosing a direction that intellectually fits you as well as your dream does. These achievers have done exactly that, and therefore probably felt little to no inner resistance in following their bliss. It was a relatively risk-free pursuit. Don't blindly walk the plank of your hopes and dreams. When you feel internal resistance, don't ignore it in the name of faith or shout over it, claiming your divinity. Hear it out. Then, with honesty, you can dispel it with certainty or adjust your headings.

How can you say that life is fair?

Life is what we think it is. And with a little thought it's not too hard to grasp that, spiritually speaking, it's impossible to fail; everything works out in our favor; the elements conspire on our behalf; there are always reasons to be happy; millions of lives are touched by ours; we can have anything we dream of; things just keep getting better; and we live for ever.

Yeah. I think "fair" works.

Actually, while I've said a number of times that life is fair, I think I misspoke in each instance. Fair presumes a 50/50 chance of *survival*. Actually, life really *isn't* "fair" when you consider that we are each inherently born to thrive and that ultimate failure is impossible. Truly, the cards are stacked in our favor!

I don't know what I should be doing with my life!

I have a two-part answer for this one.

Part I: Whatever it is you're now doing with your life is what you "should be" doing, *including asking the question you're now asking*! If you weren't where you now are, you wouldn't be seeking the answers you most need, gaining the wisdom that perhaps, in part, you've chosen this lifetime to attain.

Part II: Asking that question likely means you'd like to be doing "more" with your life, in which case, simply begin by doing more. "Like what?" you ask. Start with little things, which all on their own will grow into bigger things. Every journey begins with a first step, which is the hardest step because it seems so incredibly futile compared to where you see yourself going. But once you take it, it's easier to take the second step and then easier to take the third. Take many little steps down every remotely interesting corridor that reveals itself to you. Go ahead and spread yourself too thin—what have you got to lose? Before long, you'll know exactly what it is you should be doing with your life, and very likely you'll find you're already in the middle of doing it.

**We *are* perfect, not because we've reached a point
but because we're reaching.**

I feel troubled by the idea that we never reach perfection—that perfection is the unattainable. What am I missing?

If you define "perfect" as a destination, then I agree: no one will ever get "there." However, if you define it as a process, then I'd have to say we've all "arrived" and things will never, ever get any better than this.

You and I are adventurers on a journey through revelations, bliss, and eternity. Our own definition of exactly what we are, who we are, why we are, and where we are changes in every moment, yet we are always, and only, the perfect reflection of what we think we are. Effortlessly and automatically, we unfailingly make our own reality by the thoughts we think, whether we realize it or not. The plan that put us here is now in full effect, and *it is a perfect plan*. And the agreement we abide by is *a perfect agreement*. And as to our own awareness and evolution, they too are fluid, *progressing perfectly*.

We *are* perfect, not because we've reached a point but because we're reaching.

I don't get it. You're saying I choose to be "tormented"? Does anyone choose this? If someone is upsetting me, it's my "will"?

I get this kind of question a lot—people not understanding how or why they'd ever create hardships or horror stories within their lives. Generally, no one sets out to create horror stories before their life begins, but many of us do choose challenging circumstances, along with leanings and inclinations that may lead us into some "hot water" when combined with all the other choices we make. So while no one would choose to marry an axe murderer, they could choose to marry a deeply disturbed person, knowing what some of the consequences might be. And why would anyone want to find and fall in love with a deeply disturbed person? There'd be count-less reasons, and first among them would be a recognition of the divinity within this person and a desire to be part of his or her healing. But these decisions aren't just made before a life begins. Our so-called spiritual contracts are all remade in every moment of every life so that nothing is predestined and no one's happiness is at the mercy of their past choices.

If you look at any incident in your life as an isolated incident, you're taking it out of context.

To give you another example, I've been in several relationships that ended very painfully, at least for me. But today, with hindsight, I can see those experiences a lot more clearly, and have taken from them two great lessons. First, I've learned to be honest with myself. In each case I was well aware of the *potential* for the kind of problems that could arise long before they actually arose, yet I still stayed in the relationships and even allowed myself (pretended!) to be totally shocked and dismayed by the shenanigans that led to their unhappy endings. But here the old adage applies: if you play with fire, you're going to get burned, and it does no good, once you do get burned, to cry out your innocence.

The other realization I've had looking back is that I did indeed choose to play with fire for some really excellent reasons—reasons so compelling that even having been burned, those relationships were well worth it. What happened in the end was a small price to pay for all the good and fun that came from them, including some of the "higher" points in my life so far. All in all, I chose not just the ending of the relationship but the entire package, and as a package deal, they were well worth the ride.

If you look at any incident in your life as an isolated incident, you're taking it out of context. By looking at the bigger picture and at the events preceding and succeeding the incident, at some point you'll always be able to find its value and therefore realize that it resulted from your desire to learn and grow, to be wiser and more compassionate.

What's the catch? Why does it seem so hard? What's the magic step to making the good thoughts become things? Is it only our self-harming, limiting, self-doubting thoughts that so easily become things, even without any effort?

I think that like most seekers, you're thinking that the answers are complex, mysterious, and hard to find and apply. But that kind of thinking only perpetuates your search for answers and adds to the difficulty in finding them. So to get back to basics, the truth is that *thoughts become things*, period. There are no mitigating factors, no other laws that trump this principle. Those three words say it all; it couldn't be simpler. Now, as I said in chapter 2, "Beliefs," it's our beliefs that make us think as we do. So if you're finding that it seems your experiences are more unsatisfactory than satisfactory, it's simply because, realize it or not, that's the nature of your prevailing beliefs.

Once you start becoming aware of your limiting beliefs, the key is to begin changing them, and to do this you might begin by affirming, "It's easy, it's fun, and I know how life works," and stop saying, "It's hard, I don't know, and I'm lost." Next, start acting like life is easy, fun, and knowable.

Many people say, "Yes, I understand that my *thoughts become things*," yet they spend no time visualizing each day. Many even continue to mull over unhappy memories of their past, just projecting more of the same into the future. How many have clearly defined the life of their dreams? If you truly believed that *thoughts become things*, you'd be visualizing, focusing on the good, and defining what you want. And if you're not yet there, then really, you're still of the persuasion that life is something that happens to you, rather than fully grasping that you are its conductor.

Your challenge, just like mine, is to start living these answers; knowing about them isn't enough. Living them in the presence of our old manifestations is what's required, and it is "harder" at first, but as your life begins changing and momentum starts building, it gets easier and easier.

To me, your writings and those of others in this genre seem to contain a "blame the victim" mentality that seems very shortsighted. What am I missing?

First of all, "blame" implies fault—a very negative way to characterize responsibility. We don't typically *blame* young children when, through their own naiveté they burn themselves on a hot stove, trip and fall while running, or catch chicken pox from classmates, and similarly, we should not *blame* adults for their circumstances. Also, a belief in "victims" completely disregards the premise that we are absolute creators. We are not part-time creators, nor is "dominion overall things" conditional; therefore, no matter how challenging the concept may be, spiritually speaking, there really is no such thing as a "victim." Of course, this is rather impossible to see when we view and try to understand life with our physical senses alone, which takes any event completely out of the larger context from which it arose.

Secondly, the larger context of all events is always spiritual. *Thoughts become things* is the spiritual principle that explains matter and circumstance creation, yet it does not speak to the reasons, motivations, or lessons involved in our day-to-day focuses. Just as gravity actually makes modern day atmospheric flight possible, it explains nothing of aerodynamics or aviation.

There are countless reasons why seemingly "bad things happen to good people," some born of naiveté and others born of nobility, but just because all we may see is pain and suffering doesn't mean that mutual objectives aren't being met, and it doesn't mean that the parties involved weren't cocreators of the occurrence. *None of this, incidentally, justifies a violation, nor does it mean independent parties should stand back as neutral observers. In fact, one of the very reasons such a scenario was created may have been precisely to draw in bystanders and to inspire others to rethink old attitudes, customs, and stereotypes.*

How do you get going once you know this stuff?

Baby steps. Living the life of your dreams isn't just about dreaming; it's also about living. You have to put yourself out into the world so that the winds of change can catch your sails, you have to go out so that the Universe will have every opportunity to work its wonders and grant you new people, wonderful accidents, and crazy coincidences—none of which can happen if you just sit inside and visualize every day. You have to follow your impulses, turn over every stone, and possibly, depending on your old way of thinking, start doing things you may never have considered doing before.

For example, when we first started selling TUT T-shirts in Orlando, we had a tough time finding our first retail space until the renovated downtown marketplace offered us some outdoor pushcart space. Well, Mom, Andy, and I all felt the same: *none of us* wanted to be selling our T-shirts from an outdoor pushcart, but we also felt that it was definitely the break we needed, so we signed the lease. The point here is that none of us really "wanted" to open this cart, but we all *felt* that it was the right thing to do. Within two years (two *very* long years, I should add), that cart turned into a small store, and then that store turned into a chain of stores.

When deciding whether or not to lease that first cart, we could have easily said, "No, thanks. We don't want to bust our butts working an outdoor sidewalk; heck, our *thoughts become things*, so we're just going to visualize our way into a chain of stores." Well, all things are possible, and I'm sure there could have been other ways for us to proceed, but I really believe that in getting to where you want to go, *especially when dealing with all your old beliefs about life and success*, a lot of little steps are in order, not just one or two giant leaps. But the only way you'll be able to take a lot of little steps is if you dive into life headfirst and live it, doing what you now can, from where you now are, and using what you now have, even when your first steps don't look remotely glamorous.

The answer to every one of your questions lies within yourself. Life isn't supposed to be the ultimate mystery; it's an open book. We just have to take the time to read it. Whatever it is you want to know, begin by telling yourself that you already know it.

12

The Meaning of Life

o you realize what reading a book like this means? It's loaded with implications: it reveals your belief that the so-called mysteries of the Universe are perhaps knowable. It reveals your belief that your dreams are achievable. And perhaps most importantly, it reveals that you've taken responsibility for your life and your future. I hope you've been giving credit where credit is due. You are undoubtedly much closer than you even imagine to achieving the happiness and fulfillment you chose this lifetime to experience.

Sweet Dreams

We've covered a lot of ground, yet what I've most wanted to impress upon you is so very, very simple: There *is* a principle at play in the Universe that turns your thoughts into the things and events of your life. It's an inviolate principle and one that explains fully how you have indeed been given dominion over all things. By recognizing and understanding this principle, you can begin using it, turning your wishes into reality, and living the life of your dreams.

Whether visualizing or daydreaming, your *thoughts become things*. This isn't wishful thinking; it's the way things have always been in time and space, and it means that whatever it is that you most want truly lies only a thought away. Imagination is what sets the "mold" from which all matter and events are first cast, and to make this even more believable for you, let's continue with some deductive reasoning. First, I want to take for granted that by now you understand that time and space are illusions.

Thoughts become things!

Well, if time and space are the illusions that set the stage for this grand odyssey called life, doesn't it logically follow that all things found *within* time and space—matter and events—are also illusions?

Now, since time, space, *and matter* are all really illusions, then, as I pointed out before, in many regards—in fact, in every regard—the constructs of our lives are very much the same as the constructs of the dreams we have at night. And you don't have any problem realizing that the props and circumstances of your nighttime dreams are illusions, do you? When recalling them, you still know they're dreams even though they sure seemed real when you were dreaming them, no matter what you're dreaming. When it comes to nighttime dreams, the craziest things can happen. Cars turn into elephants, fish can fly—people can fly!—and in some we're heroes, in others we're villains. Sometimes we feel accomplished and successful, while other times we're spinning in loops and going in circles.

So let me ask you, "Would you find it impossible to believe that tonight you might have some crazy, wacky, unpredictable dreams?" No, of course not. Then would it be impossible for you to have a dream where you found yourself surrounded by wealth and abundance, health and harmony, friends and laughter? Again, of course not.

What if, in such a dream you became aware that you were dreaming? Would you protest and say, "I can't be dreaming of such splendor; I don't deserve it! This doesn't make logical sense. Stop the nonsense!" No, you wouldn't, because in your dream you would know it's all an illusion, and that worthiness, logic, and the paying of one's so-called dues (or other such limitations) would not have any bearing on the illusions around you, right? After all, it's just a dream. Nor would you think that this can't be happening, because last night you dreamed you were poor and without friends. The past doesn't matter in your dreams, does it? You're not limited in what you can dream tonight by what you dreamed last night. There are no restrictions or limits in nighttime dreams, because as real as they seem, we know they're all just illusions.

Are you getting the picture? As I said before, your life right now in time and space is no less a dream; it's every bit the illusion. It's just that since the matter in our lives is such a dense form of thought, it simply takes a little longer (but not much longer) to manipulate or change the direction of things. In your life right now, you are not subject to the limits and constraints of having to pay your dues, your past, being worthy, or even being logical! These are all just beliefs, rules you've created that needn't exist because by your mere presence here, just as in a dream, you're prequalified. As one of the founding creators of all time and space, you are deserving—deserving of anything you can imagine. You've already paid enough dues to last through eternity, and nothing can take what you've earned away from you.

You are now dreaming, fellow adventurer, and in this dream, whether you realize it yet or not, you are unlimited. You are divine. And you are powerful. Abundance, health, and harmony are only a thought away, a thought that will engage universal principles that must deliver it to you. You're not alone; the entire Universe is on your side, yearning to give you all that you have the courage to wish for.

**Thoughts don't start becoming things once
you know this stuff; the Universe doesn't start applying
its principles once you become enlightened.
The game is under way.**

As Predictable, Dependable, and Reliable as Gravity

What happens when you throw a ball into the air? About midway through its journey, it falls back down to Earth. Why? It's the law; it has to. Now, does it matter who threw it for the law to take over? Does it matter how old or young he is? Does it matter how good looking and popular he is? Does it matter how spiritual he is? Does it matter whether he's a "good" person? Does it matter how enlightened he is? Does it even matter whether or not he believes in the law or in the Universe or even in God? No! *Nothing matters* once he throws that ball, because as the ball leaves his fingertips, *the Universe and its principles take over*. And that's exactly what happens once you choose your thoughts, so choose them wisely.

Do you see what this means? Doesn't it blow your mind? Infinite possibilities—what an understatement! There is *nothing* you can't do, *nothing* you can't have, and *nothing* you can't be!

Thoughts become things, and our lives are the proof, but do you see one of the biggest ironies about this? It's that every single one of us is already living the life of our dreams; it's just that some are not too happy with what they've been dreaming. Thoughts don't start becoming things once you know this stuff; the Universe doesn't start applying its principles once you become enlightened. The game is under way, and you're now playing it.

Your thoughts have always become the things and events of your life, and that includes this very moment. You're already living the life of your dreams; this is an inescapable truth. Look about you at all that you now see and feel. This is what you've called forth. And you can change it all in the twinkling of an eye.

In every regard, you're already a master; you're already moving mountains, and throughout your entire life you've been doing the impossible. You just have to know this to the core of your being so that you can willfully direct your life and bring about deliberate change. And the fastest way to knowing this is *through knowing and understanding yourself—by being yourself, only yourself and all yourself*. You are truly the only mystery you ever have to contend with, and you're no mystery at all. Understand yourself, and you'll understand the Universe.

Your Greatest Love Affair

And where to begin? By appreciating who you already are and loving all you already have. You are unique; you are special. You know this is true. There is no one in all the world who sees things quite as you do, who has insights that rival your own, and who feels the way you feel. (I know who I'm talking to.) You wear your heart on your sleeve and you'd do just about anything for anyone except yourself ... until now, that is.

Appreciate yourself, because right now you are exactly who you're supposed to be, exactly where you're supposed to be, doing exactly what you're supposed to be doing, including asking the very questions you're now asking—which, incidentally, you wouldn't be asking had your past not unfolded *exactly* as it has. So be glad for it—for everything you've ever done, learned, and experienced, the good, the bad and the ugly—because it has all brought you to the degree of understanding you now possess, and it has given you the hunger to press on for more.

Appreciate yourself, because the more you do, the more everyone else will too, and that's not even the half of it. The more you appreciate yourself, the easier your life will get. You'll become more in demand at work, at home, and everywhere else. Your health will improve. Your "balance" will improve, and abundance will effortlessly flow to you. You'll sleep better, you'll play more; you'll fear less, you'll "know" more. And, yes, as unimportant as it may be, you'll even get better looking. Minutes and hours will actually be added to your days, and as life gets better, you'll gather momentum. In fact, you're already on a roll, and you can't be stopped. Evidence everywhere is mounting; there's no doubting it. Life is *so* awesome—and you are invincible.

You are truly the only mystery you ever have to contend with, and you're no mystery at all. Understand yourself, and you'll understand the Universe.

Somewhere in Paradise Right Now

It's easy to take ourselves and our incredible world for granted. So begin by noticing the magic everywhere, in your own backyard and splashed around the world. Right now, *at this very second*, no matter what time of day it is, somewhere in the world thundering waves are crashing at sunrise on the sparkling white sands of a tropical beach. You can almost hear them if you try. And at this very moment, there are dolphins leaping into the air, beavers building dams, and eagles soaring just beneath the sun. Somewhere right now, there's lava running down a mountainside, a new island is rising from the sea, and snow is falling silently on a countryside.

Somewhere else right now, two strangers are meeting after an unpredictable yet not accidental sequence of events, and a wonderful adventure is about to begin for both. Somewhere else, someone is healing from a horrible disease that he was told he could not survive. And right now, very possibly in your own town, someone is realizing that she's finally created enough wealth to never have to worry about money for the rest of her life, while others are laughing hysterically with friends—so hard that it feels like their sides are splitting. And as you read this very sentence, somewhere a newborn baby is filling its lungs for the first time, and the very same love that's beating its tiny little heart is beating yours, sent from a Universe that adores you, that claims you as its own precious child, and that yearns for your every happiness.

You're not beholden to life; *life is beholden to you.*

As Good As It Gets

You are the prodigal child who's lost your way, yet the Universe blesses your wandering and is anxiously preparing for your return at a moment's notice—not to some celestial heaven away from Earth but to *a heaven here* on Earth, *right now*. And though you've momentarily forgotten where you came from, the Universe has never left you, and the world remains your oyster. You're not here to experience lack, disease, or limits; you're here, in this very lifetime, to experience abundance, health, and harmony. That is your purpose: to follow and live the life of your dreams. Understand this, believe in your sovereignty, choose your thoughts accordingly, *and live your amazing, extraordinary life.*

Don't just see the magic; engage it! *Challenge* it! *Dare* it! *Dream* big, with every expectation that your dreams will manifest. *Demand* that they come true! You're not beholden to life; *life is beholden to you.* You're the master, its creator. You are its reason for being. You came first.

Remember who you are, get centered in the present, visualize, perform acts of faith, and watch what happens. At first you'll get little sparks of magic mixed into your weeks—odd little so-called coincidences or accidents that don't really make much sense—except that they will ring some sort of bell in the depths of your being. You'll see that you're worrying less, focusing more on the present, and enjoying who you already are. There may still be a "setback" or two, but you'll find that your resilience has increased as you stay in a mood of divine nonchalance. You'll understand that these "setbacks" are like remnant manifestations from your old life and your old ways of thinking, and *you'll happily dust yourself off and look ahead.*

Actually, you know exactly what I'm talking about, don't you? Everything's already begun changing in your life. Now, more than ever before, you're happy to have time alone; you enjoy just thinking about stuff, pondering, or visualizing. You're more confident and you feel the Universe present in all your affairs.

No longer do you ascribe your successes to the wonderful mortal you, though the mortal you couldn't be more splendid. Instead, you give credit entirely to the wonderful spiritual you and its connection to Divine Intelligence. You understand, at last, that you can do nothing and be nothing without this magic, and you realize that your every prior success in life came from when you engaged it. It's like you've found a long-lost friend, sometimes you feel so light—as if you could just float. Lately, you feel you could cry tears of joy virtually every single day.

In everyone, you see God; and in everyone you sense their joys, their sorrows, and their dreams. You want to reach out and help, and you almost feel guilty for your own "blessings," because you realize that you are no more special or talented than those you meet who are in pain, and you want so greatly to lighten their load. Your priorities have shifted, and what now matters most is *sharing*—with those inclined to be shown—another way of looking at life. You know this is all you can offer because they must find what you've found, by first going within and understanding themselves. So you lead by example.

Of course, you've noticed something else that's strange lately. Physical principles have begun taking a back seat to spiritual principles. Less no longer means less; logic no longer applies. You find that the more you give, the more is given to you. The more you teach, the more you're shown the way. The more you heal, the more you're healed. And everything you do seems to get simpler and easier by the day. Life seems so fair, so rich, so abundant, and love is everywhere; you wonder how it had ever escaped you before.

You're now spending more and more time every day just quieting your excited mind and contemplating how else you can spread the wealth and happiness you've attained. You plot surprises, anonymous gifts, and secret partnerships. You're on a mission, and on this mission you notice that for the first time ever you feel almost no resistance to life. You want to say "YES!" to everything and everyone.

You realize that the opportunities *and challenges* that come your way are perfect for your continued awakening, and you realize that this is no accident, nor were there ever accidents in your past. So you've given your all to each and every one, yet still you seem to have all the time in the world. It's like the more you do, the more you can do, and you realize it's because you're now engaging the magic by leveraging the Universe; you and the Universe are a team. Every day becomes such a gift that you feel like a kid again, with awe and wonder and an inexhaustible hunger to explore and play.

Fellow adventurer, ain't life grand? Wherever you now are, hang in there, because there is so much happiness in store for you. Even if you're now at the top of your game, there's still more to come—so much that you can't now comprehend it; views and vistas beyond your wildest imagination.

You are ready. You are divine. You are powerful, unlimited, and eternal. You are invincible. You are sublime. You are infinite, worthy, and so deserving. You are God. Think the good thoughts, move with them, listen to your heart and mind, feel your way, and the Universe will bring you its magic until your every cup, bucket, and tub runneth over, out the windows, down the streets, and into all the lives you touch.

Epilogue

*O*kay, *okay, that wasn't so fair. We knew all along that you were lost. Actually, we know a lot more about you than you might think.*

Listen up, old friend (older than you can even fathom): you were the brave one among us—so brave in fact, that you kind of left us in your dust. You see, none of us have even tried TIME and SPACE yet because we were wanting to see how you turned out!

Really, you haven't been gone for as long as we like to joke, but before you left we agreed to be your lifeline, your Angels, just in case you ever called. We've done our part, all right, and have been there each and every time you so much as said "Ouch!" (though we did pitch the white winged costumes you made us wear for your "Going Somewhere" party). Our point is this: you've done such a bang-up job, we're all more than a little anxious to get going with our turns, though we're afraid you'll be angry if we abandon our posts.

We've rationalized a bit and figure that at your rate of progress, you don't really need us anymore. Besides, as it turns out, there's really very little we can actually do for you here other than rant and rave from the "bleachers." You wouldn't have it any other way, remember?

What's more (and we didn't know this when you left), once we begin our own adventures, we'll remain in touch and within reach, available at your slightest call, though consciously none of us will likely know just what's going on.

Anyway, we made our decision some time ago, before you even began this lifetime, and have each planned our way into the very same TIME and SPACE where you now reside. In fact, one of us just might be that loud neighbor of yours . . . Aha! And in case you were beginning to wonder, we also arranged for your finding this book through the "simultaneosity" we spoke of earlier (we snuck into the future). You don't still believe in coincidence, do you?

So that you don't feel too put out, we smuggled in the following excerpt from one of the Illustrious One's latest memoirs, to hopefully tip the scales in your quest for understanding.

Adios amigo, and until we meet again, remember:

> *Life is not about hiding and seeking, nor is it about learning the things you've forgotten; it's not even about remembering them. It's about BEING—BEING YOURSELF! You were Born to Expand the Infinite Nature of God.*
>
> *Live only to be who you now are. You are Creation's first and last hope to fill the shoes you alone can fashion, and eternity will pass before this chance will come again.*
>
> *You are the dream of a legion before you who have passed on the torch of time and space awareness so that your mere existence could immeasurably enrich All That Is: God. By simply BEING, you will fulfill this dream, centered in the Here and Now, where all dreams come true, all truths reside, and understanding is born.*
>
> *Your sacred heart was hewn at the dawn of creation in a dance to celebrate the birth of forever; you can do no wrong. There are no "shoulds" or "shouldn'ts" and no "rights" or "wrongs." Life is not about being happy or sad, good or bad. It's not even about making your dreams come true; that much is i n e v i t a b l e .*
>
> *There is only BEING. Eternal BEING. Inescapable BEING. You are perfect; it is done. Your rare and precious light has, and will forevermore, illuminate the worlds you create—the worlds that now wait, for*

More on Mike

*B*efore becoming a teacher on life, dreams, and happiness, Mike Dooley spent sixteen years between the corporate and entrepreneurial worlds. For six years he was a CPA with Price Waterhouse in the United States and abroad, after which he cofounded Totally Unique T-shirts to begin retailing inspirational gifts and apparel. One million T-shirts later, he recorded his first audio program, *Infinite Possibilities: The Art of Living Your Dreams*, which has been a perennial bestseller since its release in 2001, selling over a quarter million CDs and evolving into this book. In the past seven years, Mike has taken his philosophies on the road, speaking in nineteen countries on six continents before tens of thousands of people, and in 2006 he was featured in the bestselling book and DVD *The Secret*. Today his daily email, "Notes from the Universe," a reminder of our power and divinity, is received by three hundred thousand people in one hundred eighty-two countries.

You can learn more about Mike and his teachings at his website, www.tut.com.

Recommended Reading

$\mathcal{T}$his is not meant to be a list of all the great books that are out there. These are just the books that have had the greatest effect on me, helping to define and confirm my own thoughts and suspicions about life. I offer them as possible suggested reading to enhance your own adventures. They're listed here in no particular order.

The Nature of Personal Reality, **by Jane Roberts**
Like all her Seth books (and they're all outstanding), this one is very deep, objective, and even a bit complex, but I consider Seth to be the "granddaddy of them all."

Discover the Power Within You: A Guide to the Unexplored Depths Within, **by Eric Butterworth**
Awesome clarity. Extremely inspirational! Lots of biblical and Christian references but explained as I believe they were originally meant, without the religious spin.

Siddhartha, **by Herman Hesse**
Profound wisdom in a timeless, world-famous story.

The Game of Life and How to Play It, **by Florence Scovel-Shinn**
Very simple and powerful advice, written in the 1920s. Easy reading for any age.

Life and Teaching of the Masters of the Far East (six-volume set),
by Baird T. Spalding
> Mind-bending! Volumes 1 and 2 are as adventurous as they are inspirational.

Illusions: The Adventures of a Reluctant Messiah and
Jonathan Livingston Seagull, both by Richard Bach
> Exhilarating, fun, and easy to read. These two novels are on almost everyone's list for good reason!

Journeys Out of the Body, by Robert Monroe
> The classic on out-of-body experiences.

Life After Life: The Investigation of a Phenomenon—Survival of Bodily Death, by Raymond A. Moody Jr. and Elisabeth Kubler-Ross
> The classic on life after life and near-death experiences.

Conversations with God: An Uncommon Dialogue,
by Neale Donald Walsch
> Each of the books in this series is a mindblower. They're also very easy and fun to read.

Emmanuel's Book: A Manual for Living Comfortably in the Cosmos,
by Pat Rodegast and Judith Stanton
> The entire series of Emmanuel books offer gentle yet powerful reminders of how angelic we all are. Wonderful.

Ramtha: The White Book, by Ramtha
> Very friendly, powerful, and inspirational. Another easy read and one of the most powerful of all the titles listed here.

The Prophet, by Kahlil Gibran
> Insight into life's most basic truths. Another perennial, international bestseller.

The Science of Getting Rich, by Wallace D. Wattle

If you've ever thought that you might like wealth, you'll love this. A truly unique and encouraging perspective.

Atlas Shrugged and *The Fountainhead,* both by Ayn Rand

Although Ayn Rand was an agnostic/atheist, in my view her books are extremely spiritual in that she considered herself a "man worshiper," and she reveled in the glory of life and our ability to have dominion over it all. Her epic novels are spellbinding, romantic, and deeply philosophical, and her talent is off the charts.

The Secret (DVD and book), by Rhonda Byrne

I'm grateful to have been one of the featured teachers in this outstanding documentary on the Law of Attraction. It's as inspirational as it is enlightening.